In *Leviathan* Thomas Hobbes defines moral philosophy as "the science of Vertue and Vice." Few modern readers take this description seriously, however, typically assuming that Hobbes's ethical views are unrelated both to his views on science and to the subject of virtue. Influential modern interpretations have portrayed Hobbes as either an amoralist, a moral contractarian, a rule-egoist, or a divine-command theorist, and not as a proponent of a science of virtue.

David Boonin-Vail challenges these standard views and defends a novel and unorthodox interpretation of Hobbes's ethics. He shows that Hobbes is best understood as embracing a theory of virtue concerned with the development of good character traits rather than with rules of behavior. He also analyzes how Hobbes grounds his theory of moral virtue in a more general science of human nature.

By focusing in a new way on Hobbes's moral theory, this book is likely to attract considerable attention among both philosophers and intellectual historians.

Thomas Hobbes and
the science of moral virtue

Thomas Hobbes and the science of moral virtue

DAVID BOONIN-VAIL

Tulane University

CAMBRIDGE
UNIVERSITY PRESS

Published by the Press Syndicate of the University of Cambridge
The Pitt Building, Trumpington Street, Cambridge CB2 1RP
40 West 20th Street, New York, NY 10011-4211, USA
10 Stamford Road, Oakleigh, Melbourne 3166, Australia

First published 1994

Printed in the United States of America

Library of Congress Cataloging-in-Publication Data

Boonin-Vail, David.
Thomas Hobbes and the science of moral virtue / David Boonin-Vail.
p. cm.
Includes bibliographical references and index.
ISBN 0-521-46209-6
1. Hobbes, Thomas, 1588–1679 – Ethics. I. Title.
B1248.E7B66 1994
171'.2 – dc20 93-48754
CIP

A catalog record for this book is available from the British Library.

ISBN 0-521-46209-6 hardback

For my parents, Leonard and Harriet Boonin,
and my wife, Martha Boonin-Vail

Contents

Acknowledgments

This study began its life as a doctoral dissertation at the University of Pittsburgh, and for their help in guiding it through to its fruition, I would like first of all to thank the members of my committee: Kurt Baier, Carol Kay, Peter Machamer, Fred Whelan, Jennifer Whiting, and especially my director, David Gauthier. Although his own contractarian reading of Hobbes's ethics constitutes one of the principal targets of the interpretation developed here, David was always a fair and generous reader. Shortly after one meeting with him in which we had discussed some textual evidence for and against my interpretation of Hobbes, I was in the graduate students' lounge when a student came in and told me that "Gauthier is walking around the department asking if anyone has seen you and waving a copy of *Leviathan* around." With some trepidation, I slowly walked down to his office, expecting to be confronted at last with the definitive rebuttal to my account, only to find that he had instead uncovered an additional piece of text in its favor. This was typical of his involvement in my work, and his constant enthusiasm for this project from its very beginning is deeply appreciated.

Several friends and colleagues also read and commented on individual chapters in progress, and I thank them, as well as anonymous referees from the Cambridge, Oxford, and Cornell university presses, who commented on the manuscript as a whole and provided a number of valuable suggestions. The finished product also benefited a great deal from discussions with others too numerous to name (I now wish that I had kept a list), and would never have been completed without the love and support of my friends, my family, and – especially – my wife, Martha, who never let her own considerable work load keep her from offering me comfort.

Hobbes is said to have boasted that if he had read as much as others, he would have known no more than others; and whether true in his case or not, it is certainly false in the case of my understanding of Hobbes. This book could not have been written without the help of the vast and often excellent secondary literature his writings have generated. My many debts are noted at the appropriate points throughout the text, but I should like to acknowledge here the contributions of two writers in particular, whose insights into Hobbes's thought were especially valuable in the early stages of my work, when on the grounds that I could find no one else who shared it, I was tempted to abandon my suspicion that virtue played a central role in Hobbes's moral thinking. One is A. E. Taylor, whose important paper on Hobbes's ethics forces the reader to confront Hobbes's often neglected discussions of the difference between just acts and just persons. The other is Bernard Gert, whose writings on Hobbes have explicitly linked him to the Aristotelian tradition of virtue ethics, and whose account of what Hobbes is up to in the laws of nature was the only one I could find that seemed congenial to my own nascent understanding. Although I ultimately depart from the accounts by Taylor and Gert in important ways, their fundamental insights served as both supports and guideposts as my own interpretation began to take shape.

I am also grateful for the teaching fellowships I received from the University of Pittsburgh in 1989–90 and 1991–92, and for a visiting teaching fellowship I received from Yale University in 1990–91, which helped support my work in a more material way.

Finally, I thank the two professors who introduced me to the pleasures of philosophy: John Ferrari, whose courses were among the highlights of my undergraduate education at Yale (and who assuaged all my doubts about majoring in philosophy by confessing to me, when I asked if he ever thought the whole subject was nothing but baloney, that he thought so all the time but found it to be such good-tasting baloney), and my father, Leonard Boonin, who read and commented on the entire manuscript at several stages and who, years before, had helped initiate me into the cult of philosophical inquiry by reading to me the stories of Curious George.

Abbreviations for Hobbes's works

"AL"	"Appendix to [the Latin edition of] *Leviathan*"
B	*Behemoth*
BR	*A Briefe of the Art of Rhetorique*
"CCA"	"Mr Hobbes Concerning ye Compression of Aire"
Co	*De Corpore*
D	*A Dialogue between a Philosopher and a Student of the Common Laws of England*
DC	*De Cive*
DH	*De Homine*
DME	*Thomas White's De Mundo Examined*
DP	*Decameron Physiologicum*
EL	*The Elements of Law*
EL I	*Human Nature* (in *The Elements of Law*)
EL II	*De Corpore Politico* (in *The Elements of Law*)
EW	*The English Works of Thomas Hobbes*
L	*Leviathan*
LC	Letter to Mr. Cavendish
LD	Letter to the Duchess of Newcastle
LEH	Letter to Edward Howard
LMM	Letter to Marin Mersenne
LN	*Of Liberty and Necessity*
LNC	*The Questions concerning Liberty, Necessity, and Chance*
LS	Letter to Lord Scudmore
LSS	Letter to Samuel Sorbière
"LTH"	"The Life of Thomas Hobbes of Malmesbury"
MH	Manuscript on the Law of Heresy
"O"	Objections to Descartes' *Meditations*
PD	*A Physical Dialogue of the Nature of the Air*
PPG	*Principia et Problemata aliquot Geometrica*
SL	*Six Lessons to the Savilian Professors of the Mathematics*
SPP	*Seven Philosophical Problems*
"ST"	"A Short Tract on First Principles"

Thomas Hobbes and the science of moral virtue

Chapter 1

Hobbes's project and its critics

1.0 PRELUDE

In 1672, at the age of eighty-four, one of the most controversial figures of the seventeenth century sat down to compose his autobiography. "The Life of Thomas Hobbes of Malmesbury," unlike the life it undertakes to record, is unremarkable and brief. The man who was vilified as the Monster of Malmesbury, whose works were condemned as atheistic and immoral, and whose very name has come to evoke the most nasty species of egoism offers hardly a single introspective thought in defense of his character. "I . . . always lived moderately," he mentions at one point, and "I love peace along with the Muses and easy companions," he says at another, but beyond this his memoir proceeds, almost without exception, in the detached (though often vivid) voice of a biographer who remains uncertain of his subject's ultimate moral worth ("LTH": 2, 1). As the narrative draws to a close, however, Hobbes provides what may serve as an explanation of this rather curious fact: "You know my character" already, he insists, addressing "all men who read my writings. For my life is not incompatible with my writings. I teach justice and I cultivate it" ("LTH": 7).[1]

Now it may at first seem somewhat peculiar that in relating his long and eventful life to his teachings, Hobbes should in the end

1 Hobbes's contemporaries seem largely to have conceded the justice of his character, though they challenged its compatibility with his writings. Edward Hyde, Earl of Clarendon, for example, opens one of the harshest attacks on *Leviathan* by admitting that Hobbes "hath been alwaies looked upon as a Man of Probity" who has lived "a life free from scandal" (1676: 3). This view, moreover, has survived through such later writers as Hume, who noted that Hobbes, while promoting a "selfish system of morals," had lived an "irreproachable" life despite the fact that he "lay not under any restraint of religion which might supply the defects of his philosophy" (1975: 296).

speak of justice as a character trait that one cultivates. This, after all, is to embrace the vocabulary of virtue, to speak the language of Aristotle, and Hobbes had vigorously persisted throughout his writings in the claim that "scarce any thing can be [said] more ignorantly, than a great part of [Aristotle's] *Ethiques*" (*L:* 687). Hobbes's name is generally associated with his defense of political authoritarianism, and one might therefore expect him to boast that in praising justice he had taught obedience to the sovereign and had practiced it. Yet the apparent affinity with the virtue ethics of Aristotle here should not be ignored, for it is far from the only place in Hobbes's writings in which it appears.[2] The present study seeks to offer a critical interpretation of Hobbes's moral science, and this requires attention to a wide variety of considerations. But Hobbes's self-assessment here should be kept in mind from the outset as a reminder of the primary conclusion of this work as a whole: that Hobbes is best understood as a sort of virtue ethicist, and a very interesting sort, one who provides a distinctive and powerful defense of the role that the virtues play in human flourishing, and of the person who by nature is disposed to do the right thing, and to enjoy doing so, not for any benefits which might thereby be gained, but simply because it is the right thing to do.

1.1 BACKGROUND

When Hobbes published *De Cive* in 1647, he explained in the preface to the reader that the book had originally been conceived as the third section of a three-part work on the elements of philosophy. "In the first," he noted, "I would have treated of *body* and its general properties; in the second of *man* and his special faculties and affections; in the third of *civil government* and the duties of subjects" (*DC:* preface).[3] While Hobbes was patiently working on the various parts of this project, however, England came to be "boiling hot with questions concerning the rights of dominion and the obedience due from subjects." And this, he explained, "was the cause which, all those other matters deferred, ripened and plucked from me this third part." For while *De Cive* had been planned as the culmination of an entire philosophical system, Hobbes recognized that "grounded on its own principles suffi-

2 The parallels between Hobbes's and Aristotle's accounts of the virtuous person are discussed in section 5.1.

3 See footnote 29 in this chapter, however, for the claim that this standard translation is misleading in a significant way.

ciently known by experience, it would not stand in need of the former sections" (*DC:* preface).

This confession has often been taken as evidence that Hobbes's pretense to system was largely superficial, since he acknowledges that one can know the principles of his civil philosophy without having to worry about his physics. But for the student of Hobbes's ethics, the passage is at least as important for what it does not say. For Hobbes does not concede that all three parts of his system can be understood independently of one another, does not allow that his treatment "of *man* and his special faculties and affections" can be detached from his physics, and does not list that discipline's treatment of such topics as "*appetite, will, good* and *evil, honest* and *dishonest,* and the like" as the subjects of his disclaimer. These topics circumscribe the domain of moral philosophy as Hobbes understands it, and thus whatever degree of separation is suggested here between natural philosophy and civil philosophy, it is not explicitly extended to the relationship between natural philosophy and ethics.[4]

This same silence characterizes Hobbes's comments about his system in *De Corpore,* which he finally published in 1655. Those "that have not learned the first part of philosophy, namely, *geometry* and *physics,*" he allowed, "may, notwithstanding, attain the principles of civil philosophy." But civil philosophy and moral philosophy are not the same thing, and, Hobbes insisted, they "do not so adhere to one another, but that they may be severed" (*Co:* 6.7). In apparently weakening the link between natural philosophy and politics, then, Hobbes again refrained from weakening the link between natural philosophy and ethics.[5] Indeed, Hobbes did not hesitate in the same work to claim that "After *physics* we must come to *moral philosophy;* in which we are to consider the motions of the mind," and to argue that "the reason why these are to be consid-

4 This distinction is often overlooked. George Shelton, for example, cites this passage from the preface to *De Cive* on the opening page of his recent work on Hobbes's moral philosophy, and avers that the "quotation shows quite clearly that [Hobbes] regarded his moral and political philosophy as a free-standing structure" (1992: 1). But Hobbes speaks explicitly here only of his political philosophy.

5 Aloysius Martinich's extensive commentary on Part I of *De Corpore* also notes this implication: "Although civil philosophy properly comes after geometry and physics, it is possible, says Hobbes, to study it before them. Hobbes does not make clear whether ethics, which falls between physics and civil philosophy, can be studied before geometry and physics or not. Hobbes's remark that civil philosophy can be detached from ethics suggests that it cannot" (1981: 425).

ered after *physics* is, that they have their causes in sense and imagination, which are the subject of *physical* contemplation" (*Co:* 6.6).

That ethics in Hobbes's system enjoyed a closer tie to natural philosophy than did politics can perhaps best be seen in the accompanying table of science that concludes Chapter 9 of *Leviathan* (*L:* 149).[6] Science, or philosophy, is immediately divided there into natural philosophy, which studies natural bodies, and political or civil philosophy, which studies political (or elsewhere "artificiall") bodies. Whereas "ETHIQUES" is therefore represented as one specific subdivision of "PHYSIQUES" which is in turn a branch of natural philosophy, the disciplines concerning the rights and duties of sovereigns and subjects are not. This is not to say that Hobbes ever abandoned the claim that his political theory was a part of his overall system of thought;[7] it is simply to acknowledge that Hobbes distinguished between political and moral philosophy, and that he was less equivocal about the systematic place of the latter. Like so

6 This is also made clear by the division of subjects in the two works known collectively as the *Elements of Law.* There the subject of the natural law, which is explicitly understood as the moral law (*EL* I: e.g., 18.1), is treated in the part "Concerning men as persons natural" (*Human Nature*), whereas the various issues concerning government are discussed in the separate part "Concerning men as a body politic" (*De Corpore Politico*). (This division is unfortunately misrepresented in the Molesworth edition, which follows the original, corrupt, and unauthorized publication of the *Elements of Law* in having *Human Nature* end after Chapter 13. The Tonnies edition, cited here, follows the original manuscript copies in presenting *Human Nature* as running through Chapter 19. For background on this, see Tonnies [1928], as well as Goldsmith [1969: vi].) The discussion of this division is admittedly less clear in *De Corpore* (*Co:* 1.9). There, as in *Leviathan,* Hobbes divides philosophy into natural philosophy, concerned with bodies that are "the work of nature," and civil philosophy, concerned with the commonwealth "made by the wills and agreement of men." He goes on to write, however, that "civil philosophy is again commonly divided into two parts, whereof one, which treats of men's dispositions and manners, is called *ethics;* and the other, which takes cognizance of their civil duties, is called *politics,* or simply *civil philosophy.*" This seems to imply that ethics is a branch of civil philosophy, rather than of natural philosophy, but this suggestion is incompatible with Hobbes's account of the distinction between natural and civil philosophy in the very same paragraph: Ethics is the study of human dispositions, and such dispositions are natural bodies, not the product of agreement.

7 The force of the *De Cive* disclaimer should not be overstated. As one writer has put it, Hobbes can allow for knowledge of politics without a foundation in physics without completely severing the two "in precisely the same sense [in which] a knowledge of the orbits of the planets may be derived from experience, from observation, without any reference to the laws of gravity" (Gray, 1978: 202).

- SCIENCE, that is, Knowledge of Consequences; which is called also PHILOSOPHY.
  - Consequences from the Accidents of Bodies Naturall; which is called NATURALL PHILOSOPHY.
    - Consequences from the Accidents common to all Bodies Naturall; which are *Quantity*, and *Motion*.
      - Consequences from Quantity, and Motion *indeterminate*; which being the Principles, or first foundation of Philosophy, is called *Philosophia Prima*. — PHILOSOPHIA PRIMA.
      - Consequences from Motion, and Quantity *determined*.
        - Consequences from Quantity, and Motion determined.
          - By Figure, . . — *Mathematiques*, — GEOMETRY.
          - By Number, . . — *Mathematiques*, — ARITHMETIQUE.
        - Consequences from the Motion, and Quantity of Bodies in *speciall*.
          - Consequences from the Motion, and Quantity of the great parts of the World, as the *Earth* and *Starres*, — *Cosmography*, — ASTRONOMY. GEOGRAPHY.
          - Consequences from the Motion of Special kinds, and Figures of Body, — *Mechaniques*, Doctrine of *Weight*, — *Science* of ENGINEERS. ARCHITECTURE. NAVIGATION.
    - PHYSIQUES, or Consequences from *Qualities*.
      - Consequences from the Qualities of Bodyes *Transient*, such as sometimes appear, sometimes vanish . . . . METEOROLOGY.
      - Consequences from the Qualities of Bodies *Permanent*.
        - Consequences from the Qualities of the *Starres*,
          - Consequences from the *Light* of the Starres. Out of this, and the Motion of the Sunne, is made the Science of . — SCIOGRAPHY.
          - Consequences from the *Influence* of the Starres . . . . ASTROLOGY.
        - Consequences of the Qualities from *Liquid* Bodies that fill the space between the Starres; such as are the *Ayre*, or substance ætheriall.
        - Consequences from the Qualities of Bodies *Terrestriall*.
          - Consequences from the parts of the Earth, that are *without Sense*,
            - Consequences from the Qualities of *Minerals*, as *Stones*, *Metalls*, &c.
            - Consequences from the Qualities of *Vegetables*.
          - Consequences from the Qualities of *Animals*.
            - Consequences from the Qualities of *Animals in generall*
              - Consequences from *Vision*, — OPTIQUES.
              - Consequences from *Sounds*, — MUSIQUE.
              - Consequences from the rest of the *Senses*.
            - Consequences from the Qualities of *Men in speciall*
              - Consequences from the *Passions* of Men . . . . . — ETHIQUES.
              - Consequences from *Speech*,
                - In *Magnifying*, *Vilifying*, &c. — POETRY.
                - In *Perswading*, — RHETHORIQUE.
                - In *Reasoning*, — LOGIQUE.
                - In *Contracting*, — The *Science* of JUST and UNJUST.
  - Consequences from the Accidents of *Politique* Bodies; which is called POLITIQUES, and CIVILL PHILOSOPHY.
    1. Of Consequences from the *Institution* of COMMON-WEALTHS, to the *Rights*, and *Duties* of the *Body Politique*, or *Soveraign*.
    2. Of Consequences from the same, to the *Duty*, and *Right* of the *Subjects*.

many other speculative thinkers of the seventeenth century,[8] Hobbes sought to construct a consistent and unified system of thought that would include a science of morals, and for many years his readers took his systematic intent seriously.

Certainly Hobbes's contemporaries treated his doctrines as a systematic, albeit reprehensible, body of thought.[9] They were offended almost exclusively by what they perceived to be his unorthodox, if not heretical, views on religion, and by his apparently relativistic view of morality. Yet they did not limit their attacks to his social and religious doctrines, often focusing instead on the philosophical foundations on which they seemed to rest. Thus Bishop Bramhall attacked Hobbes's materialism as "that main root of Atheisme, from which so many lesser branches are daily sprouting up," and Robert Boyle expressed hope that his attack on Hobbes's physics would help to undermine his positions on reli-

8 In his *Preface* to the French edition of the *Principles of Philosophy,* for example, Descartes wrote that "the whole of philosophy is like a tree. The roots are metaphysics, the trunk is physics, and the branches emerging from the trunk are all the other sciences, which may be reduced to three principal ones, namely medicine, mechanics and morals. By 'morals' I understand the highest and most perfect moral system, which presupposes a complete knowledge of the other sciences and is the ultimate level of wisdom" (1985: 186). Indeed, Descartes is so like Hobbes in this respect that when the anonymous first edition of *De Cive* first appeared, Descartes was thought by many to be its author.

9 This was not true of all of Hobbes's contemporaries, as Quentin Skinner has documented in a number of important papers. Hobbes seems to have had influential admirers on the Continent, if not in England (see, especially 1963 and 1966 for evidence of Hobbes's admirers). This fact should temper the popular picture of Hobbes's role in the history of ideas, but it nonetheless remains that the responses published during his lifetime were overwhelmingly negative. Even Skinner acknowledges that recognition of Hobbes's greatness was largely restricted during his lifetime to a "small and rather private circle of friends," and notes that private correspondence relating to Hobbes is of particular importance in tracing Hobbes's positive influence "because it happened that Hobbes's political works were to gain a sufficiently sinister reputation for any public or printed avowal of sympathy with their views to become very difficult" (1963: 160, 159); similarly, in (1966), Skinner agrees that "there are certainly signs that a man who sympathized with Hobbes's views was better able to say so in private than in any published form" (1966: 305). Hobbes himself, it is worth adding, refers to the doctrine of his own *De Cive* as "abhorrent to the views of almost everyone" in a letter to Samuel Sorbière, in which he worries that the inscription identifying him as the tutor to the Prince of Wales, which appeared beneath his portrait in that work, would be used to "bring the Royal Family into illwill with most people" (LSS: 311, 310).

gion[10] (indeed, attacks on Hobbes became most fierce when he at last published *De Corpore*).[11] The determinism of Hobbes's system was another popular (or rather, unpopular) object of scorn, since, as one preacher put it, it made men nothing but "the tennis-balls of destiny."[12] And the great mathematician John Wallis evidently hoped to undermine Hobbes's philosophical views by showing him "how little he understands the Mathematics from which he takes his courage."[13] Although we may legitimately question the extent to which Hobbes's contemporaries truly appreciated the interconnectedness of his writings and the extent to which they simply wished to avoid being associated with anything written by so odious a man, it remains undeniable that, as one historian has put it, "they considered his religious and metaphysical opinions and his political doctrines to be inseparable."[14] Finding almost nothing in his works with which they could agree, his adversaries nonetheless tacitly endorsed one of Hobbes's most cherished beliefs: that the normative claims which had made him infamous rested firmly on a larger body of philosophical thought.

Although he has come to be remembered almost entirely for his political doctrines, the view of Hobbes as a philosophical system builder has generally survived over the years. George Croom Robertson in 1886 expressed skepticism about the relation between Hobbes's science and his politics, for example, but he nonetheless emphasized that a treatment of Hobbes needed to address the

10 Bramhall in *The Catching of Leviathan* (1676) and Boyle in *An Examen of Mr T. Hobbes his Dialogus Physicus De Natura Aeris* (1662). Both quoted in Mintz (1969: 67, 87).

11 See Tuck (1993: 336).

12 Jeremy Taylor, quoted in Mintz (1969: 115).

13 Quoted in Rogow (1986: 203).

14 Mintz (1969: vii). One incident which suggests that Hobbes's contemporaries were willing to reject his works as a whole without necessarily grasping their overall structure is recounted by Hobbes's friend, Henry Stubbe. The intemperate exchanges between Hobbes and Wallis were often carried out in Latin, and each accused the other of, among other things, faulty grammar. Stubbe assisted Hobbes in this element of their debate, in an attempt, as he put it, "to vindicate Mr. Hobbes, and to show the insufferable ignorance of the puny professor, and unlearned critic [Wallis]" (*EW* VII: 426–7), but he was dismayed to find that there were people who would "make me guilty of [Hobbes's] sentiments, because I excuse his Latine" (quoted in Mintz, 1969: 148; for more on Hobbes and Stubbe, see Jacob, 1983: esp. 10–11). The conclusion of one recent writer seems apt, if somewhat understated: "The common expressions of anti-Hobbesian fervor did not necessarily represent the fruit of careful study" (Kay 1988: 24).

entire range of his thought, and conceded, somewhat equivocally, that his theoretical system as a whole "hangs (or is meant to hang) together" (1886: 76).[15] Although Leslie Stephen in 1904 questioned whether Hobbes's physics provided his "real" method for examining politics, he still insisted that understanding Hobbes's natural philosophy was "essential" to understanding his thought, and he compared Hobbes in this regard to Herbert Spencer, surely the most systematic thinker of his own era (1904: 113, 74, 73).[16] Isolated and often half-hearted doubts aside, then, the dominant view remained that Hobbes's normative views were importantly related to the other elements of his philosophy.

In 1936, however, Leo Strauss published a book from which Hobbes scholarship has never fully recovered. In *The Political Philosophy of Hobbes,* Strauss attacked the traditional view of Hobbes as a systematic philosopher, and claimed not only that Hobbes's politics were not derived from his science, but that attempting such a naturalistic foundation "would have been the ruin of his political philosophy" (1936: 29, 169). Instead, Strauss argued, Hobbes was a humanist who based his political views on a morality that could not be reduced to natural science. Hobbes eventually presented his political views in the language of science, to be sure, but this, Strauss urged, was simply a rhetorical ploy designed to appeal to his seventeenth-century audience. As Ernest Baker put the heart of the thesis in his preface to the English translation of Strauss's book, Hobbes "was a moralist rather than a scientist" (1936: viii).

This view of Hobbes as a moralist and not a scientist gained support from two other important works which appeared in the years that followed. In "The Ethical Doctrine of Hobbes,"[17] A. E. Taylor presented a picture of Hobbes that would have astonished Hobbes's contemporaries. Instead of a "Colossus lying stretched out in the sea in all his enormity, his dreadful jaws gaping fiercely,

15 Robertson also writes that Hobbes already held many of his political views before he became enamored of modern science (1886: 65), and claims that he relied on his observations of men, not matter, to ground his political philosophy (1886: 135–6), but he does not argue that the scientific theories, although an afterthought, cannot be added to form a coherent system of thought (1886: e.g., 44, 138).

16 Similarly, George E. G. Catlin, in 1922, insisted that "although [Hobbes] prepared the political coping stone of his system before cutting the blocks of its naturalistic foundations, yet those foundations are always presumed and Hobbes is incomprehensible unless his fundamental materialism be remembered" (1922: 22).

17 Taylor's article is discussed in more detail in section 3.4.

and with obscene regurgitations belching forth abominable dogma which befouls the British coastlines,"[18] Taylor's Hobbes was "a fundamentally honest man with an almost overwhelming sense of duty" who believed that a just man was honest and benevolent and was motivated to do things because they were just, and not simply because they were in his interest (1965:[19] 53, 37–8). This deontological Hobbes was very nearly Kant, and his ethical doctrine was seen to rest ultimately on the obligation to obey God's commands, and not on a scientific materialism (1965: 50).[20] Taylor's understanding of Hobbes's ethics differed in important respects from Strauss's, but they held in common the view that whatever Hobbes's ethical views were, they were in no way dependent on his science.

The other important work which contributed to this view of the Hobbesian corpus was Howard Warrender's *Political Philosophy of Hobbes*. In this lengthy book, Warrender rejected Taylor's deontological reading of Hobbes's ethics, but he endorsed and greatly elaborated on the view that God, and not science, lay at the foundation of Hobbes's normative claims. Hobbes, according to Warrender, believed that men had moral obligations even in the state of nature, but that these obligations arose only because God commanded obedience to the laws of nature. These laws could be viewed as prudential theorems revealed by reason, and in this respect they might prove somehow related to Hobbes's mechanistic psychology, but they had no moral character whatsoever until they were acknowledged as divine commands (1957: e.g., 99, 232, 252).[21] Warrender remained uncertain as to why Hobbes thought men were obligated to obey God – perhaps out of self-interest, perhaps just because He is God – but for Warrender the point remained that Hobbes was a moralist in the natural law tradition, and not a representative of the new science.

Although neither Strauss's book nor the Taylor-Warrender thesis ever became standard interpretations, their various rejections of

18 Charles Robotham, quoted in Mintz (1969: 56).

19 Taylor's article was originally published in 1938, but references are to the version in Taylor 1965.

20 Taylor expresses the view that Hobbes's politics and ethics are independent of his materialism and science more explicitly in (1908). Although written thirty years before his important article, and contradicting it on some points (see, e.g., 1908: 81), this otherwise slight volume seems to me to anticipate the Strauss thesis as pronouncedly as do those of Robertson and Stephen.

21 For a similar view, see also Wilson (1979: esp. 50–1).

Hobbes's systematic pretenses came to be widely shared. Even Richard Peters's 1956 book, *Hobbes*, which offered a relatively systematic and sympathetic examination of all aspects of Hobbes's thought, ended with the harsh conclusion that Hobbes's use of science had been nothing but "window dressing" for an "insecure dogmatist" (1956: 214).[22] Hobbes's prized reputation as the paradigmatic system builder had apparently been repudiated, and this helped pave the way for the avalanche of increasingly specialized Hobbes scholarship that followed.

Amid the torrent of such works that has appeared over the past thirty years, three books in particular have attempted to rebut the view that Hobbes was a moralist and not a scientist. The works of J. W. N. Watkins (1965), M. M. Goldsmith (1966), and Thomas A. Spragens, Jr. (1973), all take Strauss as their primary target, and all urge us to be more mindful of Hobbes's systematic intent, and to take his repeated declarations of this intent seriously.

Watkins argues that Hobbes adopted the resolutive-compositive method of science championed especially at the University of Padua, and that this had important consequences for his political philosophy. The method of Galileo (whom Hobbes praises as having "opened to us the gate of natural philosophy universal" [*Co:* viii]) involved resolving an object of study down to its primary components, and then studying how they are composed back into the original whole. Watkins claims that Hobbes applied this method to the study of politics, and that the result was his analysis of the state of nature, and his defense of the social contract. Insofar as this renders Hobbes's science important to his politics, it represents a response to the attack led by Strauss. But Watkins goes on to explain that the conclusions Hobbes thereby reached are in no sense moral conclusions, and that the rules prescribed by the laws of nature have no moral character (1965: esp. 51–7). Watkins's Hobbes is a value-free social scientist, investigating and explaining human activity, but offering no moral evaluation of it. Thus, although Watkins self-consciously takes Strauss to be his fundamental adversary, he ultimately capitulates to the central claim Strauss defended in its purest form: Hobbes's scientific and moral claims

22 T. S. Eliot reached much the same conclusion in his 1927 essay on Bramhall: Hobbes's "theory of government has no philosophic basis: it is merely a collection of discrete opinions, prejudices, and genuine reflections upon experience which are given a spurious unity by a shadowy metaphysics," the sort of "specious effect of unity" which "appears to be intellectual but is really emotional, and therefore very soothing to lazy minds" (1964: 313, 317).

are incompatible, so he must be either a scientist or a moralist, but not both. Watkins's contention that Hobbes can say everything he is saying without using the vocabulary of morality (1965: 56) is thus but the mirror image of Peters's claim that Hobbes has no need to use the vocabulary of science.

Goldsmith's book covers much the same ground as Watkins's and reaches much the same conclusion. Hobbes is again presented as a social scientist, applying the Galilean method to the body politic, and although this also renders Goldsmith a critic of Strauss, he follows Watkins in tacitly accepting the Straussian framework: Hobbes can be a scientist or a moralist, but he cannot be both. The laws of nature, on Goldsmith's account, are mere hypothetical imperatives lacking moral character, and the state of nature "describes that area in which morality does not exist" (1966: 173).[23]

Spragens's book, heavily influenced by Kuhn's writings on the role of paradigms in science, is in some respects interestingly different from the books of Watkins and Goldsmith. Spragens is concerned to show that, despite Hobbes's self-avowed rejection of Aristotelian science, he is not so much rejecting it as transforming it. Hobbes, according to Spragens, applied the new Galilean understanding of motion to the older philosophical framework, and came up with a new cosmological paradigm. This paradigm influenced Hobbes's political philosophy not by serving as a foundation for it, but rather by serving as a heuristic, a source of inspiration. This renders the link between science and politics weaker in Spragens's Hobbes than in the Hobbes of Watkins or Goldsmith; Spragens's position is not so much a philosophical claim about the nature of Hobbes's system of thought, as a psychological claim about the influences that inspired Hobbes to create it. This would seem to make Spragens's case difficult if not impossible to establish by reading Hobbes's texts,[24] and in any event, to the extent that

23 Andrzej Rapaczynski has more recently defended much the same view as that of Watkins and Goldsmith, arguing that Hobbes realized that "political philosophy in the seventeenth century had to be grounded in *modern* natural science, with its mechanistic approach," but maintaining that this can be understood only by insisting that Hobbes was engaged "in a purely descriptive and scientific, rather than a normative, inquiry" and that Hobbes must thus be understood as "a positivist" rather than a "moralist" (1987: 28, 61, 23).

24 Peter Machamer and Spyros Sakellariadis offer some useful criticisms of Spragens's position along these lines in section IV of (1989). The difficulty of establishing such a claim about heuristical influences within Hobbes's thinking is also reflected in the fact that one could account for much of the same textual evidence and reach precisely the opposite conclusion: that Hobbes's political

Spragens does read Hobbes as a systematic writer, he also ultimately agrees that Hobbes has no substantive moral theory. Hobbes does, according to Spragens, have a theory about morality, but it is the purely emotivist theory that all moral judgments are purely subjective. Thus Spragens, like Watkins and Goldsmith, allows Hobbes to be a scientist only at the cost of denying that he is a moralist.[25]

Tom Sorell's recent work is also motivated by the attempt to take Hobbes's systematic intentions seriously. Unlike Watkins, Goldsmith, and Spragens, Sorell seems willing to allow that Hobbes has a genuine moral theory and to insist that it constitutes a component of Hobbes's science. But Sorell's account of what Hobbes means by the claim that ethics is a science seems better suited to Hobbes's science of politics than to his science of morals. Thus Sorell, too, ultimately fails to give a satisfactory account on which Hobbes is both a scientist and a moralist.

In his book, *Hobbes,* and in a subsequent series of papers, Sorell rejects the claim that Hobbes "attempted a *reduction* of politics to physics," that "the strictly scientific content of Hobbes's politics [is] contributed by the inference from the passions, and its links with Hobbes's mechanistic psychology," the claim, in short, that "Hobbes's politics is scientific because of its deductive links with the natural sciences of psychology, physiology, and physics" (1988a: 524; 1990: 348; 1988b: 70). As Sorell points out, and as was noted at the outset of this section, Hobbes acknowledges that his civil philosophy can be understood independently of his natural philosophy, and so is in this sense autonomous (e.g., 1988b: 70–1; 1986: 7–

thinking served as a heuristic for his scientific thinking. A concern with order and disorder at the social level might inspire one to posit a mechanical model of motion at the scientific level. Thus, William T. Lynch has argued (with about the same degree of plausibility as Spragens) that "a pre-existing political *agenda* influenced the position that Hobbes would take in mechanical issues," that "the motivation for [Hobbes's mechanical] heuristic is politically rooted," that "we should think of Hobbes's political agenda as a kind of heuristic that a bounded rational agent could use to impose order on disparate fields of inquiry," and that Hobbes's system of thought presents "an example of politics enabling science" (1991: 298, 315, 319, 299).

25 Michel Verdon offers an interesting variation on Spragens's thesis, agreeing that the unity between Hobbes's science and politics is "analogical" but arguing that they rest on a Cartesian rather than Galilean transformation of Aristotle's theory of motion. Like Spragens, Goldsmith, Watkins, and Rapaczynski, though, Verdon, too, insists that as a result, Hobbes does not have a substantive moral theory but instead demonstrates "the relativity of morals" (1982: 653, 663).

13). In the table of philosophy from *Leviathan*, natural philosophy and civil philosophy are pictured as entirely independent, having in common only the fact that both are branches of philosophy, or science (*L:* 149). This is what motivates Sorell's alternative account of the sense in which Hobbes's civil philosophy retains a scientific status: It is scientific because of the deductive form of its argument, not because its conclusions rest in any way on the conclusions of natural science. For Hobbes, Sorell argues, "it is deductive structure that is crucial for the scientific status of a doctrine" (1990: 349). And this seems best to reflect Hobbes's analysis as reflected in the table of science.

Sorell, however, attempts to extend this analysis of the science of Hobbes's politics to the science of Hobbes's ethics, and this is where his analysis goes awry. Hobbes, on this account, does not base the scientific status of his ethics on "any content it shares with the natural sciences. In particular, he need not trade on any overlap between a mechanistic physics and ethics, though he thinks such an overlap exists." Instead, Sorell argues, what physics and ethics have in common on Hobbes's account "can only be described at a fairly high level of generality": It is simply that "they are both specimens of science. They both result from the exercise of the same cognitive capacity, namely the capacity for reasoning. They both result from reasoning guided by method" (1986: 12, 26).

This analysis is plausible if moral philosophy is viewed as a part of civil philosophy, and it is clear that this is how Sorell views Hobbes's understanding of the relationship between the two. Hobbes, he writes, "maintained that moral and political knowledge could be acquired by someone quite ignorant of geometry and physics. So he allowed for a kind of independence of civil science from the rest of science" (1988a: 520). But, as was also noted above, Hobbes distinguishes moral knowledge from political knowledge, and whereas the knowledge of "POLITIQUES" is indeed to be found in civil philosophy, the knowledge of "ETHIQUES" is to be found in natural philosophy (*L:* 149). Sorell overlooks this important distinction, and this undermines the plausibility of his account of Hobbes's science of morals. Although Sorell's account does identify a kind of unity between ethics and natural science, it is, as on Spragens's account, a largely analogical affinity. Ethics is taken to be similar to physics, in that both employ roughly the same sort of reasoning, rather than a branch of physics, as the table of sciences following Chapter 9 of *Leviathan* (*L:* 149) unambiguously indicates.

The existing literature on Hobbes, as this abbreviated but representative survey makes clear, offers essentially two alternatives: Hobbes is a scientist who uses the language of morality as window dressing, or he is a moralist who uses the language of science as window dressing. The attempt to vindicate his science of politics has proved a tacit repudiation of his science of morals. Thus, in his attack on the traditional view of Hobbes as a systematic thinker, Strauss may have lost the battle, but he is, at least to this point, clearly winning the war.[26]

1.2 OVERVIEW

A guiding thought behind this work is that to understand Hobbes as a moralist one must also understand him as a scientist. Hobbes's project is to defend a theory of moral virtue by grounding it in a science of human nature, to justify a largely familiar doctrine of morality in a largely unfamiliar way. The tasks of this study are to explain how Hobbes accomplishes this and to suggest that his project merits consideration by those who recognize the importance of virtue to moral philosophy. Although an important feature of this enterprise is that it can thereby vindicate Hobbes's reputation as a systematic thinker, this vindication is not in itself an immediate goal. I am concerned to defend a particular interpretation of Hobbes's moral theory, one that understands his ethics to culminate in a theory of moral virtue, but in doing so I hope also to illustrate the soundness of the broader claim that Hobbes is best understood as a moral scientist.

In accord with this guiding orientation, the body of the book takes the following shape: Chapter 2 offers an account of Hobbes's science of human nature, beginning with his understanding of scientific method and focusing on those elements of his view of human nature that are most relevant to his pursuit of a moral science. Chapter 3 addresses the problem of interpreting Hobbes's moral theory, and after considering some of the perspectives prom-

26 This seems to be the case even among works on Hobbes that attack the Strauss thesis only peripherally. Sheldon Wolin, for example, limits his critique of Strauss's "brilliant but overly ingenious book" to a single endnote. Although Wolin therefore follows Watkins and others in emphasizing the connection between Hobbes's science and politics, he too denies that Hobbes has a genuine moral theory: The laws of nature, he insists, "were not designed to make Hobbesian men moral in any sense except in a tautologically political one. [They] were not intended to disclose the 'nature of things' or the substance of morality, but only to prescribe how men ought to act within a system of rules" (1960: 478–9, n. 124, 268).

inent in the literature, concludes that it is best understood as a theory of moral virtue. Chapter 4 examines Hobbes's attempt to justify this moral theory by grounding it in his science of human nature. This is shown to involve two independent and complementary arguments which lead from the desirability of avoiding anarchy to the value of cultivating the moral virtues. Chapter 5 initiates the project of assessing the merits of Hobbesian virtue ethics by asking how it would answer some of the questions posed by those who have sought in recent years to revive the tradition of giving virtue a central place in moral philosophy.

Before we can turn to the task of examining the descriptive and normative components of Hobbes's system and offering an account of their relationship, however, a few preliminary points must be made. The first is that, for Hobbes, science and philosophy are one and the same thing, the body of the knowledge of consequences. "The Registers of Science," he says in the *Leviathan,* "are such *Books* as contain the *Demonstrations* of Consequences of one Affirmation, to another; and are commonly called *books of Philosophy*" (*L:* 148).[27] When we interpret Hobbes as a moral scientist, we must be careful not to import our own views of science uncritically into Hobbes's worldview. To say that Hobbes is a moral scientist is to say that, for him, ethics is a branch of natural philosophy, of the study of the consequences of the accidents of natural bodies. A study of Hobbes's ethics must therefore begin with a study of his views of science and human nature, and although the account offered in Chapter 2 does not pretend to novelty at every point, it is nonetheless important to the novelty of the interpretation of Hobbes that emerges from this study: that he seeks to defend a largely traditional set of moral virtues in a largely untraditional way.

A second point, though a simple one, is often obscured in discussions of Hobbes's philosophical system:[28] The claim that Hobbes's moral philosophy is a part of his natural philosophy is distinct from, and independent of, the claim that he developed his natural philosophy before he developed his moral philosophy. Even if Hobbes's normative writings enjoy a temporal priority among his works, this tells us nothing about the content of his normative writings or how it is related to the content of his writings in natural philosophy.

The fact that the three sections of Hobbes's *Elements of Philosophy*

27 See also, e.g., the treatment of philosophy in *Co:* 1.2ff.

28 See, e.g., Strauss (1936: 29).

were published out of order may nonetheless generate some psychological resistance to the view of Hobbes as a moral scientist. It is therefore worth pointing out that the order in which Hobbes's works were first published does not establish the order in which they were first developed. Recent historical scholarship by Richard Tuck has in fact provided an impressive array of evidence for the view that "all three *sectiones* of [the *Elements of Philosophy*] were drafted by 1640" and that "Hobbes had actually written up his general philosophy in almost as detailed a form as his civil philosophy by 1641" (1988a: 26, 16).[29] Even after *De Cive* was published in 1647, many people continued to think of Hobbes as primarily a scientist, though the figure of Hobbes as a natural philosopher, as one recent work has noted, has since all but "disappeared from the literature" (Shapin and Schaffer [1985: 21]).[30] Even if it were true that Hobbes had not written on such subjects as motion and causation before publishing his first works on ethics and politics, this would not show that he had not been thinking about such issues.[31] Although we might be tempted to endorse the dubious view that a

29 As part of his case, Tuck argues that the English translation of Hobbes's preface to *De Cive* cited at the beginning of section 1.1 is misleading. Rather than describing what he "would have" discussed in the first and second sections of the *Elements*, Tuck insists that Hobbes simply says what Section One "contains" and what Section Two "deals with," thereby emphasizing that the other sections already existed "a few years before the Civil War" (1988a: 19–20). Although Tuck does not note this, his position also makes sense of the fact that Hobbes says that circumstances "ripened and plucked from me this third part," implying not that the other sections were nonexistent at this time but, rather, that none of the three was yet fully ready for consumption. Tuck's claims about the authenticity of the piece attributed to Hobbes and published as the "Short Tract on First Principles" are discussed in Chapter 2, footnote 5.

30 For evidence that "in the late 1640s [Hobbes] was thought of by many people principally as a scientist," see Malcolm (1988: 51ff). In an earlier paper, Malcolm offers the intriguing (though largely speculative) suggestion that Hobbes's interests in science may be traced back as far as his involvement with the Virginia Company in the early 1620s (1981: 316–17). That Hobbes was held in high esteem as a natural philosopher by his contemporaries is perhaps best attested to by the testimony of Samuel de Sorbière, who provides the only independent contemporary account of Hobbes's relationship with the Royal Society. Sorbière writes that it was agreed "on all hands, that if Mr Hobbes were not so very dogmatical, he would be very useful and necessary to the Royal Society, for there are few people that can see further into things then he, or have applied themselves so long to the study of natural philosophy" (quoted in Skinner 1969: 222).

31 One reason to suppose that he had been thinking about such issues may well lie in his first published work, the 1628 translation of Thucydides. The topic of

moral scientist must begin with natural philosophy before turning to ethics, we cannot confidently exploit this prejudice to discredit the reading of Hobbes as a moral scientist.

An ambiguity may arise from the fact that this work seeks both to interpret and, to a certain extent, to promote the merits of another's writings. The outside reader of G. E. Moore's dissertation on Kant, for example, noted with some frustration that it was often difficult to determine "whether Mr. Moore is interpreting Kant, or expressing his own views,"[32] and although I have tried to avoid it, the same ambiguity may at times frustrate the reader of this work with respect to my own views and those I attribute to Hobbes. In Chapters 2 through 4, I am concerned to interpret Hobbes's ethics, and in Chapter 5, I try to show that Hobbes may have an important contribution to make to the recent revival of virtue ethics. This study does, therefore, endorse the merits of a Hobbesian approach to virtue ethics, at least to the extent of recommending it as deserving of more attention than it has to this point received, but in doing so it is not committed to defending every detail of the theory as Hobbes presents it. In this respect, when the book attempts to speak for Hobbes, it does not thereby speak for me. I must also register a certain tentativeness with respect to this evaluation, which I take to be part of an ongoing project. My hope is that I may have carried out the task of attributing a novel theory of virtue to Hobbes with enough success to encourage others to join me in assessing the merits of the theory itself.

A fourth preliminary point must also be acknowledged: To call a moral theory a virtue theory can mean a number of things. A complete explanation of what this amounts to in the case of Hobbes can only emerge after Hobbes's theory has been explained

Thucydides' *History* is *kinesis,* "the greatest commotion that ever happened amongst the Grecians" (*EW* VIII: 2). Thucydides' conception of motion has been described as linear, and thus "quite 'Galilean' in the larger sense of the word," and at least one recent writer has therefore suggested that "Hobbes's praise of Thucydides indicates that his views on motion, sequence, time, cause, and, hence, power, were well formed before his discovery of Euclid and Galilieo" (Brown 1989: 226, 216). For the argument that Hobbes valued Thucydides' work primarily for its methodological focus on identifying causes, and that "in translating Thucydides, Hobbes had already displayed a concern with an ideal of scientific knowledge," see also Gigliola Rossini (1987: 310; see esp. secs. I–II). Laurie M. Johnson attempts to undermine the apparent affinities between Thucydides and Hobbes in her recent study (1993).

32 Edward Caird, quoted in Tom Regan (1986: 87).

in some detail.[33] To avoid confusion as we proceed, it may be useful to state that, according to the interpretation defended here, Hobbes is not saying merely that traits of character should be included in the class of objects to be assessed by morality as good and bad, nor is he insisting that traits of character should be the only objects included in that class. What Hobbes maintains is that vindicating the goodness of certain traits of character is the ultimate task of moral philosophy, and that although moral philosophy must concern itself with such subjects as actions and rules for actions in order successfully to accomplish this principal task, such concerns are important to the extent that they contribute to this task, to the vindication of the moral virtues. Hobbes's theory, on this account, is agent-centered in the sense that evaluating an agent's character is understood to be the central task of ethics, but it is not agent-centered in what has come to be a more technical sense of the term: He does not claim that the notion of a just person is more fundamental than that of a just act. The notion of a just act, according to the account of Hobbes offered here, is not derivative from the notion of a just person, but rather subordinate to it. Hobbes's moral theory is concerned to illuminate the nature of just acts, so it can illuminate the importance of being a just person.

Finally, a few words must be said about which parts of the Hobbesian corpus should serve as the focus of our attempt to understand Hobbes's moral theory. *Leviathan* is Hobbes's best-known work, and many have treated it as the primary if not exclusive source material in examining Hobbes's considered normative views.[34] Other writers have disdained *Leviathan* as a merely polemical popular statement of doctrines more carefully and satisfactorily elaborated in other works, especially in *De Cive*.[35] There are, no

33 See Chapter 5 and, in particular, section 5.2.

34 The presumption that "the English text of *Leviathan* contains the definitive presentation of Hobbes's civil philosophy" is often accepted without argument, but F. C. Hood presents an extensive defense of it in (1964: 41–56).

35 Bernard Gert, for example, argues that although "as literature *De Cive* does not rival *Leviathan*, which is a masterpiece of English prose style, it is superior to it as philosophy" (1978: 3). Sterling Lamprecht maintains that "*Leviathan* is [Hobbes's] greatest contribution to *belles lettres* . . . But intellectually and philosophically it is not as fine as the *De cive*" (1940: 35). A. E. Taylor insists that *Leviathan*, though "far the most readable and amusing of [Hobbes's] works" is "a rhetorical and, in many ways, a popular *Streitschrift*," and Taylor relies almost exclusively on evidence from *De Cive* in defending his own interpretation of Hobbes (1965: 36, 35). It is also worth noting that among some of

doubt, differences in tone, emphasis, and (at least on some specific matters) substance among Hobbes's various works, but this need not force a choice on us in our present task. The components of the moral theory here attributed to Hobbes are to be found in essentially the same form in *Leviathan* and *De Cive*, as well as in *De Homine* and the *Elements of Law*, and evidence for the interpretation will therefore be cited when appropriate from a wide variety of Hobbes's texts.

This more inclusive approach has the advantage of making a fuller use of Hobbes's writings than is often done in studies of his ethics, but it is not without its problems. As William James complained in a letter to the author of a dissertation dealing similarly with his own philosophy,[36] "You take utterances of mine written at different dates for different audiences belonging to different universes of discourse, and string them together as the abstract elements of a total philosophy which you then show to be inwardly incoherent. This is splendid philology, but is it live criticism of anyone's *Weltanschauung?*" Hobbes also wrote over a long period of time, for different audiences, in different forms, in different languages, and for different purposes, and the artificial nature of reading his entire works as a single text must surely be acknowledged.

But if it is in a sense unfair to Hobbes to collapse all his writings into a single whole, it is even more misleading to dwell on only a few of his works, as if the many others did not exist. As Hobbes himself writes in *Leviathan*, "it is not the bare Words, but the Scope of the writer that giveth the true light, by which any writing is to bee interpreted; and they that insist upon single Texts, without considering the main Designe, can derive no thing from them cleerly" (*L:* 626). And, as James also understood, the hazards of this more eclectic approach need not prove insurmountable: "The whole Ph.D. industry of building up an author's meaning out of separate texts leads nowhere," he warned, "unless you have first grasped his center of vision, by an act of imagination." If the approach taken to Hobbes's writings in the following chapters is justified, it is on the grounds that in attending to both their bare words and their main design, it does reveal such a vision on the part of

Hobbes's earliest admirers, his now largely neglected work on *Human Nature* was considered to be his greatest achievement (Tonnies cites James Harrington and Diderot as two such examples in 1928: xi).

36 The letter is cited by James Collins in (1972: 401).

Hobbes, a vision that follows him throughout his many guises: social scientist, historian, classicist, literary critic, moralist, polemicist, humanist, author, translator, Christian, philosopher, citizen. That vision is one of the importance and value of the moral virtues, the essential contribution they make to human flourishing, and the genuine wisdom of those who cultivate them for their own sake.

Chapter 2

The science of human nature

2.0 OVERVIEW

Natural philosophy is concerned with propositions about natural bodies, and ethics, according to Hobbes's table of science, is a branch of natural philosophy. It follows that the domain of ethics is some subset of the universe of natural bodies, and in particular, the subset of human beings. To say that Hobbes's ethics constitute a moral science, then, is to say that he is an ethical naturalist of sorts, that his normative conclusions are the consequences of propositions about "the Qualities of *Men in Speciall*" and in particular about their passions, the "*Interiour Beginnings of Voluntary Motions*" that he also calls "endeavour" (*L:* 149, 118, 119). An account of Hobbes's moral theory must, on this view, begin with an account of these distinctively human qualities. This chapter therefore attempts to offer an account of Hobbes's science of human nature, beginning with his view of scientific method in general and then focusing on those elements of human nature that are most relevant to the treatment of his moral theory that follows in Chapter 3. After offering a brief account of Hobbes's materialism, the chapter develops an account of Hobbes's views of human desires (or "endeavours"), reason, and mortality. This chapter and the one that follows thus set the stage for Chapter 4, which analyzes Hobbes's attempt to ground his theory of moral virtue in his science of human nature.

2.1 SCIENTIFIC METHOD

The various statements about scientific methodology that are scattered throughout Hobbes's writings are at times confusing and, when taken as a whole, can seem wildly inconsistent. Depending on which passages have been emphasized (and on how they have been read), Hobbes has been portrayed as claiming that the propositions of science are purely *a priori*, and as insisting that they must rest on a body of verifiable evidence, as holding that the truths of science are demonstrable and certain, and that they are hypothetical and probabilistic, as maintaining that the great scientists in history are the great experimentalists, and that experiments play no meaningful role in scientific inquiry. It is possible that Hobbes is simply confused in what he says about natural philosophy, and that he has no single view of scientific method.[1] It must be conceded that on this, as on many other subjects, Hobbes's texts are not always entirely consistent, but his overall view of science may nonetheless prove more coherent than it might at first seem. There are, in a sense, two sides to Hobbes's philosophy of science, one geometrical, the other experimental, but in the end they seem to come together more cleanly than might be suspected, at least by those whose interests in Hobbes have not led them to examine his scientific writings directly.

2.1.1 Hobbes's love affair with geometry, as well as the fortuitous origin of their courtship, are well known:

> Being in a Gentleman's Library, Euclid's Elements lay open, and 'twas the 47 *El. libri* I. He read the Proposition. *By G*____, sayd he . . . *this is impossible!* So he reads the Demonstration of it, which referred him back to such a Proposition; which proposition he read. That referred him back to another, which he also read. *Et sic deinceps* [and so on] that at last he was demonstratively convinced of that trueth. This made him in love with Geometry. (Aubrey 1957: 150)

As Aubrey's story suggests, it was Euclid's demonstrative method, rather than his substantive conclusions, that attracted Hobbes to geometry.[2] As Hobbes makes clear in a number of passages, it was to the grounding of geometric proofs in clear definitions, in particular, that he attributed the power of that method. Since truth, on

1 F. S. McNeilly, for one, attributes all these views to Hobbes, arguing that "Hobbes did not adopt a single and consistent doctrine either of truth or of scientific method, but in different works – and sometimes in different parts of the same work – expressed a number of quite different and mutually incompatible views" (1968: 4).

2 Hobbes has more than a few unkind words for Euclid in his *Six Lessons to the Professors of the Mathematics*, deeming some of his definitions "inexcusable" and "intolerable," and maintaining that in his geometry "there be some few great holes" (*SL*: 202, 207, 245). The significance of the fact that, on Hobbes's view, geometrical definitions can prove to be mistaken is examined in section 2.1.3.

Hobbes's account, "consisteth in the right ordering of names in our affirmations, a man that seeketh precise *truth*, had need to remember what every name he uses stands for." Therefore, he concluded, "in Geometry, (which is the onely Science that it hath pleased God hitherto to bestow on mankind,) men begin at settling the significations of their words; which settling of significations, they call *Definitions;* and place them in the beginning of their reckoning" (*L:* 105). Definitions are thus the key to geometry and geometry is the model for science.

Hobbes's insistence that science follow geometry's axiomatic method is often taken to suggest that he means to maintain what is sometimes called a conventionalist view of science. As F. S. McNeilly puts it, "so far as the universal propositions of science are concerned . . . Hobbes seems to be asserting that they are true by virtue just of the definitions of their terms" (1968: 67).[3] When geometers "settle" on the "significations of their words," on this account, they simply agree to endow terms with meanings that are essentially arbitrary; when they prove that the internal angles of every triangle add up to 180 degrees, therefore, they are not uncovering a new fact about the world, but simply proving a proposition that is true by virtue of the definitions of the terms they have chosen. When Hobbes seeks to extend the geometrical method to the natural sciences, on this account, he therefore takes the same view of scientific propositions. As a more recent writer has put it in taking this view of Hobbes's science, "Like geometrical propositions, those of any other science are universal and abstract. Their truth is dependent upon the logical interconnections between them, not upon the extent to which they 'fit' or correspond to empirical reality" (Johnston 1986: 52). Geometry does seem, nonetheless, to provide knowledge that is useful in manipulating the natural world,[4] and, this view of Hobbes maintains, it would be understandable for Hobbes to think that other useful sciences could therefore be founded in the same way.

The conventionalist account of science thus often inferred from Hobbes's infatuation with geometry, moreover, seems to be borne out by a number of passages in his scientific writings. Much

3 Though, as noted above, McNeilly does not see this as the only view of science to be found in Hobbes's texts.

4 In the dedication prefacing *De Cive,* Hobbes boldly claims that all the improvements by which "this present age doth differ from the rude simpleness of antiquity, we must acknowledge to be a debt which we owe merely to geometry."

(though not all) of his early "Short Tract on First Principles," for example, proceeds (or tries to proceed) from stipulative definitions of terms to substantive conclusions about the natural world. Thus, after defining substance as "that which hath being not in another, so as it may be of it self" and accident as "that which hath being in another, so as, without that other it could not be," he concludes, from the meaning of these terms, that in nature, "everything is eyther Substance or Accident."[5] In the section on reasoning in *De Corpore,* he writes that "these three single names, *body, animated, rational,* are in speech compounded into this one name, *body-animated-rational,* or *man,*" and argues that "In like manner, of the several conceptions of *four sides, equality of sides,* and *right angles,* is compounded the conception of a *square,*" as if men and squares can equally be understood as the mere products of convention (*Co:* 1.3).[6] And in *Thomas White's De Mundo Examined,* Hobbes again seems to suggest that facts about the world can be uncovered merely by tracing deductive arguments back to the definitions of their terms:

5 "ST": 152–3. Richard Tuck has recently argued that "there is actually no evidence whatsoever that the Short Tract is by Hobbes" and has suggested, in light of the Tract's divergences from Hobbes's published views on optics, that it was more likely written by Robert Payne, a member of the Cavendish circle (1988a: 16–18). Tuck's argument has elicited a mixed response in the works on Hobbes that have since appeared. Robert Kraynak, for example, calls Tuck's position "plausible" in his recent study (1990: 133n.), but Perez Zagorin dismisses Tuck's claim as "groundless," his evidence as "remarkably slight" and his arguments as "mistaken and devoid of substance" (1993: 512, 508, 506), and Jean Bernhardt labels Tuck's scholarship on this matter "un modèle de ce qu'il faut éviter" [a model of what one must avoid] (1990: 23).

Tuck's argument would seem to be inconclusive at best, but the largely accepted view among scholars who have examined the relevant materials seems to remain that Hobbes did indeed write the "Short Tract," although when he did so is unclear (the consensus is that it was written between 1630 and 1636). So far as its content is concerned, William Sacksteder, a leading bibliographer as well as scholar of Hobbes, says that "I see no reason to think the ['Short Tract'] not to be from the same hand as the major works, nor to think it not to form part of the systematic thinking (despite revisions) for a very systematically committed philosopher" (correspondence with the author, 10 August 1990). Noting that its authenticity has been questioned but not clearly repudiated, I cite evidence from the "Short Tract" when it seems relevant, but I draw no conclusions from it that cannot be confirmed by at least two of Hobbes's other works.

6 He later says that "primary propositions" such as "*man is a body, animated, rational*" are "nothing but definitions, or parts of definitions, and these only are the principles of demonstration, being truths constituted arbitrarily by the inventors of speech, and therefore not to be demonstrated" (*Co:* 3.9).

If, when we state: 'The world is finite', what we say is true, then the world *is* finite; if the same applies with [the word] 'infinite', then the world is infinite. . . . Suppose the word 'world' also implies 'finite', that is, from something's being called 'world' the same thing is necessarily called 'finite'. Then we know that the world is finite; . . . If, however, the word 'world' also signifies 'infinite', then we know that the world is infinite. [Again], if 'world' signifies neither ['finite' nor 'infinite'], we do not know whether the world is finite or not; this is discoverable only by defining our terms. (*DME:* 28–9, bracketed words in original)[7]

The proposition "the world is finite" is true, Hobbes seems clearly to recognize at the beginning of this passage, if it correctly describes the world. But, he seems also to promise, its truth-value can nonetheless be discovered simply by attending carefully to the meaning of words.

The problem with the conventionalist methodology often attributed to Hobbes is obvious.[8] Truth, according to Hobbes, is a property of propositions, not of the objects to which they refer (e.g., *Co:* 3.7), but the propositions of philosophy are themselves propositions about bodies (e.g., *Co:* 1.8; *L:* 149), and whether the proposition that a particular body has a particular property is true or not would seem to be a problem that must be settled by examining the body itself, not by examining the definitions of the words which purport to refer to it. When Hobbes disputes the claim that man is a social animal, for example, he clearly believes that there is a fact of the matter about which he is right and Aristotle is wrong (*DC:* 1.2). If this is the case, then, as Hobbes in this instance seems to recognize, the matter must be settled by looking at people and not by looking at words. Yet Hobbes's insistence that science is the "knowledge of the truth of propositions, and how things are called" and that it is "the experience men have of the proper use of names in language" (*EL* I: 6.1) seems on the face of it to rule out such appeals to empirical facts. It makes it seem that the truths of science must all be analytically true, and this is the source of the charge, common from his day to the present, that although Hobbes praises (and compares himself to) such scientists as Galileo and

7 It is worth noting that Hobbes eventually concludes that the question is one for faith and not for science (*DME:* 32). It should be kept in mind that this text was first made public in 1973, and was thus unavailable to, for example, Watkins, Goldsmith, and McNeilly.

8 To say that the conventionalist methodology is flawed is not to show that Hobbes does not endorse it, but the fact that Hobbes seems to recognize its inadequacy should make more plausible the notion that this is not his considered view.

Harvey, his own view of science cannot accommodate the experimental methods by which their great successes were achieved.[9]

2.1.2 Readers familiar with this picture of the scientific Hobbes, whose laboratory is the armchair and whose only instrument for research is the dictionary, may be surprised by the chapter on "the principles and method of natural philosophy" in the *Decameron Physiologicum*. In it, *B* responds to *A*'s desire "to know the causes of the effects or phenomena of nature" by leading him through a series of simple definitions (e.g., motion, place, time) and basic axioms (e.g., "Two bodies, at the same time, cannot be in one place") which are to serve as the foundational principles of his reasoning (*DP:* 82–7). When *A* then asks if this is "all the preparation I am to make" in order to satisfy his curiosity about the natural world, *B* says no. For in addition to all of this, he insists that

> you must furnish yourself with as many experiments (which they call phenomenon) as you can. And supposing some motion for the cause of your phenomenon, try, if by evident consequence, without contradiction to any other manifest truth or experiment, you can derive the cause you seek for from your supposition. If you can, it is all that is expected, as to that one question, from philosophy. For there is no effect in nature which the Author of nature cannot bring to pass by more ways than one. (*DP:* 88)

Here we have a picture of both the nature of scientific propositions and the method by which they are established that differs significantly from the one at times attributed to the geometrical Hobbes. Instead of being universal statements that are true by virtue of the meanings of their terms, scientific claims are presented as hypothetical explanations that can only be asserted as possible (or at best probable) causes of natural phenomena. And the claims themselves are justified not by simply examining the meanings of the

9 One of the earliest of Hobbes's critics to take this view was Robert Boyle, who charged that Hobbes "endeavoured to disparage unobvious experiments themselves, and to discourage others from making them." The passage is cited by Shapin and Schaffer, who characterize Boyle's concern as the worry that "laboratory labour might be undone by armchair criticisms" (1985: 174). Among the more recent writers to maintain such a view are David Johnston: "Hobbes took almost no interest in the possibility of experimental falsification or verification, even in physical science" (1986: 51); Ralph P. Forsberg: "Hobbes came to conceive of science as deductive and non-empirical, and he scorned the use of experience or history in science as unreliable" (1990: 9); and Laurie M. Johnson: "Because science [according to Hobbes] involves the geometrical calculation of words alone, the test for truth is not its empirical verification but the soundness of its internal logic and its utility" (1993: 21).

terms they contain but by gathering as much experimental information as possible and seeing whether any of it falsifies them.

With respect to the first half of this view, despite the fact that Hobbes's science has at times been portrayed as deductive and certain, he is clear throughout his scientific writings that the propositions of natural philosophy are hypothetical and probabilistic.[10] Hobbes introduces the treatment of physics in *De Corpore,* for example, by saying that he is now turning to the part of philosophy "which is the finding out by the appearances or effects of nature, which we know by sense, some ways and means by which they *may* be, I *do not say they are,* generated" (*Co:* 25.1, emphasis added). And he concludes the work by reiterating that in the part on physics, "I have assumed no hypotheses, which is not both possible and easy to be comprehended; and seeing also that I have reasoned aright from those assumptions, I have withal sufficiently demonstrated that they *may* be the true causes; which is the end of physical contemplation" (*Co:* 30.15, emphasis added).[11] In *Seven Philosophical Problems,* he acknowledges that "The doctrine of natural causes hath not infallible and evident principles," and that "In natural causes all you are to expect, is but probability" (*SPP:* 3, 11). In the "Epistle Dedicatory" to *Six Lessons to the Professors of the Mathematics,* he recognizes that "because of natural bodies we know not the construction, but seek it from the effects, there lies no demonstration of what the causes be we seek for, but only of what they may be" (*SL:* 184). In the *Physical Dialogue of the Nature of the Air,* he allows that the role of the philosopher who studies natural phenomena is "to find the true or at least very probable causes of such things" (*PD:* 356). In the *Tractatus Opticus,* he writes that "nothing further is required in Physics . . . than that the motions we suppose or imagine are conceivable, that the necessity of the Phenomenon can be demonstrated from them, and that nothing false can be derived from them."[12] In the unpublished manuscript

10 This has also been clear in works focusing on Hobbes's natural philosophy, though often overlooked by others, at least since Brandt: "The positively characteristic feature of Hobbes' physics is in the first place that he seeks to demonstrate the *possible* causes of the natural phenomena, and this demonstration is based entirely upon geometrico-mechanical premises" (1928: 371, original in italics).

11 See also the author's epistle dedicatory: "In the three former parts of this book all that I have said is sufficiently demonstrated from definitions; and all in the fourth part from suppositions not absurd."

12 Cited and translated by Richard Tuck, in (1988b: 252).

"Mr Hobbes Concerning ye Compression of Aire" Hobbes avers that "further than possibility no man can goe in ye assigning of Naturall Causes" ("CCA": 275–98, 297).[13] A July 1636 letter from Hobbes to the Earl of Newcastle, which predates Hobbes's published writings on natural phenomena, includes the recognition that in "the greatest part of naturall philosophy, as dependinge upon the motion of bodies so subtile as they are invisible, such as ayre and spirits, the most that can be atteyned unto is to have such opinions, as no certayne experience can confute, and from which can be deduced by lawfull argumentation, no absurdity."[14] Although it is necessary that the natural philosopher "reason aright" from premises that are clear and sensible, this guarantees only that the resulting explanation of observed phenomena will be possible, not that it will be correct.

Much the same can be said about the second half of the view of scientific method represented in *B*'s response to *A* in the *Decameron Physiologicum:* Despite the somewhat familiar view that Hobbes has no use for experiments, he is clear throughout his scientific writings that experiments can be of great value. To rebut an argument of Thomas White's that seems to assume that fire always produces smoke, for example, Hobbes in his critique of *De Mundo* cites "an easy experiment to show that there can be fire without smoke" (*DME:* 84–5).[15] In *De Corpore,* he freely admits that his explanation of gravity is susceptible to empirical falsification, noting that "a certain consequent" of his account is that "heavy bodies descend with less and less velocity, as they are more and more remote from the equator," and agreeing that whether or not this is so is something that "experience must determine" (*Co:* 30.4). He concludes a lengthy consideration of various experiments concerning the behavior of water in the *Decameron* by having *B* declare that, "As for mean and common experiments, I think them a great deal better witnesses of nature, than those that are forced by fire, and known

13 The precise dating of the manuscript is unclear, but see the text of Schaffer's accompanying article for evidence dating it to 1664.

14 Quoted in Tuck (1988b: 250).

15 Although it must be admitted that the experiment is somewhat obscure: "If you place a burning-mirror opposite the sun, no smoke is seen before you move some dense matter to the combustion-point, and yet fire was present there before you do so" (*DME:* 85). In the same work, Hobbes also criticizes armchair scientists who "dare to philosophise about the skies" for acting as if "without looking into the heavens one could learn the 'natural qualities' of the firmament!" (*DME:* 96).

but to very few" (*DP:* 117).[16] He acknowledges in the dedicatory letter prefacing the *Physical Dialogue of the Nature of the Air* that as a result of the numerous experiments performed by the Royal Society, "it is not to be doubted that there may be some great consequence for the advancement of the sciences from their meeting" (*PD:* 347).[17] In the text of that work, Hobbes's strategy in disputing Boyle's claim to have produced a vacuum is not to deny the legitimacy of Boyle's reliance on experiment, but to accept and even to exploit it.[18] Thus, Hobbes tacitly concedes that alternative explanations of the experimental data used by Boyle to support the vacuum must be provided by the plenists, and he attempts to provide them himself (of the behavior of the air-pump itself, e.g., *PD:* 354–5; of the deaths of animals placed inside it, *PD:* 366–7).[19] Hobbes

16 The reference here is clearly to the Royal Society, which Hobbes elsewhere criticizes for not making its proceedings open to the public (e.g., *PD:* 350). That Hobbes attacks what he takes to be secret experiments, however, in no way suggests that he questions the value of experiment itself. The fact that he praises common experiments as "better witnesses of nature" indicates that he holds experiment itself to be of value, and only unverifiable and cumbersome experiments to be suspect.

17 Hobbes, it must be acknowledged, does insist at the same time that "they may meet and confer in study and make as many experiments as they like, yet unless they use my principles they will advance nothing." But the fact that Hobbes denies that experiments *alone* can produce scientific progress in no way suggests that experiments do not contribute to such progress.

18 That Hobbes's attack on Boyle constitutes an implicit attack on the experimental method itself is often assumed by those who have taken note of it. Quentin Skinner, for example, characterizes Hobbes's dialogue as an attack on "both Boyle and the experimental approach generally" (1969: 221). In a more recent survey of writings on Hobbes, Perez Zagorin writes that "Hobbes challenged the scientific findings based on Boyle's air pump and thereby also impugned the validity of the experimental method of which Boyle's invention was the symbol" (1990: 321). This is a mistake, however; Hobbes challenges Boyle's findings largely by showing they are not warranted by the experimental method, not by challenging the validity of the method itself. This assessment of Hobbes's response to Boyle also differs from that offered by Shapin and Schaffer in (1985). Although the picture of Hobbes developed in that work might broadly be described as antiexperimentalist, it is important to note that Shapin and Schaffer do not attribute to Hobbes the view that experiment is of no value at all: "The point to be made is not that Hobbes 'despised' experiment, nor that he argued that experiments ought not to be performed, nor even that experiments had no significant place in a properly constituted philosophy of nature. What Hobbes was claiming, however, was that the systematic doing of experiments was not to be equated with philosophy" (1985: 129).

19 Hobbes exploits the same strategy in the cited manuscript "Concerning ye Compression of Aire", discussing two recent experiments which had been

criticizes one of Boyle's experiments on the ground that it was poorly designed, and suggests how it might be improved (*PD:* 369); and he appropriates another for his own purposes, arguing that "no stronger or more evident argument could be devised against those who assert the vacuum than this experiment" (*PD:* 374). Even the treatise on *Human Nature* appeals to experimental evidence as proof of such claims as that color does not inhere in external objects (*EL* I: 2.5–2.7). In all this Hobbes assumes, and certainly never denies, that experiments are relevant to establishing scientific claims about nature. Indeed, when Descartes claimed in his *Dioptrics* that refracted light acts like a bullet fired at an angle into a solid surface, Hobbes did what any experimentalist worth his salt would do: He got himself an air gun and tested the theory.[20] Thus, despite the antiexperimentalist reputation Hobbes's writings at times seem to invite (an invitation all too often accepted), there is more than enough evidence to support the conclusion reached by Watkins: "The popular idea that Hobbes despised experiments . . . is incorrect. He only despised haphazard experimenting" (1965: 46n).[21]

cited as evidence of the compressibility of air and explaining how the results of each could be accounted for without assuming such compressibility ("CCA": 296). The same approach characterizes a 1648 letter from Hobbes to Mersenne: "Toutes les experiences faites par vous et d'autres, avec l'argent vif ne concluent pas qu'il y a du vuide, parceque la matiere subtile qui est dans l'air estant pressée passera a travers l'argent vif et travers tout autre cors fluide, ou fondu que ce soit. Comme la fumée passe a travers l'eau." [All the experiments done by you and others with mercury do not conclude that there is a vacuum, because fine matter which is in the air and being compressed will pass through the mercury and through all the other fluid bodies or melted material as the case may be. Just as smoke passes through water.] (LMM: 312). Hobbes appreciated the need to respond to the experimental evidence of Boyle and others on their own terms, and as at least one writer has recognized "[I]n the struggle of the mechanical philosophy against scholastic modes of explanation, Hobbes and Boyle stood side by side" (Applebaum 1964: 119).

20 Hobbes reports this in his *Tractatus Opticus*. Noel Malcolm notes this, along with the facts that Hobbes owned an impressive collection of telescopes and microscopes (including two telescopes by Torricelli), was the first person to give the correct dynamic explanation of the sine law of refraction, and performed dissections with William Petty (and possibly also with William Harvey), as evidence that Hobbes "was far from refusing to dirty his hands in practical science" (1988: 47). On the influence of Hobbes's optics in the seventeenth century, see Alan E. Shapiro (1973), which also offers an account of Hobbes's derivation of the sine law of refraction (1973: app. I).

21 Watkins was not the first writer to recognize this. Laird, for example, notes that "Hobbes did not despise experimental investigations" (1934: 116).

2.1.3 It is not difficult to see why Hobbes's readers have sometimes come away confused from his discussions of scientific method. He seems to want science to embody the analytic purity of geometry and at the same time accommodate the empirical relevance of experimentalism, to want scientific propositions to be both certain and probabilistic, *a priori* and *a posteriori*. Part of the problem, it must be conceded, can be attributed to Hobbes himself, whose writings are not entirely consistent. But a good deal of the blame must also be borne by Hobbes's readers, who have all too readily seized on his fascination with geometry without really considering what he has to say about it. The idea that geometrical definitions are purely arbitrary constructs, in particular, is alien to Hobbes's conception of geometry, and in this lies the key to reconciling the two faces of his scientific method.

Mathematical definitions, Hobbes writes in the *Principia et Problemata aliquot Geometrica,* "must not only be true, but likewise accurate." And "to define well," he adds, "that is so to circumscribe with Words the Thing in Hand, and that clearly, and with as much Bevity [sic] as can be, that no Ambiguity be left, is a very difficult Task, and not so much a Work of Art, as of the natural Intellect" (*PPG:* 113).[22] Far from being arbitrary constructs, therefore, definitions, according to Hobbes's account, even in geometry, are fixed by the nature of the "Thing in Hand" that is to be defined. As he puts it in *De Corpore,* "the nature of a definition consists in this, that it exhibit a clear idea of the thing defined" (*Co:* 6.15). Definitions can be clear or unclear, better or worse, right or wrong, true or false, depending on how well they correspond to the phenomenon they attempt to describe, and Hobbes does not hesitate to speak of definitions in this way throughout his scientific writings. In the critique of *De Mundo,* to take just one example, he argues that "The Aristotelian definition of place . . . is not true" (*DME:* 44). Strictly speaking, on Hobbes's view, only a proposition can be true or false, but his characterization here merely reinforces the view that, for Hobbes, a definition in a sense *is* a proposition: the proposition that a given set of criteria accurately captures the phenomenon named by the term being defined.[23] As he puts it in *De Corpore,*

22 See also footnote 2.

23 Thus Hobbes argues in *Leviathan* that "The Definition of the *Will,* given commonly by the Schooles, that it is a *Rational Appetite,* is not good. For if it were, then could there be no Voluntary Act against Reason" (*L:* 127). The definition is faulty because it fails accurately to circumscribe the phenomenon it purports to

definitions of universals "are nothing but the explication of our simple conceptions," so that, for example, "he that has a true conception of *place*, cannot be ignorant of this definition, *place is that space which is possessed or filled adequately by some body;* and so, he that conceives *motion* aright, cannot but know that *motion is the privation of one place, and the acquisition of another*" (*Co:* 6.6). This conception of a definition as a proposition whose truth depends on its correspondence to reality is clearly revealed in one of the extremely rare displays of humility in Hobbes's writings. "I confess," he admits in his *Six Lessons to the Professors of the Mathematics*, "your exception to my universal definition of parallels to be just" (although Hobbes cannot resist adding that it was "insolently set down") (*SL:* 254). Hobbes's original definition, he concedes, "is not, as it stands, universally true," and he proceeds to amend it so that "it is both true and universal" (*SL:* 254–5). The definition of parallel lines, on Hobbes's account, cannot simply be stipulated, for in that case there could be no such mistake for the author of the definition to make. Rather, the definition must be sought in, and tested against, the phenomenon it purports to define, and must be revised if it is found to come up short.

Finally, it is important to note that Hobbes maintains this approach to definition when he comes to consider the various properties of human beings. Hobbes begins his attempt to define reason in Chapter 5 of *Leviathan*, for example, by discerning (or at least claiming to discern) a common feature of arithmetical, geometrical, logical, political, and legal reasoning. In each case, he claims, the reasoner proceeds by adding and subtracting, though the object of these operations varies from discipline to discipline. After making these observations, he concludes: "Out of all which we may define, (that is to say determine,) what that is, which is meant by this word *Reason*, when wee reckon it amongst the Faculties of the mind. For REASON, in this sense, is nothing but *Reckoning* (that is, Adding and Substracting) of the Consequences of generall names agreed upon, for the *marking* and *signifying* of our thoughts" (*L:* 111).

Note the form of Hobbes's argument here. When we wish to define reason, we begin not with stipulation, but with observation. We observe the various operations that are called reasoning, that is, and we try to detect what they all have in common, what feature renders them all forms of reasoning, and not merely independent

define, accounting for only voluntary acts in accordance with reason instead of all voluntary acts.

and unrelated activities of the mind. If we look carefully (according to Hobbes, at least), we find that they all amount to different forms of adding and subtracting, and it is only "out of all" this that we are permitted to advance our definition with confidence. Definitions, that is, must ultimately be rooted in facts about the world, facts which can only be uncovered by observation. Once definitions are properly settled on, they can be combined with the sorts of axioms that *B* describes in the *Decameron,* and used in the sort of deductive reasoning that Hobbes's science seeks to borrow from geometry. The definitions in science, that is, the elementary propositions about natural bodies, must remain open to revision in light of new evidence, but the scientist can nonetheless "reason aright" from those definitions that best fit the evidence to find conclusions that follow inexorably from them. In this way, Hobbes can reasonably claim to maintain a view of science that benefits from the example of geometry without becoming detached from empirical reality.

What is the significance of all this for Hobbes's attempt to develop a science of morals? In *De Homine,* Hobbes speaks of "the evidence on which rests the science of causes; in truth, natural history for physics and also civil histories for civil and moral science" (*DH:* 11.10). In Part I of *De Corpore,* he allows that whereas *"history,* as well *natural* as *political"* is not itself science, it is nonetheless "most useful (nay necessary) to philosophy" (*Co:* 1.8). The propositions of moral science must be arrived at by "right reasoning" which begins with the "Qualities of *Men in Speciall,*" but these qualities cannot simply be agreed to by stipulation; they must be uncovered by investigation. Everyone knows which bodies are picked out by the name "human," and defining the term is a matter not of fiat, but of providing a clear and salient set of criteria that accurately picks out those bodies, and only those bodies.[24] Thus Hobbes criticizes those who "either suppose, or require us or beg of us to believe, that man is a creature born fit for society." Such theorists defend a view of human beings by simply assuming or stipulating that sociability is a part of human nature, and thus, although "on this foundation they so build up the doctrine of civil society," the "axiom" from which they begin is "certainly false; and an error proceeding from our too slight contemplation of human nature" (*DC:* 1.2).

It is true that Hobbes frequently likens his moral science to ge-

24 Although this is not true in borderline cases: "Upon the occasion of some strange and deformed birth, it shall not be decided by Aristotle, or the philosophers, whether the same be a man or no, but by the laws" (*EL* II: 10.10).

ometry, and this has sometimes been taken to mean that his moral science cannot justifiably draw on the sort of empirical considerations that he here acknowledges to be necessary.[25] But the apparent tension between the geometrical and empirical elements of Hobbes's approach to science disappears when we realize that he would say precisely the same thing of a mistaken geometer that he here says of the mistaken social scientist. An axiom defining parallel lines, like one defining human beings, is capable of being wrong when it is built from an inadequate understanding of the true nature of the phenomenon it seeks to circumscribe, and whatever conclusions about parallel lines derived from it are for that reason suspect. If Hobbes must similarly refer to experience, introspective or otherwise, to ground the picture of human nature that serves as the foundation for his moral science, then, this is not (as Strauss and others often seem to suggest)[26] a sign that his argument is departing from his scientific method. As at least one writer has noted, "the idea that [Hobbes's science] was strictly deductive and *a priori* – a view so often attributed to Hobbes – . . . is mistaken. Hobbes insisted that his knowledge began from his observations of men and manners and thus was, in principle, accessible to anyone able to look at the world and follow, with Hobbes, the steps of his analysis" (Danford 1978: 11). In defending the content of the science of human nature to which we must now turn, we should not be surprised to see this sort of combination of *a priori* and empirical considerations at work. "If you will be a philosopher in good earnest," as Hobbes says in *De Corpore*'s epistle to the reader, "let your reason move upon the deep of your own cogitations and experience."

2.2 BODY

To say, as Hobbes does, that ethics is the branch of natural philosophy concerned with the passions of human beings, is to say that

25 Johnston's book, although reliable in many respects, again provides a clear example of this view: "Like that of a geometrical theorem, the truth of a scientific proposition about human nature was not dependent, for [Hobbes], upon its accuracy as a representation of empirical reality" (1986: 122).

26 Strauss, for example, writes that "Hobbes's political philosophy . . . is not derived from natural science but is founded on first-hand experience of human life," as if the use of first-hand empirical evidence is excluded from Hobbes's account of natural science (1936: 29).

the inner workings of human beings can be understood as natural bodies. Hobbes was aware of Descartes's famous denial of this claim, so it is not surprising that the defense of his own position is intimately connected with his reasons for finding Descartes's views unconvincing. The claim that human beings are thoroughly material creatures forms the foundation for Hobbes's science of human nature – "body," after all, comes first in Hobbes's equation of "man" with "body-animated-rational" – and thus a brief treatment of his rejection of Descartes's dualism is at the same time an introduction to his own understanding of human nature. The claim that human beings can be understood in purely material terms, moreover, is not incidental to the defense of his moral science, despite the fact that commentators on Hobbes's ethics have rarely paused to consider it. The claim is important in a general sense, since the treatment of the mind as a complex physical object allows it to be treated as something that can be subsumed under general natural laws. And it is important in a more specific sense: It provides the foundation for Hobbes's analysis of habituation, which in turn plays an important role in his defense of virtue.[27]

Hobbes accepts the Cartesian inference from "I think" to "I am," and he does not object to Descartes's description of himself as "a thinking thing." When Descartes amplifies this characterization by adding "that is, I am a mind, or intelligence, or intellect or reason," however, he implicitly introduces the contention that this thinking thing is also a noncorporeal thing, and at this point Hobbes identifies a problem: "It does not seem to be a valid argument to say, 'I am thinking, therefore I am thought' or 'I am using my intellect, hence I am an intellect.' I might just as well say 'I am walking, therefore I am a walk'" ("O": 122). There is a difference, Hobbes sensibly insists, between a subject that performs a given action and the faculty or property in virtue of which it is able to do so. He therefore concludes, "it may be that the thing that thinks is the subject to which mind, reason or intellect belong; and this subject may thus be something corporeal. The contrary is assumed, not proved" ("O": 122). The fact that I think does not establish that I am a nonmaterial entity, and Hobbes goes on to argue that, if anything, it suggests the opposite: "We cannot conceive of jumping without a jumper, of knowing without a knower, or of thinking without a thinker. It seems to follow from this that a thinking thing

27 See section 4.4.

is something corporeal" ("O": 122). This suggestion is inconclusive at best,[28] but his overall objection raises an important doubt about the foundation of Descartes's ontological dualism, and it establishes early in Hobbes's published writings that he is inclined to understand mental phenomena materialistically.

Hobbes stands by and develops his claim that humans are purely material mechanisms throughout his philosophical works, and as we might expect from the above analysis of his views on method, the argument in defense of this basic tenet of his science of human nature rests on a combination of *a priori* reasoning and empirical considerations. In *De Corpore,* for example, where the argument is perhaps most fully developed, Hobbes's position rests largely on the claim that "it is necessary that mutation can be nothing else but motion of the parts of that body which is changed" (*Co:* 9.9).[29] That this is to be understood as a purely analytic truth is suggested by both Hobbes's description of its content as "necessary" and the fact that it is treated in Part II, on "The First Grounds of Philosophy," in which Hobbes later insists "I have affirmed nothing . . . which is not sufficiently demonstrated to all those, that agree with me in the use of words and appellations" (*Co:* 25.1). Both these comments suggest that the truth of the claim that "all change is motion of the parts of the body changed" can be discerned simply by attending to the meaning of its various terms.

The analytic status of this proposition is also confirmed by Hobbes's attempt to demonstrate its truth. For although the demonstration itself is somewhat unclear and perhaps question-begging, it is nonetheless clear that the premises on which it is meant to rest are themselves supposed to be analytically true. Hobbes describes the first of these as "we do not say anything is changed, but that which appears to our senses otherwise than it appeared formerly," and the first four words here betray the claim's stipulative character: If an object does not appear to us to be in any sense different, then we do not say that it is changed. For the second, Hobbes refers to an earlier claim that can be summarized as follows: If body A acts on body B at t_1 and again at t_2, and if all parts of A and all parts of B are in the same state at t_1 as they are at t_2, then the effect

28 As Descartes replies, "It may be that the subject of any act can be understood only in terms of a substance . . . but it does not follow that it must be understood in terms of a [material] body" (1984: 124).

29 This foundational principle appears throughout Hobbes's scientific writings (e.g., *DP:* 129).

of *A* on *B* will be identical at both times (*Co:* 9.8). Hobbes treats this claim as "manifest of itself" and does not offer a more elaborate explanation, but it seems likely from his comments in defense of the principle of inertia (see *Co:* 8.19) that he has in mind what would now be called the principle of sufficient reason: *A*'s effect on *B* at t_2 is not different from its effects at t_1 because there is no reason for it to be different. For *A*'s effect on *B* to be different at the two times would thus amount to there being an effect without a cause, something Hobbes treats as essentially a contradiction in terms.[30]

Hobbes cites these two avowedly analytical propositions as grounds for the claim that all change is motion of the parts of bodies, and his argument, though not entirely clear, seems to be this (*Co:* 9.9): Suppose something changes. Then, by the first proposition, it follows that something is now appearing to me in a way that it was not appearing to me before. So this something is producing an effect on me that is different from the effect it was producing on me before. Now, by the second proposition, if all the parts of this something and all the parts of me are in the same place as they were before, then the effect produced on me by this thing will be the same. The effect, however, is not the same, and it follows that some part of the object or of me (or of both) is not where it was before. This "relinquishing of one place, and acquiring of another" by some body or its parts is motion (*Co:* 8.10).[31] Change, therefore, is motion of the parts of the body changed.

Although Hobbes's defense of the claim that all change is motion of bodies proceeds without depending on empirical evidence, the claim represents only half of his defense of his mechanistic treatment of the mental. To the claim that all change is motion of bodies, he must add the claim that our ideas or mental phantasms do, in fact, change. This claim is clearly an empirical one. We know that it is true that "our phantasms or ideas are not always the same," he says, because this is something "we may observe" (*Co:* 25.1). Hobbes's defense of materialism, like Descartes's rejection of it, thus turns crucially on the thinker's unavoidable recognition that he or she is thinking. But unlike Descartes, Hobbes insists on a

30 It is also possible that Hobbes instead (or in addition) has in mind something more like the principle of the uniformity of nature, and is assuming that observed regularities in nature justify the conclusion.

31 The complete definition also stipulates that motion is a "continual" relinquishing of location, but this requirement, by which Hobbes means to exclude the possibility of quantum movements, is not relevant to the present discussion.

second conclusion from which even the most radical skeptic cannot escape: Thoughts change.[32] From this fundamental feature of the phenomena of our mental life, Hobbes concludes that "it is manifest, that they are some change or mutation in the sentient" (*Co:* 25.1). With this, Hobbes is ready to conclude his argument. For referring back to his earlier conclusion,[33] Hobbes now makes essentially the following argument (*Co:* 25.2): All change is motion of the (physical) parts of the thing changed; ideas are properties which change in the person experiencing them; therefore, ideas are (physical) parts of the person experiencing them. As Hobbes puts it, "Sense, therefore, in the sentient, can be nothing else but motion in some of the internal parts of the sentient."

In *De Corpore,* exploiting the combination of empirical and a priori considerations that characterizes his scientific method, Hobbes establishes the materialistic foundation for his science of human nature, and more fully defends his earlier claim in reply to Descartes that "it seems that the correct inference [from 'I am thinking'] is that the thinking thing is material rather than immaterial" ("O": 123). The famous *cogito ergo sum* is subtly but radically transformed: I think, therefore I am matter.

2.3 ANIMATED BODY

Man, according to Hobbes's definition, is not only a material body but also an animated body; the branch in his table of science passes from physics through "Consequences from the Qualities of *Animals*" before finally arriving at the particular domain of bodies with which ethics is concerned (*L:* 149). Having briefly examined Hobbes's fundamental claim that man is a body, we must next consider what he understands by the claim that man is also an animal. "There be in Animals two sorts of *Motions* peculiar to them," Hobbes maintains (*L:* 118), and we must take account of what these distinctively animal motions are, how they are related, and what this implies about the nature of animal, and thus about the nature of human, desires.

2.3.1 The two sorts of motions which Hobbes identifies as distinguishing animals from all other bodies are vital motion, and

32 As Tuck observes in a slightly different context, "Descartes did in a way depict [the skeptic] as someone contemplating a single image in front of his mind's eye rather than the moving pictures postulated by Hobbes" (1989: 44).

33 Although in the Molesworth edition, at least, the text erroneously refers back to Chapter VIII instead of to IX.

animal or voluntary motion.[34] The vital motions of animate bodies are described as those "begun in generation, and continued without interruption through their whole life" and to which "there needs no help of Imagination." These are the motions that are necessary to life and that persist independent of the will. In *Leviathan,* Hobbes identifies these with "the *course* of the *Bloud,* the *Pulse,* the *Breathing,* the *Concoction, Nutrition, Excretion,* &c" (*L:* 118). In *De Corpore,* where Hobbes identifies the vital motion exclusively with "the motion of the blood, perpetually circulating . . . in the veins and arteries," he adds that this "hath been shown from many infallible signs and marks by Doctor Harvey, the first observer of it" (*Co:* 25.12). Thus, although Hobbes says little more in either work about the nature of the vital motions themselves, he is clear that they are known through observation and experience, and must thus be credited to the empirical side of his science of human nature.

The circulation of the blood may be established through observation, but Hobbes recognizes that the same cannot be said of any motion "where the thing moved is invisible; or the space it is moved in, is (for the shortnesse of it) insensible" (*L:* 118–9). This is precisely the case with the "small beginnings of [voluntary] Motion" that Hobbes identifies as "endeavour," and his treatment of voluntary motion therefore differs from his treatment of vital motion (*L:* 119). Hobbes initially describes voluntary motion in *Leviathan* as "to *go,* to *speak,* to *move* any of our limbes, in such manner as is first fancied in our minds," but this first characterization is potentially misleading. I might imagine being pushed out of a window immediately before being pushed out of it, for example, but this would not, in Hobbes's sense, qualify my plunge as a voluntary motion. There must be not merely a temporal, but a causal relationship between my first thinking of moving and my then moving, and this is more clearly indicated in Hobbes's subsequent claim that voluntary motions *"depend* alwayes upon a precedent thought" (*L:* 118, emphasis added). The salient difference between vital and voluntary motion is that voluntary motions are caused by the imagination, whereas vital motions are not.

34 Although Hobbes relies more on the term "animal motion" in *De Corpore* (*Co:* 25.12) and treats *"Voluntary motion"* merely as what *"Animall motion"* is "otherwise called" in *Leviathan* (*L:* 118), I use the term "voluntary motion" exclusively here, since it points more saliently to the feature that distinguishes it from vital motion, and since both vital motion and voluntary motion are, in a sense, forms of animal motion.

This causal relationship between imagination and voluntary motion is also crucial to what is, in *Leviathan,* Hobbes's very brief argument for the claim that the "endeavours" from which voluntary motions arise are to be understood literally, and not merely metaphorically, as the motions of bodies. Hobbes says that since voluntary motions depend on a prior thought "of *whither, which way,* and *what;* it is evident, that the Imagination is the first internall beginning of all Voluntary Motion," and that the invisibility of such tiny motions does not prove that they do not exist (*L:* 118–19). The argument from the claim that voluntary motions are ultimately caused by endeavors to the conclusion that these endeavors are bodies in motion is incomplete. Hobbes presumably means the conclusion to rest as well on the view found throughout his works, that only a body can cause another body to move. In *De Corpore,* for example, he writes that "Whatsoever is at rest, will always be at rest, unless there be some other body besides it, which, by endeavouring to get into its place by motion, suffers it no longer to remain at rest" (*Co:* 8.19, original in italics). In the *Decameron Physiologicum,* he describes as an "axiom" the principle that "whatsoever body being at rest is afterwards moved, hath for its immediate movement some other body which is in motion and toucheth it" (*DP:* 86).[35] Hobbes attempts to defend this axiom, as he did the axiom that all motion is change, without depending on empirical considerations; self-movement is treated as impossible, indeed as inconceivable; without an external body endeavoring to move it, a body at rest has no reason to move one way rather than any other. That imagination is the beginning of voluntary motion Hobbes presumably thinks can be discerned by all through simple introspection. But that it must therefore be composed of bodies in motion is not easily seen by "unstudied men" and can be shown only by reference to his axioms of motion. His analysis of voluntary motion, like his argument against Descartes, exemplifies the full range of his scientific method: Substantive conclusions are reached by combining basic observations with simple, self-evident axioms.

2.3.2 Both vital and voluntary motion, Hobbes insists, are to be

35 Hobbes holds this position as early as the "Short Tract," although it is spelled out there in different terms. He writes, "That which now resteth, cannot be moved, unless it be touched by some Agent," and "Whatsoever is Agent or Patient, is Substance," and his definition of "substance" as "that which hath being not in another, so as it may be of it self" comes close to his later conception of body (e.g., *Co:* 8.1) as *"a thing subsisting of itself"* and *"having no dependance upon our thought"* ("ST": 152–3).

understood literally as physical motions peculiar to animate bodies. How are the two related? In *De Corpore,* Hobbes offers the following account (*Co:* 25.12): Vital motion is influenced by the interaction between the agent and the external world. "For the original of life being in the heart," he argues, "that motion in the sentient, which is propagated to the heart, must necessarily make some alteration or diversion of vital motion, namely, by quickening or slackening, helping or hindering the same." External motions are translated into internal motions, that is, and Hobbes identifies the results with pleasure and pain. "Now when it helpeth, it is pleasure; and when it hindereth, it is pain, trouble, grief, &c." Pleasure and pain, in turn, provide the essential link between vital and voluntary motion. For the voluntary motions all originate with an endeavor. The endeavor is called appetite when toward something and aversion when away from something. A voluntary motion toward or away from something, therefore, is the external manifestation of the inner desire for or aversion to it, which is in turn a tiny motion generated in response to its helping or hindering of the vital motion.

Hobbes offers essentially the same account of voluntary motion, endeavor, appetite and aversion in *Leviathan,* although he says this time only that appetite "seemeth to be, a corroboration of Vitall motion, and a help thereunto," not that it in fact is (*L:* 122). This formulation seems more appropriate, since it brings Hobbes's description of his claims more closely in line with his stated method. Strictly speaking, his claim about the causal relation between vital and voluntary motions must remain conjectural, since, as we have seen, Hobbes is well aware that in nature effects might be produced by different causes. The study of animate bodies is one branch of the study of physics, that is, and the caveat with which Hobbes concludes the section on physics in *De Corpore* must therefore be kept in mind: that Hobbes has depended on hypotheses in developing his account, that the account must be taken only as an account of how things may be and not how they in fact are, and that "If any other man from other hypotheses shall demonstrate the same or greater things, there will be greater praise and thanks due to him than I demand for myself, provided," as Hobbes characteristically adds, "his hypotheses be such as are conceivable" (*Co:* 30.15).

The *Leviathan* account of animal motions differs from the account found in *De Corpore* more substantively in that Hobbes here spells out explicitly the relationship between endeavor and good and evil. Endeavor toward an object is appetite or desire, and away from it is aversion, and, Hobbes now adds, "whatsoever is the object of any mans Appetite or Desire; that is it, which he for his part calleth *Good:* And the object of his Hate, and Aversion, *Evill;* And of his Contempt [i.e., indifference], *Vile,* and *Inconsiderable*" (*L:* 120). Good and evil are introduced as subjective terms[36] that are "ever used with relation to the person that useth them," and with the chain of terms running from animal motion through good and evil now spelled out, our brief overview of Hobbes's account of animate bodies is in a sense complete.

2.3.3 The claim that all our voluntary motions are determined by and evaluated according to the extent to which they help or hinder our vital motions, however, leads inevitably to one of the truly perennial questions of Hobbes scholarship: Is Hobbes a psychological egoist? The answer depends largely on what one means by psychological egoism.

One commonsense definition of psychological egoism might run something like this: People[37] always act to satisfy their own desires. In this sense, Hobbes's analysis of animate bodies commits him to psychological egoism. Every voluntary act is causally determined by an originating endeavor which, when it is toward an object, Hobbes identifies as desire. A voluntary act, then, can be seen as an effort to satisfy a desire (where this is understood to include the desire to avoid things to which the agent is averse) by examining the meanings of the terms involved in the claim. Since Hobbes has further equated good and evil with what is and is not desired by the agent, this analytic status can also be extended to the correlative formulation that people always seek what they consider good (and avoid what they consider evil). These claims about people are analytically true on Hobbes's account, and the position they represent might thus best be described as "tautological egoism."[38]

Although tautological egoism may at first glance seem to capture the sense of selfishness that psychological egoism is typically taken to represent, in fact it says nothing about selfishness at all. For although it insists that people always act to satisfy their desires, it

36 As we shall see in section 3.1.1, this characterization of Hobbes's conception of good and evil as subjective is incomplete. His account leaves room for the possibility of a moral law that is objectively good for all people.

37 The formulations of psychological egoism which follow are expressed in terms of human beings, but they are meant to apply equally to all animals.

38 Bernard Gert (1978: 7) uses this term; see also Gert (1967).

says nothing at all about the content of those desires. As Bernard Gert has pointed out, it is perfectly consistent with tautological egoism for a person "to desire to help another, that is, to act from charity or benevolence. It is also possible for a man to desire to act justly, i.e., to act out of a moral sense" (1978: 7). It is equally consistent with a person's acting from an utter dislike for his own well-being. Tautological egoism may therefore be comfortably derived from Hobbes's science of animate bodies, but this fact cannot be used to burden Hobbes with the implausible view that people always act with an exclusive concern for their own welfare.

Yet this stronger form of psychological egoism is often understood to form an important corollary to Hobbes's analysis of the causes of voluntary motions,[39] and Hobbes does indeed seem to embrace such a view in a number of well-known passages. He is often portrayed, particularly in historical surveys of philosophy, as the founder of this view, as the father of economic man, the rational calculator concerned exclusively with maximizing his ability to serve his own interests. The claim that this picture of human selfishness follows from Hobbes's analysis of the cause of voluntary motions is often illustrated by a story Aubrey tells of Hobbes:

> One time, I remember, goeing in the Strand, a poore and infirme old man craved his Almes. He, beholding him with eies of pitty and compassion, putt his hand in his pocket and gave him 6d. Sayd a Divine that stood by, Would you have donne this, if it had not been Christ's command? Yea, sayd he. Why? quoth the other. Because, sayd he, I was in paine to consider the miserable condition of the old man; and now my almes, giving him some reliefe, doth also ease me. (Aubrey 1957: 157)

Alasdair MacIntyre calls Hobbes's reply to the vicar "a lie told in the interests of saving the face of a theory," and the theory he attributes to Hobbes is that "any regard for the welfare of others is secondary to a regard for, and indeed is only a means to, my own welfare" (1966: 136).

MacIntyre's analysis paints a familiar picture of Hobbes, and suggests that Hobbes means to draw the following lesson about his own nature (and by extension about human nature in general) from his encounter: I am concerned only with my own well-being, and not at all with the well-being of the old man. In considering

39 For example, David Gauthier (1969: 7) maintains that "From this account of vital and voluntary motion, it follows that each man seeks, and seeks only, to preserve and to strengthen himself. A concern for continued well-being is both the necessary and the sufficient ground of human action. Hence man is necessarily selfish."

whether to give him money, I ask only whether doing so will serve my interests, not whether it will serve his. I find that his misery causes pain to me. It is in my own interest to avoid such pain, and I decide to give him the money solely on these grounds. Thus, I am a psychological egoist in a sense stronger than that of tautological egoism. Not only do I always act to satisfy my own desires, but my only desire is to serve my own welfare. My desires are always, and entirely, self-regarding.

It is easy to see how this interpretation of Aubrey's story might be reached, but it is less easy to see how it can be sustained. Aubrey, for one, understood the story to show something altogether different about Hobbes: that Hobbes was a genuinely charitable man who was generous with "those that were true objects of his Bounty" (1957: 157).[40] And, contrary to MacIntyre's assertion that Hobbes is trying to protect a theory that would render such a motive impossible, nothing about Hobbes's reply undermines this view. Hobbes does not deny that his desire was the other-regarding desire to give some relief to the old man. His response is perfectly consistent with this desire. Rather, Hobbes offers a claim about what the cause of the desire he acted on was, namely, the pain caused by considering the old man's condition. Hobbes does not say he acted as he did because he sought to fulfill a desire to rid himself of pain; rather, he claims that the desire he acted on was caused by his own pain. But as far as Hobbes's comment is concerned, his pain caused him to so act by causing in him a desire which is itself an other-regarding desire: the simple desire to help another in distress. The relation between vital and voluntary motion, therefore, the fact that on Hobbes's account desires are caused by their ability to strengthen the vital motion in the agent and thus produce pleasure, in no way commits him to the view that the desires themselves must always be self-regarding.[41]

40 Aubrey also attributes Hobbes's willingness to "doe some good to the Towne where he was borne" not to any self-regarding desire but to his "publique and charitable Intention" (1957: 153).

41 This treatment of Hobbes's psychology owes a great deal to Jean Hampton's especially clear and illuminating discussion, which emphasizes the need to make "a sharp distinction between desires, on the one hand, and the cause of desires, on the other hand," and which concludes that Hobbes does not maintain that all desires are self-regarding (1986: 23). Bernard Gert makes much the same point in an important article on the relationship between Hobbes's mechanistic account of human nature and his allegedly egoistic psychology: "From the fact that whenever anything benefits my vital motion, this causes me to desire it, it does not follow that I desire it because I *believe* that it will benefit my

In addition to acknowledging that Hobbes's science of human nature does not commit him to this stronger form of psychological egoism, it is important to note some of the passages in which he explicitly disavows it. In *Leviathan,* for example, he considers the different passions which correspond to different objects of desire and aversion. "*Desire* of good to another" he calls benevolence, and desire of good "to man generally" he calls good nature (*L:* 123). In neither case does he state or imply that the object of desire is anything other than the good for another. Hobbes also defines pity in the same work as "*Grief,* for the Calamity of another," and although he claims that it "ariseth from the imagination that the like calamity may befall himselfe," this is again a claim about the cause of the agent's state of mind, not about the object of his unhappiness, which remains the suffering of the other (*L:* 126).[42] Nor is Hobbes's recognition of genuinely other-regarding desires limited, as some would have it, to the pages of *Leviathan.* In *Human Nature,* for example (first circulated around 1640), Hobbes identifies charity as the "desire to assist and advance others" and is careful to note that this excludes cases where the donor acts out of a desire "to purchase friendship, or . . . to purchase peace" (*EL* I: 9.17).[43] Hobbes does not spend a great deal of time discussing friendship or familial ties in his writings, but he does on occasion recognize "the natural affection of parents to their children" (*EL* I: 9.17), offer such comments as that "by the judgment of nature, next in blood is next in love; and next in love is next to preferment" (*EL* II: 4.16), and acknowledge the sacrifices people will make for their friends or their relatives, all of which again suggest that people may have genuinely other-regarding desires.[44]

vital motion. . . . Although Hobbes does maintain that our desiring a thing is caused by its benefiting our vital motion, he never claims that whatever we desire we desire because we *believe* it will benefit our vital motion" (1965: 346).

42 That Hobbes refers to the imaginative placing of oneself in the situation of the sufferer in the definition of pity should not be taken to suggest that it in any way constitutes the feeling of pity as opposed to being its cause. As Hobbes says of definitions in *De Corpore,* "Definitions of things, which may be understood to have some cause, must consist of such names as express the cause or manner of their generation" (*Co:* 6.13).

43 Even in his work *Of Liberty and Necessity,* Hobbes acknowledges that a person can "giveth money voluntarily to another" not in exchange for some perceived benefit, but simply "out of affection" (*LN:* 243).

44 In *De Cive,* for example, he says of the contract not to assist those who are to be punished by the sovereign that "men observe [it] well enough, for the most part, till either themselves or their near friends are to suffer" (*DC:* 6.5). In *Leviathan,* he argues that a desire for posthumous fame is not in vain because

In addition, Hobbes allows room for desires which are neither self-regarding nor other-regarding. Man is distinguished from other animals, for example, in part by his curiosity, which Hobbes defines as the desire "to know why, and how" (*L:* 124). The curious person, that is, seeks knowledge not because it is good for himself or because it is good for others, but simply for the sake of knowledge itself. And as we shall see in more detail in Chapter 3, Hobbes insists throughout his normative writings on the existence of the just man who is motivated to do the right thing not because it serves his interests or because it serves the interests of others, but simply because it is right.

How, then, shall we answer the question of whether Hobbes is a psychological egoist in this stronger sense? Many critics from Hume on have concluded that he is.[45] Others, including Gert, Watkins, and Hampton, have insisted that he is not.[46] Still others have suggested that in some works he is and in others he is not.[47] There is a reason why some questions in Hobbes scholarship are perennial, and we might do best at this point to concede that the texts are at times inconsistent and the question has no clear answer.[48] But the question of what Hobbes says about the content of human desires is not the same as the question of what his science of animate bodies commits him to saying about the content of human desires. The fact remains that his analysis of animal motions does not commit him to the position that all human desires are self-regarding and that, at the very least, he does not consistently assert that they are. In addition, Hobbes, as we have seen, insists that a scientific account of human nature must prove capable of accommodating empirical evidence. It seems highly unlikely

those who work to earn a reputation can take delight in "the benefit that may rebound thereby to their posterity" (*L:* 162).

45 Hume attributes to the "Hobbist" the attempt to "explain every affection to be self-love, twisted and moulded, by a particular turn of imagination, into a variety of appearances" (1975: 297).

46 Although Hampton generally restricts this evaluation to "the Hobbes who wrote *Leviathan*" (1986: 21).

47 Most notably F. S. McNeilly, who argues that Hobbes defends this form of egoism in his earlier works but abandons it in *Leviathan*. See also Ross Rudolph (1986: esp. 74–82) for a version of this view. For a concise, useful critique of the claim that Hobbes's accounts of pity and charity become progressively less egoistic throughout his writings, see Kemp (1982: 57–62).

48 Thus our evaluation comes closest to that of Kavka, who concludes that "having noted what the considerations are on both sides of the question, it is difficult to see what further illumination might be gained by simply attaching an egoistic or nonegoistic label to *Leviathan*" (1986: 51).

that a picture of human beings as purely self-interested creatures can do so. Our concern here is with the science of human nature that Hobbes considers the foundation for his science of moral virtue, and that foundation does not include the claim that all human desires must be self-regarding.

Hobbes's analysis of the motions distinctive of animate bodies does not commit him to the view that all desires are self-regarding; it must be conceded nonetheless that Hobbes does not usually paint a particularly rosy picture of human nature. Although he does not insist that all human desires are entirely self-regarding, he maintains that most human desires are largely self-regarding. This does not follow directly from his analysis of vital and voluntary motion, but he does presumably think that it is confirmed by the experiences of people past and present. The view, therefore, can easily be incorporated into his science of human nature since Hobbes freely admits that history is necessary to science, that it provides the evidence on which science must rest. From this portion of Hobbes's conception of human nature, we may take the view that humans tend to be primarily concerned with their own welfare, but not the view that they are concerned with nothing else.

2.4 RATIONAL ANIMATED BODY

The view often attributed to Hobbes that man is a "rational animal" suggests a creature of sustained, dispassionate logic, incapable of flights of irrationality, and Hobbes's own characterization of man as "body-animated-rational" certainly encourages this reading. Yet in discussing reason, Hobbes is always careful to treat it as a faculty humans are capable of developing, not as an innate power that governs them perfectly and immutably. "Reason," he says in *Leviathan*, "is not as Sense, and Memory, borne with us; nor gotten by Experience onely; as Prudence is; but attayned by Industry" (*L:* 115). Even in the *Six Lessons to the Professors of the Mathematics*, which deals only peripherally with human nature, he is clear that "the essence of a man is his *capacity* of reasoning" (*SL:* 221, emphasis added). Hobbes is thus far from insisting on the complete rationality of human beings; indeed, if there is one theme that runs most strikingly throughout his many observations on humanity, it is the endless variety of ways in which people continue to succumb to irrational and superstitious beliefs. Reason is, nonetheless, the feature Hobbes believes most clearly distinguishes humans from other animate bodies, and we must thus try to understand both what Hobbes takes reason to be, and what this entails for his attempt to develop a science of morals.

2.4.1 As we saw in section 2.1.3, reason for Hobbes is simply a matter of calculation: "in what matter soever there is place for *addition* and *substraction*, there also is place for *Reason;* and where these have no place, there *Reason* has nothing at all to do" (*L:* 110–11).[49] Reason is a form of calculation involving words, and thus Hobbes notes approvingly that the Greeks "have but one word *logos,* for both *Speech* and *Reason;* not that they thought there was no Speech without Reason; but no Reasoning without Speech" (*L:* 106). Hobbes also notes with approval the fact that "the act of reasoning they called *Syllogisme,*" although the identification of reasoning with syllogistic thinking can prove misleading. Hobbes himself uses the term "syllogism" narrowly in the traditional sense of an argument consisting of two premises and a conclusion (*Co:* 4.1), but he does not insist that all reasoning is syllogistic in this technical sense. Rather, he notes that the etymology of the term reflects the more general notion of the "summing up of the consequences of one saying to another" (*L:* 106–7).[50] Thus reason, for Hobbes, is the process by which statements or collections of statements are seen to entail, often through long and complex deductive arguments, conclusions.

2.4.2 Two features of this distinctively human characteristic are particularly relevant to the discussion of Hobbes's moral science developed in the following chapters. One is that reason, because it produces conclusions that follow from long chains of considerations, permits humans to distinguish between what Hobbes calls "real" and "apparent" good:

49 See also, e.g. (*Co:* 1.2): "By RATIOCINATION, I mean *computation*. . . . all ratiocination is comprehended in these two operations of the mind, addition and substraction."

50 As the philosopher notes in Hobbes's *Dialogue of the Common Laws,* "Etymologies are no Definitions, and yet when they are true they give much light towards the finding out of a Definition" (*D:* 110). The *Oxford English Dictionary* (1971: 3205) acknowledges as one possible etymology the sort of explanation suggested here by Hobbes, noting that some have interpreted "to syllogize" as "to add up, make a sum of." It also confirms that "syllogism" was commonly used in the seventeenth century to refer to noninductive reasoning in general, and cites Bacon (for whom Hobbes at one time worked as an amanuensis and who praised Hobbes as performing this task "better then any one els about him" [Aubrey 1957: 9]) as one who used the term in this way.

> In many things, whereof part is good and part evil, there is sometimes such a necessary connexion between the parts that they cannot be separated. Therefore, though in each one of them there be so much good, or so much evil; nevertheless the chain as a whole is partly good and partly evil. And whenever the major part be good, the series is said to be good, and is desired; on the contrary, if the major part be evil, and moreover, if it be known to be so, the whole is rejected. Whence it happens that inexperienced men that do not look closely enough at the long-term consequences of things, accept what appears to be good, not seeing the evil annexed to it; afterwards they experience damage. And this is what is meant by those who distinguish good and evil as *real* and *apparent*. (*DH:* 11.5)

Note that, for Hobbes, discerning the real good from the apparent is a matter of calculating consequences. An action might appear to be good because of its immediate rewards, yet prove to be bad in light of further costs which it imposes and which "cannot be separated" from it. Arriving at an accurate understanding of consequences is the province of reason, and in reaffirming that "the real good must be sought in the long term," Hobbes later insists that this search "is the job of reason" (*DH:* 12.1). Reason distinguishes humans from other animals by providing them with a way of understanding what is really good, as opposed to what merely appears to be good. Those who do not take advantage of reason to do so, as we shall see in the following chapters, are simply "Fooles."

A second feature of reason that merits attention is that it enables man to "reduce the consequences he findes to generall Rules, called *Theoremes,* or *Aphorismes;* that is, he can Reason, or reckon, not onely in number; but in all other things, whereof one may be added unto, or substracted from another" (*L:* 113). Reason, on Hobbes's account, is a capacity for accurately determining the implications of propositions, but these implications can in turn be used to ground general rules or principles. Hobbes claims that this is the goal of philosophy: Grounded in "true ratiocination," he argues, its "profession is . . . to establish universal rules concerning the properties of things" (*Co:* 1.2, 4.7). These two features of reason, its ability to distinguish the real good from the apparent and its ability to assist in the formulating of general rules, suggest the role reason may play in the founding of Hobbes's moral science. It provides human beings with the capacity to discern general principles concerning what is really, and not merely apparently, good for them.

2.4.3 Since human beings, according to Hobbes's account, are rational, animate bodies, and since reason provides them with the means for discovering truths that help them to achieve what is good, it might seem that in making moral science possible, Hobbes's analysis at the same time shows it to be unnecessary. What could a moral scientist say about good and evil that would not be equally apparent to every rational being?

At this point we must remember that, for Hobbes, reason is definitively human only in the sense that all have the capacity to develop and perfect it. As one writer has put it, although the individual on Hobbes's account "is capable of thinking and of constructing trains of thought, he is all too prone to fantasy, illusion, and absurdity" (Wolin 1970: 24). As Hobbes perhaps best explains in an important passage in *De Homine,* the reason for this is that humans are passionate, as well as rational, animals:[51] The emotions, he argues, "are called *perturbations* because they frequently obstruct right reasoning. They obstruct right reasoning in this, that they militate against the real good and in favor of the apparent and most immediate good, which turns out frequently to be evil when everything associated with it hath been considered" (*DH:* 12.1). The fact that everyone has the potential to make accurate calculations of long-term consequences does not alter the fact that "the good or evill effect [of their actions] dependeth on the foresight of a long chain of consequences, of which very seldome any man is able to see to the end" (*L:* 129). The passions frequently prevent people from reasoning properly, and Hobbes's analysis therefore leaves open the possibility that there is a "good and evil, which not every man in passion calleth so, but all men by reason" (*EL* I: 17.14). The goal of his science of morals is to bring this possibility to fruition, and the role of the passions in his science of human nature shows this to be no small task.

2.5 MORTAL RATIONAL ANIMATED BODY

Man, according to Hobbes's definition, is a rational animated body. From the fact that he is a body, it follows that his behavior can be exhaustively subsumed under the study of physics; from the fact that he is animate, it follows that he has desires and aversions, that he considers some things to be good and others to be evil; and from

51 In the Epistle Dedicatory to *Human Nature,* he refers to reason and passion as "the two principal parts of our nature" (*EL* I: xvii).

the fact that he is (potentially) rational, it follows that he is capable of discovering general rules or principles that will help him distinguish what is good according to reason from what merely appears to be good as a result of the interference of the passions. These features begin to set the stage for a consideration of Hobbes's moral science, but one more feature of human nature requires discussion first. For man is not only a rational animated body; he is also a mortal one.

2.5.1 In one of his best-known statements on the subject of mortality, Hobbes argues at the outset of *De Cive* that "every man is desirous of what is good for him, and shuns what is evil, but chiefly the chiefest of natural evils, which is death; and this he doth by a certain impulsion of nature, no less than that whereby a stone moves downward" (*DC:* 1.7). Hobbes's language here, as in comparable passages in his other works,[52] suggests that people seek to avoid their own death because they are in some sense compelled to do so. The comparison of the death-averse human with the falling stone, in particular, suggests that the source of this natural compulsion is some sort of motion. This suggestion fits in well with Hobbes's view that life itself is nothing but matter in motion, and when this is combined with his clear advocacy of the law of inertia, an apparently straightforward argument seems to emerge from his texts: Life is nothing but matter in motion; matter once in motion tends to stay in motion and cannot of its own volition cease motion; therefore, humans by their very nature endeavor to continue living and are incapable of trying to end their lives. Understood as natural bodies, human beings are not only rational and animate but also self-perpetuating mechanisms.

This argument has several merits as a potential component of Hobbes's system of thought. It attempts to justify an important feature of human nature, as Hobbes's stated method requires, by appealing to more fundamental elements of his science. The conclusion it reaches about human beings is universal, and is thus capable of playing the sort of role Hobbes will later call on it to play. As we have already seen, the argument itself seems to be easily located in Hobbes's writings. It is, therefore, not surprising that it is often attributed to Hobbes by those who seek to emphasize the

52 In *Human Nature,* for example, he writes that "necessity of nature maketh men to will and desire bonum sibi, that which is good for themselves, and to avoid that which is hurtful; but most of all that terrible enemy of nature, death" (*EL* I: 14.6).

systematic nature of his thought. Thomas Spragens, for example, argues that "Hobbes' fundamental psychological model is a human equivalent of the law of inertia," and that the primary striving for self-preservation he posits is grounded in the "universal tendency" of inertial motion (1973: 189, 130–3). Lisa T. Sarasohn similarly maintains that Hobbes's "theory of psychology is modelled on inertial natural motion. Just as an object continues in its motion, a human strives to continue the pleasurable state of living, and avoid the ultimate pain, death, which is the cessation of movement" (1985: 375).[53] Hobbes does speak of people avoiding death by "a certain impulsion of nature," and reading this as one instantiation of the universal law of inertia seems to be the most sensible way of understanding what he means by this.

2.5.2 Despite the evidently straightforward nature of this account of Hobbes's position, and despite the fact that it fits so well with the view of Hobbes as a systematic thinker, the argument from inertia presents a few problems not easily resolved. One problem is that it is not clear that the argument really establishes its conclusion. From the fact that life is motion (and the fact of the law of inertia) it might follow that a living being is naturally inclined to continue living, that its motion will not end without interference from some other body. But this need not entail the further claim that such a being must seek to avoid its own destruction at all costs when it does come into contact with other bodies. It is one thing to say that a person will not spontaneously and without provocation seek to commit suicide and another to say that people always hold their own preservation to be of supreme value, that there is nothing for which they will ever sacrifice their life. To say that death is always the greatest evil is to say more than that it is never a good; yet Hobbes clearly wants to say more than that death is not a good, and the argument that attempts to justify his position by appealing to inertial motion does not seem able to do this.

A second problem with the argument from inertia is that its conclusion is patently false. The argument entails that it is a matter of fact that human beings cannot seek to commit suicide. Some human beings, however, do in fact seek to commit suicide, and it

53 Although the language of inertia in particular is often absent, the view remains largely the same on other accounts of Hobbes's argument. Jean Hampton, for example, writes that Hobbes grounds the importance of self-preservation in "the fact that we are naturally averse to anything that hinders our internal vital motions, above all, death, insofar as it is the complete cessation of vital motion" (1986: 14–15).

plainly follows from this that they can seek to do so. Furthermore, the conclusion that the argument must attempt to reach from this position – that it is therefore impossible for human beings to value anything over their own survival – is also patently false. People sometimes willingly sacrifice their lives for friends or strangers, pride or principles, God or country, and from all of this it again follows that it is possible for them to do so. Hobbes's method, as we have seen, does require claims about human nature to reflect the facts about people accurately. It does not seem possible for the argument from inertia to allow him to do so.

Finally, the argument from inertia is suspect as an interpretation of Hobbes because Hobbes himself, in a number of places in his writings, clearly recognizes that people do not in fact always value their preservation above all else. In *De Cive,* he says that "most men would rather lose their lives (that I say not, their peace) than suffer slander" and that "a son will rather die than live infamous and hated of all the world" (*DC:* 3.12, 6.13). In *Human Nature,* he says that "many a man had rather die" than admit his mistake (*EL* I: 9.6). In *Leviathan,* he claims that "most men choose rather to hazard their life, than not to be revenged" (*L:* 210–11). This suggests that Hobbes is keenly aware that human passions, particularly vanity, can lead people to value their reputation over their preservation. In addition, Hobbes is extremely worried throughout his writings that people can be led to fear eternal damnation more than death. In *Leviathan,* for example, he cites the "Counsel of our Saviour" in Matthew 10:20: "Fear not those that kill the body, but cannot kill the soule" (*L:* 610; it is interesting that he omits the remainder of the sentence: "fear him rather who can destroy both body and soul in hell"). In *De Cive,* he argues that a man is "more a master, whom we believe we are to obey for fear of damnation, than he whom we obey for fear of temporal death" (*DC:* 6.11). In *Behemoth* he worries that "as much as eternal torture is more terrible than death, so much [people] would fear the clergy more than the King" (*B:* 14–15).[54] The argument from inertia entails that a

54 *Behemoth* presents an especially wide assortment of passages in which Hobbes's understanding of human motivations cannot easily be reconciled with the claim that individuals always value their own preservation above all else. Stephen Holmes defends the work's significance largely on the ground that "it explodes one of the most common and persistent errors of Hobbes scholarship. Even today, commentators continue to assert that Hobbes conceived man as an animal propelled exclusively by a desire for self-preservation. . . . But the entire work testifies to Hobbes's extraordinarily rich understanding of the human

person could never choose death over slander, or even nonexistence over eternal torture, yet Hobbes plainly recognizes that people can, and do, make such choices. We therefore stand in need of a better understanding of Hobbes's position on death.

2.5.3 Bernard Gert offers a radically different version of Hobbes's argument. Acknowledging Hobbes's claim that "every man by reasoning, seeks out the means to the end which he propounds to himself" (*DC:* 14.16), Gert maintains that Hobbes also believes that "reason does more than this, it has an end of its own, avoidance of violent death." Reason, on Gert's account of Hobbes's position, "is very complex; it has a goal, lasting preservation, it discovers the means to this goal." For Hobbes, Gert insists, "reason is not, or at least should not be, the slave of the passions, rather the passions are to be controlled by reason." Gert goes so far as to claim that "the failure to recognize that the avoidance of violent death is the end of reason has distorted almost all accounts of Hobbes's moral and political philosophy" (1978: 13, 14). In stark contrast to the argument from inertia, which portrays death avoidance as an instinctive and ineradicable reflex, Gert insists that it is an imperative of reason.

Gert's position, as he presents it, is unacceptable. Reason for Hobbes, as we saw in section 2.4, is nothing but calculation. When given premises to work with, it can generate a conclusion by discerning the consequences implicit within them, but it cannot produce any conclusions by itself. Like a complicated slide rule or abacus, it can be used to serve various ends, but it can have no ends of its own. Where there is no place for addition and subtraction, as Hobbes puts it, "*Reason* has nothing at all to do" (*L:* 111).

Yet there seems to be something to Gert's position despite all this. As Gert points out, Hobbes says in the Epistle Dedicatory to *De Cive* that it is the rational part of human nature that "teaches every man to fly a contra-natural dissolution as the greatest mischief that can arrive to nature." The laws of nature, which help preserve the life of the agent who follows them, are described consistently throughout Hobbes's writings as dictates, or precepts, or theorems, of reason. In *Leviathan,* for example, a law of nature is defined as "a Precept, or generall Rule, found out by Reason, by which a man is forbidden to do, that, which is destructive of his

psyche. Human motivations are much too disorderly and perverse to be reduced to self-preservation or the rational pursuit of private advantage" (Holmes 1990: [x]–[xi]).

life, or taketh away the means of preserving the same; and to omit, that, by which he thinketh it may be best preserved" (*L:* 189). Hobbes does not say that these laws explain how to avoid death and are thus rational for those particular agents who have chosen death avoidance as an aim; he says that the laws of reason forbid human beings to do that which is self-destructive. This seems to suggest that the goal of self-preservation is generated by reason itself. As Gert also points out, although Hobbes acknowledges that people may, for example, prefer death to slander, he "does not say if you would rather avoid slander than death, it is rational to do so" (1978: 15).[55] There does seem to be a sense in which Hobbes wants to say that the rational person does not prefer death to suffering slander, that reason recommends self-preservation. The question is how Hobbes can say this, given his limited view of what reason is.

The answer, I believe, begins with the inertial view of Hobbes's position, although it does not end there. Desires and aversions are created, as we saw in section 2.3, by the effect that their satisfaction has upon the vital motions. There is no limit to the extent to which the vital motions can be assisted. Hence there is, according to Hobbes's account, no limit to the desires that can be had and no greatest good to be sought after. In addition, there is no natural uniformity to what will assist the vital motions in different people. What pleases me greatly may please you little or not at all, so that there need be no one thing that all by nature consider good. But there is nonetheless a limit to the extent to which the vital motions can be hindered, for they can be extinguished altogether. There is, in addition, one object of desire or aversion that has this effect on every human being: death. Although there is no *summum bonum* in Hobbes's system, therefore, there is still a *summum malum*.[56] The emphasis on inertial motion does get us at least this far: From the fact that each individual's ability to satisfy her desires (whatever those desires might be) depends on the continuation of her vital motions, and the fact that death is the cessation of the vital mo-

55 Similarly, when Hobbes acknowledges that the pains of life may be so great that "they may lead men to number death among the goods," he does not say that they are right to number death among the goods, only that they sometimes do (*DH:* 11.6).

56 Thus, although Hobbes's insistence that death is the greatest evil is often portrayed as the natural extension of his general view on egoism, it is the only exception to that view. His general view is that good and evil are whatever help and hinder the agent's vital motions, and that these vary from person to person. Death is the only exception to this rule, since its effect on the vital motions is the same for all.

tions, it follows that death is the elimination of all future desire-satisfaction, and is thus the greatest evil for each individual.

It does not follow from this that each individual, as a matter of fact, always seeks to avoid death at all costs. As we have seen, Hobbes acknowledges that people are capable of preferring death to humiliation and to damnation. This is where reason must enter the picture, and Gert is right to insist that it must play a role in Hobbes's account of death aversion even if he offers a misleading account of what that role must be. For as we have already seen, Hobbes argues that there is a distinction between the real good and the apparent, and that "the real good must be sought in the long term, which is the job of reason" (*DH:* 12.1). Reason discerns the real good from the apparent good, not because it has any ends of its own, however, but because it is the faculty concerned with determining the consequences of things, and because what is apparently good can be shown to be really evil only by discerning all its consequences. The salient consequence of death is the cessation of the vital motions it necessarily brings about, foreclosing all future opportunities for happiness. In choosing death over life, the person who fails to keep this in mind does so because some passion, some "perturbation of the mind," has obstructed his right reasoning. The person who thinks it better to die than to suffer slander is so swept up by emotions that he cannot make the most elementary rational judgment about the effects his death will have on him.[57] Hobbes's position is thus best explained, as at least one writer has tentatively suggested, as follows: "the fact that some men prefer to sacrifice life itself in order to avoid humiliation or the possibility of eternal damnation could be construed as one of the absurd results of the human ability to misreckon in spectacular fashion" (Johnston 1986: 56).[58] This makes the best sense of Hobbes's

57 The situation is somewhat more complex in the case of the person who chooses death over eternal damnation. Hobbes is careful never to endorse the rationality of the person who chooses death over humiliation, always simply noting that some people will "rather" die, or will "choose" to die. When the choice is between death and damnation, however, Hobbes allows (indeed, insists upon) the rationality of choosing death. This can be rendered consistent with the present analysis when we follow Hobbes in recasting the choice as one between a temporary death and an eternal death. The sovereign may guarantee earthly death as punishment for disobeying his commands, but "if the command be such, as cannot be obeyed, without being damned to Eternall Death, then it were madnesse to obey it" (*L:* 610).

58 Paul J. Johnson's remarks about the sacrifices people are sometimes willing to make in the name of ideology can also be taken as support for this sort of

recognition that it is possible for a person to kill himself and his insistence at the same time that "if he kill himself, it is to be presumed that he is not *compos mentis*" (*D:* 116). Most people, most of the time, are *compos mentis*, so it is perfectly consistent for Hobbes to maintain at the same time that most people, most of the time, do in fact rank their own deaths as the greatest possible evil. The conclusion of Hobbes's treatment of death is, therefore, that self-preservation and its opposite constitute "that good and evil, which not every man in passion calleth so, but all men by reason" (*EL* I: 17.14).

Having set out the salient elements of Hobbes's science of human nature, we are now in a position to consider his attempt to derive from it the science of "the *Passions* of Men" that he calls "ETHIQUES" (*L:* 149). Although the science of human nature is one branch of the science of physics, and must for that reason remain essentially conjectural, Hobbes's method nonetheless permits him to "reason arightly" from his premises to conclusions that must hold as certain so long as the premises are maintained. Hobbes must allow that his picture of people as animate, potentially rational bodies for whom death is the greatest evil is subject to revision, but he can nonetheless claim to derive from it a system of morals that is certain so long as this picture of humans is upheld. The task of Hobbes's moral theory is to justify what morality must be if people really are as Hobbes has described them, and our task is therefore to analyze and assess the justification of ethics that Hobbes offers. One problem, however, prevents us from moving directly to this task. There is substantial disagreement over what moral theory Hobbes means to be defending, or whether he even means to be defending one at all. The following chapter is therefore devoted to the problem of interpreting Hobbes's moral theory, and upon its conclusion we can turn in Chapter 4 to the question of how Hobbes means to justify it.

analysis. From the point of view of one whose ideological agenda is threatened, Johnson notes, "My very sense of who and what I am is threatened. . . . My life as I conceive it is threatened" (1989: 75). Although Johnson offers these remarks to show that Hobbes himself underestimates the force of ideological commitments (Hobbes tends to view the willingness to fight for ideology as a form of vanity, in which the ideologue is ultimately motivated by a perceived threat to his self-esteem), they seem naturally to support the view of Hobbes's notion of death taken here: The ideologue prefers death to the defeat of his cause because he believes that a threat to his cause is a threat to him, to his life as he conceives it. But according to Hobbes's account, he is wrong about this. Only a threat to his physical body is a threat to his life. On Hobbes's account people can be led to prefer death to other alternatives by "misreckoning."

Chapter 3

The theory of moral virtue

3.0 OVERVIEW

Having considered Hobbes's science of human nature in some detail, we must now turn to the question of what his moral theory is, or whether he even had one. A number of interpretations of Hobbes's moral theory (or of his lack of such a theory) have been set forth in recent years, but contrary to the views prevalent in the literature, this work contends that Hobbes is best understood as a sort of virtue ethicist, one for whom moral evaluations of actions and rules for actions are ultimately subordinate to moral evaluations of traits of character, and one who exhorts us to emulate the person who is disposed to do the right thing and to enjoy doing so simply because it is right. The chapter begins by considering two important views which provide the most direct challenge to this interpretation: the view that Hobbes has no moral theory at all, and the view that he is a contractarian for whom morality is entirely a product of human convention. Both views are rejected; there is no good reason to deny that Hobbes has a moral theory, and the theory that he does in fact have is one whose moral standards claim a validity independent of human convention. The problem becomes one of giving an adequate account of what this moral theory is, and this leads to discussions of two of the most important alternatives to the account defended here: Kavka's recent rule-egoist interpretation and the well-known, though often maligned, Taylor thesis, with the divine-command interpretive tradition it has inspired. Both Kavka's and Taylor's views contain considerable insight into Hobbes's thought, but both are found to suffer difficulties which ultimately render them unacceptable. The process of uncovering the difficulties with the views of Hobbes's moral theory prominent in the literature is at the same time the process of uncovering the elements of Hobbes's theory of moral virtue. The final section therefore brings the various considerations of the chapter together in an attempt to offer an account of Hobbes's moral theory as a theory of moral virtue, an account that accommodates the strengths of other interpretations without succumbing to their weaknesses. This in turn sets the stage for the next chapter, which examines Hobbes's attempt to defend this theory by grounding it in his science of human nature.

3.1 DID HOBBES HAVE A MORAL THEORY?

That Hobbes had a moral theory at all has been denied on a number of grounds, some of them quite plausible. In a sense the claim that "for Hobbes there is no such thing as . . . morality" (Roesch 1963: 65) can be refuted only by identifying and articulating the moral theory that he does, in fact, have. In this sense, our refutation must be deferred until the end of this chapter if not later. It is nonetheless important to begin our pursuit of Hobbes's moral theory by considering why so many people have insisted that it does not exist. For this suspicion is far from groundless, and our eventual interpretation of Hobbes must prove capable of taking its great appeal into account.

3.1.1 The most common argument against Hobbes's having a moral theory rests on the claim that he is a moral relativist. Miriam Reik, for example, has argued that "objective, absolute, ethical norms . . . simply do not exist" in Hobbes's system (1977: 90). Richard Tuck has written that the "grimmest version of sceptical relativism seems . . . to be the only possible ethical vision" that Hobbes can have (1989: 64). These statements reflect a common view among modern Hobbes scholars and, indeed, among nearly all of Hobbes's contemporaries. The seventeenth-century concern that Hobbes was an ethical relativist was second perhaps only to the related charge that he was an atheist. A moral relativist believes that there are no universally true or valid moral judgments, and if Hobbes is a moral relativist, it must therefore be admitted that it is difficult to see how he can make room for a genuine moral theory.[1] But is Hobbes a moral relativist?

1 Moral relativism is a theory about morality that might plausibly be called a moral theory. To avoid confusion, our concern here might also be stated as follows: Does Hobbes have a moral theory that allows him to identify genuine, objective moral standards? The interpretation of Hobbes as a moral relativist denies this.

Tuck's statement seems best to express the view of those who would answer in the affirmative: Hobbes is a moral relativist because moral relativism is the only view open to him, and the evidence most frequently cited in defense of this claim is Hobbes's own definition of good and evil:

> But whatsoever is the object of any mans Appetite or Desire; that is it, which he for his part calleth *Good:* And the object of his Hate, and Aversion, *Evill;* And of his Contempt, *Vile,* and *Inconsiderable.* For these words of Good, Evill, and Contemptible, are ever used with relation to the person that useth them: There being nothing simply and absolutely so. (*L:* 120)

Hobbes's position seems incontrovertibly relativistic. There is no such thing as good or evil; there is only good-for-this person (that is, desired by this person) and evil-for-that person (hated by that person). That nothing is absolutely good or evil is the cardinal tenet of moral relativism, and Hobbes apparently endorses it here without qualification. The case for Hobbes's having a substantive moral theory would seem to be at an end, therefore, before it even has a chance to begin.

But Hobbes's crucial definition of good and evil is often quoted incompletely. When it is considered in its entirety, a subtly different point emerges. The passage continues as follows:

> nor any common Rule of Good and Evill, *to be taken from the nature of the objects themselves;* but from the Person of the man (where there is no Common-wealth;) or, (in a Common-wealth,) from the Person that representeth it; or from an Arbitrator or Judge, whom men disagreeing shall by consent set up, and make his sentence the Rule thereof. (*L:* 120–1, emphasis added)

Hobbes's central claim is thus not that good and evil are terms that refer to nothing objective in the world. Rather, his point is that they do not refer to properties of the objects of people's appetites. To say that nothing is simply and absolutely good, that is, is just to say that goodness does not inhere in the objects themselves. It is not to say that there can be no common standards of good and evil. Hobbes explicitly countenances the possibility that such common principles do exist. His claim is merely that, as natural standards of good and evil, they cannot be grounded in facts about the objects themselves, but must instead be grounded in facts about human beings. Hobbes's subjective conception of value need not preclude the possibility of his articulating a theory of good and evil that would provide standards applicable to all.[2]

A parallel that Hobbes himself suggests (*L:* 121) may help to make this point more clear. According to Hobbes's theory of sense perception (e.g., *L:* 85–6), color, like goodness, is not a property that inheres in visible objects. When we see an object as red, and are tempted to attribute redness to it, what is really happening is that the mediated transmission of motion from the object through our eyes to our brain and heart is creating a motion in us which constitutes the "seeming" or "fancy" of a red object. The Scholastic doctrine attributing such visible qualities as color to objects, Hobbes therefore insists, is mistaken: Nothing is simply and absolutely red. But the fact that no object is simply red does not, for Hobbes, imply that the term "red" cannot be applied correctly and objectively. In his list of the causes of faulty reasoning color terms are not invoked as examples of insignificant words like "hypostatical" and "transubstantiate"; they are used to exemplify the fallacy of attributing to external objects properties which are in fact accidents of our own bodies (*L:* 114–15). Similarly, the fact that, on Hobbes's account, no object is simply good need not imply that the term "good" cannot be applied correctly and objectively. Just as we can identify objective common rules for distinguishing red from green, so might we also identify objective common rules for distinguishing good from evil. Just as a person whose eyes were not functioning properly might see grass as red without undermining our confidence in a common standard identifying grass as green, so a person whose reasoning was not functioning properly (such as Hobbes's Foole) could perceive injustice as good without undermining our confidence in a common standard identifying injustice as evil. There is no guarantee that common rational standards of good and evil will be discovered; the point is that Hobbes's understanding of good and evil provides no guarantee that they will not.

Hobbes does, indeed, endorse a subjective conception of value. Good is the object of desire and bad is the object of aversion. Hobbes commentators have been right to notice that this stance prevents him from defending a certain kind of moral objectivism. Having declared that nothing is absolutely good, for example, he cannot go on to claim that it is good to be honest because honesty is

2 For another way of accounting for Hobbes's remarks here without attributing a relativist position to him, see Lloyd (1993: 254–60).

absolutely good. But the fact that Hobbes is deprived of this extreme form of objectivism need not force him to embrace the opposite extreme of moral relativism. It remains open for him to attempt to identify common rules of good and evil by deriving them from basic features of human nature, rather than taking them "from the nature of the objects themselves." Although we must avoid attributing to Hobbes a moral theory that would undermine his subjectivism of value, this does not mean that we must avoid attributing a moral theory to him at all.

3.1.2 A second argument often marshaled in defense of the claim that Hobbes does not have a moral theory holds that his theory of human action is (merely) one of prudence and (thus) not one of morals. In *The Logic of Leviathan*, for example, David Gauthier expresses the suspicion that "something distinctively moral is lacking from Hobbes's arguments," and concludes that "Hobbes's 'moral' system is nothing more than a system of common, or universal, prudence" (1969: 91, 98).[3] Watkins, acknowledging that Hobbes often describes the laws of nature as moral laws, nonetheless avers that "to take such remarks to mean that these laws have a moral as distinct from a prudential character would be like taking Copernicus's use of the term 'sunrise' to indicate that he had given up his heliocentric hypothesis" (1965: 83).

As we saw in section 2.3.3, Hobbes does not insist that people have no other-regarding desires, so if the claim is that Hobbes could not have had a moral theory because he believed people can act only out of a direct concern for their own welfare, then, strictly speaking, the claim is false. But it must nonetheless be admitted that other-regarding desires are unlikely to play a central role in grounding Hobbes's moral theory, and that his moral theory must therefore rest in some way on the claim that living ethically contributes to the agent's well-being. This is a weaker claim than the claim that agents always act with an exclusive concern for their own welfare, but it remains a troubling one nonetheless; it seems to suggest that in recommending morality, Hobbes can be doing nothing more than advising people about how better to satisfy their own desires (including their other-regarding desires), which would in turn seem to render his theory merely one of prudence. It would remain open for Hobbes to claim that the prudent thing for humans to do is to behave morally, but this would leave no discernibly independent role for moral reasoning to play. As Gauthier

3 Gauthier's more recent views on Hobbes are discussed in section 3.2.

puts the point in his more recent work, "Why appeal to right or wrong, to good or evil, to obligation or to duty, if instead we may appeal to desire or aversion, to benefit or cost, to interests or to advantage?" (1986: 1).

It is tempting to conclude that Hobbes could not therefore offer a genuine moral theory, but the temptation should be resisted. Its apparent force derives from a failure to distinguish between two different senses in which one could claim that it is prudent to be moral. One way, which might be called the direct approach, would be to claim that the answer to the question "What (morally) ought I to do?" is always the same as the answer to the question "What (prudently) ought I to do?" Although the two questions might have different meanings, through a happy coincidence of interests they consistently advise the same course of action. But a theorist attempting to ground morality in prudence might also take a more indirect approach which would allow that in many cases the answers to these two normative questions can and do diverge. The claim would be that a person who acts directly out of a concern for prudence would behave differently from one who acts out of a respect for morality, but that in the long run the latter would fare better than the former from the standpoint of prudence. The indirect theorist, in other words, would argue that an agent best promotes her well-being by not always directly seeking to promote it.

If Hobbes's theory proves to be of the direct sort, we indeed have identified a serious reason to doubt that it should count as a moral theory. Such a theory, after all, allows us to answer every ought question that we can face without having to consider what we morally ought to do. This seems to be the justifiable concern behind the suspicion that a theory grounded in a concern for the agent's well-being cannot be a genuine moral theory. Gauthier's concern about Hobbes's position, for example, is grounded in the claim that "In no system of rational prudence, in which all reasons for acting must reduce to considerations of what, *in each situation,* is most advantageous for the agent, can moral obligation be introduced" (1969: 97, emphasis added).[4] But if Hobbes's theory proves to be of the indirect sort, it is far less clear that we will have sufficient grounds for denying its status as a moral theory. Moral considerations must be introduced, on such an account, precisely

4 Gauthier has made much the same point more recently by claiming that "[Hobbes's] egoistic psychology allows the internalization of no standard other than that of *direct* concern with individual preservation and contentment" (1986: 163, emphasis added).

because it proves inimicable to the agent's well-being to act on the considerations of what, in each situation, is most advantageous for the agent. Rather than allowing us to ignore the consideration of what we morally ought to do, therefore, the indirect approach implores us to heed it. And this seems much more characteristic of a genuine moral theory.[5]

We could, of course, continue to deny that Hobbes has a moral theory because even an indirect approach such as this ultimately ties morality to human well-being. But this would seem to be, as Gregory Kavka has maintained, "a rather arbitrary verbal move" (1986: 368) that would implausibly force us to insist that much of the work in the virtue ethic tradition, for example, is not really ethics. Plato's *Republic,* after all, is largely an attempt to demonstrate that it is in one's interest to be a just person, but as Julia Annas has noted, to insist that morality exclude pure selfishness does not show that it must exclude all reference to the agent's interests. "The claim that it *must* do so, and that therefore the *Republic*'s main argument is not a *moral* one, is sheer dogmatism" (1981: 324). That Hobbes seems committed to defending morality in terms of human well-being thus raises a legitimate worry about whether he could truly espouse a moral theory; but if the theory we finally attribute to him is more like the indirect approach than the direct one, we may, at least for the time being, put the worry to rest.

3.1.3 Even if we concede that Hobbes defends a theory that urges us to do more than act from reasons of self-interest, it might still be argued that the counsel it offers does not qualify it as a moral theory. The objection, one made by a wide variety of writers, would be that Hobbes's normative system departs too greatly from our own intuitions about morality. Richard Peters, for example, argues that Hobbes cannot justify calling his theory a moral theory because it does not incorporate the ideal of impartiality which Peters takes to be a necessary feature of any moral theory (1956: 173–4). Others have contended that Hobbes's concerns with promise-keeping and obedience to authority are too narrow to capture the full scope of what we ought to demand from a moral theory. Even writers concerned to defend Hobbes's views have largely conceded

5 This account would also seem to overcome Thomas Nagel's reason for denying Hobbes's theory the status of a moral theory. Nagel insists: "Nothing could be called a moral obligation which in principle never conflicted with self-interest," but on the indirect approach, a particular moral dictate can conflict with self-interest (1959: 74).

that "much of traditional morality will not be accommodated by Hobbes's theory" (Gauthier 1979: 558).[6]

Intuitions about morality are notoriously varied, however, and which intuitions, if any, are violated by Hobbes's theory will depend on what moral intuitions we choose to endorse and on what interpretation of Hobbes we ultimately accept. In this respect, we cannot fully assess the charge that Hobbes's theory is unacceptably counterintuitive until we have determined more specifically what the theory is. It may nonetheless prove useful at the outset to note that the fact that a particular moral theory violates a particular moral intuition can be used to support at least three different conclusions: the intuition is misguided, the theory is not a good enough moral theory, or the theory is not a moral theory at all. This last evaluation is an extreme one, and it seems reasonable to suppose that it ought to be reserved for extreme cases. Although we each at some point need to consider our own intuitions in passing final judgment on Hobbes, we need not suppose that every potential violation of our intuitions we encounter along the way will pose a threat to the status of Hobbes's theory as a moral theory. Given that Hobbes's theory, on the account developed here, is concerned to defend a largely traditional understanding of what it is to be a just person, it seems unlikely that it will prove as counterintuitive as it has on some interpretations seemed to be.

3.1.4 Finally, it is often supposed that Hobbes does not have a moral theory for the simple reason that he cannot have a moral theory. The foundations of his theory, that is, are nonmoral premises describing bodies in motion, and it is argued that one cannot arrive at a moral theory from such premises. This conclusion is implicit in the views of many commentators and is perhaps best made explicit by A. E. Taylor's claim that "from the axiom that neither within nor without is there any reality but motion there is, in truth, no road to moral and political science" (1908: 56). Even Gary Herbert, who is sympathetic to the view that Hobbes is a systematic moral philosopher, insists that no truly moral theory could be made to rest on a mechanical view of nature (1989: e.g., 56, 63). Hobbes, as we have seen, does develop an essentially mechanical view of nature, including human nature, and if he is to

6 This article is reprinted in Gauthier's most recent book, the introduction to which reiterates the view that Hobbes offers "those foundations for morality which we can accept" but not "the richer moral conclusions that we wish" (1990a: 3). The article is discussed in more detail in section 3.2.

construct a moral theory on it, it is clearly meant to rest on nonmoral premises. How shall we respond to the claim that this cannot be done?

The argument against Hobbes, put most simply, is that he could defend a moral theory only by committing some form of the naturalistic fallacy, illicitly crossing the uncrossable chasm said to separate fact from value, "is" from "ought."[7] Many writers have maintained that this is precisely what Hobbes has done, although he is often forgiven his transgression on ex post facto grounds, since it was committed a century before Hume deemed it a sin.[8] Others have pronounced Hobbes innocent of the fallacy, but only by claiming that his moral conclusions are not truly supported by his descriptive claims,[9] or that they apply only to a certain kind of market society[10] or by insisting that his premises are not really nonnormative,[11] or that his conclusions are not really normative.[12] The naturalistic fallacy (and whether it truly is a fallacy) is a subject too large to be pursued in detail here. But conceding for the moment that no "is" statement can logically entail an "ought" statement, it must be acknowledged that there are ways for premises to lend support to conclusions other than by logically entailing them.[13] We have no good reason to suppose ahead of time that Hobbes cannot construct his theory along some such alternative lines, and thus no reason to endorse the claim that he has no moral theory because he

7 The is/ought problem is now commonly referred to as the naturalistic fallacy, although it is worth pointing out that it is not clear that this is what G. E. Moore meant by the term "naturalistic fallacy" when he introduced it (see [1903: 9–10]).

8 Peters and Henri Tajfel, for example, conclude that it is "understandable" that Hobbes would make such a mistake, "for he lived before Hume and Kant had shown the logical impossibility of deducing statements about what ought to be from statements about what is the case" (1972: 183). C. B. Macpherson demands "Why should we impose on Hobbes logical canons which are post-Hobbesian?" (1962: 14). Tuck allows that if this is the final verdict, then "so be it" (1989: 108).

9 Martin Bertman takes this approach in claiming that the "is-ought problem . . . does not arise for Hobbes." Bertman argues that for Hobbes the natural and the artificial represent distinct "explanatory frameworks" which "themselves do not intelligibly interpenetrate," so that factual and moral judgments are never illegitimately intertwined in Hobbes's argument (1979: 156, 157).

10 "When Hobbes's theory is . . . seen as a statement of what kind of political obligation is possible and necessary in a possessive market society, his deduction of obligation from fact may be allowed to be valid" (Macpherson 1962: 87; see esp. secs. 4.v and 5.i).

11 For a useful defense of this view, see King (1974: chap. 12, esp. 166ff).

12 See, e.g., Stephen (1904: 156–7), and Watkins (1965: 51).

13 Gauthier persuasively presses this point (1969: 21–2).

cannot have one. That Hobbes must at some point try to move from "is" to "ought" justifies our detailed scrutiny of his argument, but it cannot justify our a priori rejection of it.

Hobbes is more often thought of as a political theorist than as a moral theorist, in part because of the importance of his political theory, but largely because it is so often believed that he is not a moral theorist at all. Whether because of his comments about good and evil, his emphasis on human interests, his insistence on arguing from avowedly nonmoral premises, or the controversial nature of his conclusions, many people have argued that Hobbes prevents himself from developing a recognizably moral philosophy. We have seen that the foundation from which Hobbes begins places certain restrictions on the kinds of arguments he can make and on the kinds of conclusions he can reach, but none of these limits seems severe enough to rule out in advance the possibility of success. Having argued that Hobbes has indeed left himself sufficient space within which to develop a moral theory, we must now move on to see how successfully he takes advantage of it. We must focus not on whether he had a moral theory but on what moral theory he had.

3.2 HOBBES AS MORAL CONTRACTARIAN

One important school of thought maintains that Hobbes was a moral contractarian.[14] According to this account, Hobbes believed

14 This understanding, in one form or another, was common among Hobbes's contemporaries. As one writer put it, Hobbes makes "all Justice, Honesty, Morality, Goodness and Vertue, the consequences only of a civil government; as if, where there were no Civil Magistrate, these things had no being" (Shafte 1673: preface). A critical but nonetheless flattering elegy to Hobbes published upon his death ends by attributing to him the view that:

> . . . Vice and Vertue both were our Opinion,
> And vari'd with the Laws of each Dominion.
> To which who did conform was understood,
> As their Modes differ'd to be bad or good. (Anonymous 1679)

John Bowle endorses the view that "for Hobbes, government created moral values" and lists it as one of the primary sources of Hobbes's unpopularity among his contemporaries (1951: 186).

This view of Hobbes, moreover, remained influential through the years, and found its way into many of the most important works on ethics that followed. A century later, for example, Adam Smith would write that Hobbes's "odious" doctrine was "offensive to all sound moralists, as it supposed that there was no natural distinction between right and wrong, that these were mutable and that morality is an artificial construct introduced to further human ends. Life in the state of nature proves unacceptably brutal, and its inhabitants therefore devise a variety of rules to constrain their selfish behavior. These rules are detailed in Hobbes's laws of nature, which provide, among other things, that people keep their covenants and treat others as equals.[15] Their desire for peace leads them to embrace a code of behavior that at least superficially begins to sound something like a moral code. David Gauthier has defended this interpretation of Hobbes in an important paper repudiating his earlier view that Hobbes had no moral theory at all.[16] Hobbes, he argues, establishes "a place for morality as a conventional constraint on our natural behavior" (1979: 547). By nature we are led to act purely out of self-interest, but by agreement we adhere to limits on our selfishness. Hobbes's argument takes us "from nonmoral nature to moral convention" (1979: 548).

3.2.1 Three significant virtues recommend the contractarian interpretation of Hobbes. One is that it clearly renders Hobbes's moral theory compatible with his subjective theory of value. As we noted, Hobbes insists that nothing in the world is simply and absolutely good, and this has often been taken as sufficient evidence that he cannot construct a genuine moral theory. According to the contractarian interpretation, however, the subjective theory of good and evil generates no inconsistency with Hobbes's claim to be pursuing moral philosophy. Nothing is by nature good or bad, the contractarian can agree, thus acknowledging Hobbes's theory of value, but some things are rendered good or bad by the artifice of human convention. At least in part because nothing is by nature good or bad, people find themselves compelled to create artificial standards in the first place.[17] Any interpretation of Hobbes as a

changeable, and depended upon the mere arbitrary will of the civil magistrate" (1976: 318).

15 The third and ninth laws, respectively, as they are enumerated in *Leviathan*.

16 A kind of "contractual ethics" is also attributed to Hobbes in Shelton's recent study (1992: 166).

17 They create these standards in order to escape the state of nature, and Hobbes argues that the state of nature is a state of war because people are "so long in the state of war, as by reason of the diversity of the present appetites, they mete good and evil by diverse measures" (*DC:* 3.31). Hobbes also claims that "all controversies are bred from hence, that the opinions of men differ concerning *meum* and *tuum, just* and *unjust, profitable* and *unprofitable, good* and *evil, honest* and *dishonest*, and the like; which every man esteems according to his own judgment" (*DC:* 6.9). The causes of conflict in the state of nature are treated more fully in section 4.1.

moral theorist must somehow account for his indisputably subjective theory of value, and the contractarian interpretation does so in the most straightforward manner possible: it embraces it.

Gauthier champions this feature not simply as a virtue of this interpretation of Hobbes, but as one of the most significant virtues of Hobbes's moral theory. The majority of moral philosophers, he notes, have resorted to predicating their theories on the rejection of one of three presumptions: that value is subjective, that rationality is essentially maximizing, or that interests are nontuistic. Hobbes, Gauthier argues, takes the "bolder course" by accepting the assumptions and finding, nonetheless, room to construct a defensible moral theory (1979: 547). It is not always true that the majority of moral philosophers are mistaken, and they may in this instance be right in rejecting the dogmas of contemporary social science. Although its bold embrace of value subjectivism might therefore prove more a liability than a virtue for moral contractarianism as a normative theory, it nonetheless remains an important point in its favor as an interpretation of Hobbes.

A second significant merit of reading Hobbes as a moral contractarian is that it renders his moral theory parallel with, and complementary to, his political theory. In Hobbes's political theory, there are no political distinctions in the state of nature, no established offices of ruler and ruled, no meaningful applications of the concepts of political authority or obligation. In the state of nature, all are politically equal. The severe shortcomings of this anarchic condition lead people to abandon it by creating a sovereign whom all agree to obey. The transcendence of the state of nature is thus at the same time the creation of political rights and powers, responsibilities and obligations. The political distinctions these concepts represent are real, but they are also artificial. No one is simply and absolutely a sovereign; a sovereign is one only by a convention introduced precisely in order to escape the evils inherent in the state of nature. Hobbes's political theory teaches that the absence of natural political distinctions creates difficulties so severe that they prompt people to introduce artificial ones.

The parallel between Hobbes's political theory and his moral theory, understood as a contractarian moral theory, should therefore be clear. On this account, there are also no moral distinctions in the state of nature, no established moral authorities, no meaningful applications of the concepts of right or wrong, justice or injustice, good or evil. In the state of nature, all are morally equal. But just as the drawbacks of political anarchy lead people to create political distinctions, the drawbacks of moral anarchy lead them to create moral distinctions. The transcendence of the state of nature, therefore, is the creation not only of political, but of moral obligation. People voluntarily bind themselves not only to a political authority, but to a set of moral standards. In both cases, their motivation in embracing these artificial creations is to escape the consequences of the fact that they are not provided by nature. We cannot assume that Hobbes's moral philosophy will parallel his political philosophy, but the tight correspondence established by the contractarian interpretation appears to count as a point in its favor.[18]

Last, and certainly not least, it must be acknowledged that the contractarian reading of Hobbes can justifiably claim a substantial degree of textual support from a wide range of Hobbes's writings. Hobbes does, after all, famously declare in the *Leviathan* that in the "warre of every man against every man this also is consequent; that nothing can be Unjust. The notions of Right and Wrong, Justice and Injustice have there no place. Where there is no common Power, there is no Law: where no Law, no Injustice" (*L:* 188). In *De Cive,* he insists that "there are no authentical doctrines concerning right and wrong, good and evil, besides the constituted laws in each realm and government" (*DC:* preface), and in *De Corpore Politico* he maintains that only the sovereign has the power "to set forth and make known the common measure by which every man is to know what is his, and what another's; what is good, and what bad; and what he ought to do, and what not" (*EL* II: 1.10). *The Questions Concerning Liberty, Necessity, and Chance* contains the claim that the sovereign's law "is the infallible rule of moral goodness," and that we have "set up over ourselves a sovereign governor, and agreed that his laws shall . . . dictate to us what is really good" (*LNC:* 193–4). Even his *Decameron Physiologicum* includes the assertion that "the laws of commonwealth . . . are the ground and measure of all true morality" (*DP:* 75–6). The apparent abundance of textual evidence in its favor, combined with its other significant virtues, establishes a powerful presumption in favor of the view that Hobbes was a moral contractarian.

3.2.2 Despite these substantial merits, however, the contrac-

18 The force of the point should not be overstated: As we saw in section 1.1, moral philosophy and political philosophy are two distinct enterprises on Hobbes's account, so there would be no inconsistency in their developing in different directions.

tarian interpretation of Hobbes is ultimately susceptible to two devastating objections. The first arises from the fact that its insistence that Hobbes views morality as a purely artificial convention commits it to the position that, as Gauthier puts it, "there are no *moral* distinctions within the state of nature" (1979: 550).[19] Although Hobbes does appear to say this at times, a great number of important passages in his writings conclusively demonstrate that this is not his considered view. In particular, Hobbes's doctrine of the laws of nature, so prominent in all his normative writings, shows that, for him, there are indeed moral standards in the state of nature. The laws of nature provide standards of behavior to govern human interaction, standards that exist and that may be discovered by reason, prior to the establishment of a civil sovereign. If it can be shown that Hobbes accepts the existence of moral standards in the state of nature, then the contractarian interpretation must be abandoned, and the laws of nature seem clearly to establish that he does.

There are two ways in which the contractarian could try to maneuver around this objection. One would be to concede that the laws of nature govern human conduct in the state of nature but to deny that they are moral laws. Thus Gauthier identifies the laws of nature as the foundation of Hobbes's moral theory, but insists that "they are not themselves moral principles" (1979: 551). This position would, indeed, solve the contractarian's dilemma, but it is overwhelmingly refuted by Hobbes's texts. Although his justification for the claim varies somewhat from passage to passage, Hobbes frequently and explicitly insists that the natural law is also the moral law. "The law of nature, which is also the morall law," Hobbes argues in *De Corpore Politico,* "is the law of the author of nature, God Almighty; and the law of God, taught by our Saviour Christ, is the moral law" (*EL* II: 10.7). He endorses the claim that "the natural law is the same with the moral" in *De Cive,* arguing that "the [natural] law . . . in the means to peace, commands also good manners, or the practice of virtue; and therefore it is called *moral*" (*DC:* 3.31). In *Human Nature* he claims that "the laws of nature [are] also moral laws, because they concern men's manners and conversation one towards another" (*EL* I: 18.1). In *Leviathan,* he concludes that "the true Doctrine of the Lawes of Nature, is the

19 Gauthier has continued to defend this interpretation in his most recent published writings on Hobbes: "Hobbes recognizes the fundamental absence of morality from our natural condition" (1990b: 18).

true Morall Philosophie" (*L:* 216). The identification of the natural law with the moral is reiterated elsewhere (e.g., *L:* 330; *DC:* 3.32; *EL* II: 6.11); any interpretation of Hobbes that denies this identification thus becomes unacceptable.

The other way for the contractarian to account for Hobbes's natural law doctrine is to allow that the laws of nature are, indeed, moral laws, but to deny that they apply in the state of nature. If the laws of nature themselves underwrite no moral judgments in the state of nature, it can remain true that morality is purely conventional despite the fact that the natural law is moral. This approach is somewhat more plausible than the first, since Hobbes does allow that "The Lawes of Nature oblige *in foro interno;* that is to say, they bind to a desire they should take place: but *in foro externo;* that is, to the putting them in act, not alwayes." In particular, Hobbes argues that the laws of nature do not require a person to follow them in his behavior when the refusal of others to do so would "but make himselfe a prey to others" (*L:* 215). In the state of nature, no one can enjoy the security of knowing that others will heed the laws; although genuinely moral in character, they impose no moral duties on people outside civil society. This could render Hobbes's views on the laws of nature consistent with a contractarian moral theory.

The problem with this response is that it tacitly assumes that if the laws of nature do not pass moral judgment on entire classes of actions in the state of nature, then they do not pass moral judgment on people in the state of nature at all. But Hobbes insists in a variety of passages that people can be judged immoral in the state of nature, and that they can be so judged by standards independent of any human convention. In *De Cive,* for example, he argues that *"The laws of nature are immutable and eternal:* what they forbid, can never be lawful; what they command, can never be unlawful." The "virtues of the mind" they represent, he insists, "cannot be abrogated by any custom or law whatsoever" (*DC:* 3.29). In an important footnote to his discussion of the laws of nature in that work, he adds that

> in the state of nature, what is just and unjust, is not to be esteemed by the actions but by the counsel and conscience of the actor. That which is done out of necessity, out of endeavour for peace, for the preservation of ourselves, is done with right, otherwise every damage done to a man would be a breach of the natural law, and an injury against God. (*DC:* 3.27n)

Here, clearly, Hobbes does believe that justice and injustice have an important place in the state of nature. They may apply to the conscience rather than the act, but they apply nonetheless. They do so, moreover, in a manner perfectly consistent with Hobbes's claim that in the state of nature each person's right of nature is unlimited. For Hobbes treats the right of nature as "the Liberty each man hath, to use his own power, as he will himselfe, for the preservation of his own Nature; that is to say, of his own Life; and consequently, of doing any thing, which *in his own judgment, and Reason,* hee shall conceive to be the aptest means thereunto" (*L:* 189, emphasis added). The right of nature, in other words, allows me to do anything and is in this sense unlimited, but it allows it only if I truly judge it to be a means toward preserving my life. If I harm another without believing that doing so helps to protect me, then I am unjust. Thus Gauthier is wrong to conclude that "an unlimited permissive right implies the absence of all obligation or duty – of all moral constraint" in the state of nature, or, perhaps more precisely, he is wrong to characterize the right of nature as unlimited, as a "blank check" (1979: 550). In the state of nature, the right of nature might best be understood as a check that can be written in any amount, but only under certain conditions. If we try to draw on the right when those conditions are not met – when, that is, we do not truly believe we are acting to preserve our lives – then the check is void.[20]

Because it is so often denied that Hobbes believed any moral evaluations can be made of people in the state of nature,[21] it is worth considering a few additional passages that support the contention that he did. In one note, Hobbes reiterates that "if any man pretend somewhat to tend necessarily to his preservation, which yet he himself doth not confidently believe so, he may offend against the laws of nature" (*DC:* 1.10n).[22] In *Human Nature* he considers one such law in some detail: "thus much the law of nature

20 Hobbes is equally clear on this point in a number of other works. In his *Dialogue of the Common Laws of England,* for example, he writes that "Without law, every thing is in such sort every man's, as he may take, possess, and enjoy, without wrong to any man; every thing, lands, beasts, fruits, and even the bodies of other men, *if his reason tell him he cannot otherwise live securely*" (*D:* 58, emphasis added). The importance of the role of individual judgment in Hobbes's discussion of natural right is brought out well by D. J. C. Carmichael (1988).

21 Thus a typical introductory text on ethics states that "it is impossible in [Hobbes's] state of nature to do anything morally wrong" and that the "laws of nature, as Hobbes views them, are not moral rules" (Taylor 1975: 48).

22 See Richard Tuck (1979: 125ff.), however, for the claim that although this notion is consistently present in Hobbes's writings from *De Cive* on, it is an innovation absent from his earliest political works.

commandeth in war: that men satiate not the cruelty of their present passions, whereby in their own conscience they foresee no benefit to come. For that betrayeth not a necessity, but a disposition of the mind to war, which is against the law of nature." Hobbes relates this claim to an "old time" when rapine was a common way of life, and notes that many of those who practiced it "did not only spare the lives of those they invaded, but left them also such things, as were necessary to preserve that life which they had given them . . . And as the rapine itself was warranted in the law of nature, by the want of security otherwise to maintain themselves; so the exercise of cruelty was forbidden by the same law of nature, unless fear suggested anything to the contrary" (*EL* I: 19.2).[23]

The examples thus far considered have focused on those "other" laws of nature so often passed over by those concerned exclusively with Hobbes's analysis of contract. It is therefore worth noting that even with respect to the morality of keeping our covenants, Hobbes does not give those in the state of nature a blank check. In *De Cive*, for example, he argues that "the covenants which are made in contract of mutual trust, neither party performing out of hand, *if there arise a just suspicion in either of them*, are in the state of nature invalid" (*DC:* 2.11, emphasis added). Hobbes thus carefully avoids maintaining that all covenants in the state of nature are invalid. He allows that if one party comes to doubt that the other will comply, then the first may justly renege; but the first may renege only if such a doubt arises. In an important footnote to this passage, Hobbes elaborates on his claim that this suspicion must arise after the covenant has been made: "For, except there appear some new cause of fear, either from somewhat done, or some other token of the will not to perform from the other part, it cannot be judged to be a just fear; for the cause which was not sufficient to keep him from making compact, must not suffice to authorize the breach of it, being made" (*DC:* 2.11n).[24]

23 It should in fairness be noted that Hobbes's treatment of rapine is somewhat more ambiguous in *De Cive*. He begins by stating that in a state of war the laws of nature are silent "provided they be referred not to the mind, but to the actions of men," but he concludes that those who refrained from unnecessary cruelty against their victims were not "bound to do thus by the law of nature" (*DC:* 5.2).

24 Hobbes repeats this point nearly verbatim in *Leviathan:* "The cause of feare, which maketh such a Covenant invalid, must be always something arising after the Covenant made; as some new fact, or other signe of the Will not to performe: else it cannot make the Covenant voyd. For that which could not hinder

A second example of Hobbes's explicit insistence that there can be valid covenants in the state of nature concerns agreements in which a person promises to pay ransom in the future in exchange for being spared during a time of war. In *Human Nature*, Hobbes allows that "in some cases such covenant may be void," but only because "after the introduction of policy and laws, the case may alter" if the established government decides to prohibit the performance of such agreements (*EL* I: 15.13). The implicit rule to which this is presented as the exception is that before any such government is established, the agreement is "obligatory."[25] This feature of Hobbes's position is brought out even more directly in his analysis in *Leviathan* of the claim that "Prisoners of warre, if trusted with the payment of their Ransome, are obliged to pay it": "Covenants entred into by fear, in the condition of meer Nature, are obligatory" (*L:* 198).[26]

In one of the most frequently discussed passages in *Leviathan*, his response to the Foole, Hobbes outlines yet another sense in which the justice of covenant keeping applies even in the state of nature. The Foole maintains that "there is no such thing as Justice" (*L:* 203), and in his reply to this claim, Hobbes insists that "either where one of the parties has performed already; *or* where there is a Power to make him performe; there is the question whether it be against reason, that is, against the benefit of the other to performe, or not. And I say it is not against reason" (*L:* 204, emphasis added). The details of Hobbes's response to the Foole will be considered in sections 4.1 and 4.3, but for now it suffices to note that the first half of this disjunction clearly entails that one must comply with one's agreements when the other party complies first even when there is no civil power to enforce such compliance.[27] This demonstrates yet again that under at least some circumstances, justice can require one to keep one's agreements even in the state of nature.

Finally, it is worth briefly noting Hobbes's views on parental

a man from promising, ought not to be admitted as a hindrance of performing" (*L:* 196–7).

25 This is also suggested by Hobbes's comment in *De Cive*: "We are obliged . . . by promises proceeding from fear, except the civil law forbid them" (*DC:* 2.16).

26 See also Hobbes's comments on this issue in *De Corpore Politico*, esp. *EL* II: 1.16, 3.3. For a useful discussion of this aspect of Hobbes's thought, see Golding (1989).

27 This is often overlooked in discussions of Hobbes's reply to the Foole. Thomas Scally's analysis, for example, proceeds on the assumption that the Foole is "not himself in the state of nature" and "is not acting in the natural condition" (1981: 678, 677).

dominion over children in the state of nature. In *De Corpore Politico,* he argues: "Considering men again dissolved from all covenants one with another, and that every man by the law of nature, hath right or propriety to his own body, the child ought rather to be the propriety of the mother (of whose body it is part, till the time of separation) than of the father" (*EL* II: 4.1). In *Leviathan,* his justification is different, but the conclusion remains the same: "in the condition of meer Nature, where there are no Matrimoniall lawes, it cannot be known who is the Father, unlesse it be declared by the Mother: and therefore the right of Dominion over the Child dependeth on her will, and is consequently hers" (*L:* 254).[28] Still differently in *De Cive: "by right of nature* the conqueror is lord of the conquered. By the right therefore of *nature,* the dominion over the infant first belongs to him who first hath him in his power. But it is manifest that he who is newly born is in the *mother's* power before any others" (*DC:* 9.2). There is, therefore, at least this one important application of *meum* and *tuum* in the state of nature: The child rightfully belongs to the mother.[29]

The variety of textual evidence considered here, with more evidence that can be found throughout Hobbes's writings,[30] con-

28 Hobbes's discussion of parental dominion in *Leviathan* provides yet another example of a contract he insists is binding even in the state of nature: "In this condition of meer Nature, either the Parents between themselves dispose of the dominion over the Child by Contract; or do not dispose thereof at all. If they dispose thereof, the right passeth according to the Contract" (*L:* 253–4).

29 Hobbes's insistence on this point is all the more striking in light of the fact that most of his contemporaries (including Suarez, Grotius, and Filmer) denied it. That its novelty was readily apparent is reflected in Gabriel Towerson's comment that it was unclear whether Hobbes's position was due to "his kindness to the Female Sex, or rather to new and uncouth Opinions" (quoted in Sommerville [1992: 72; see also 70–4]). If Hobbes were merely repeating a familiar claim here, it might be dismissed as an incidental nod to orthodoxy, irrelevant to understanding his own doctrine, but since he is clearly staking out an original position, it seems reasonable to suppose that he has given it some thought, and that an adequate interpretation of Hobbes's theory must be able to take it into account. It is also worth noting that Hobbes's position is disputed in one of the earliest published critiques of his work written by a woman. "Mr. Hobbes will rather advance any absurdity, than own that power has its rights from reasonable causes. [The right of parents over their children] proceeds only from the tender feelings which are inseparable from the quality of parents" (Graham 1767: 16). For a more recent critique of Hobbes's position, see King (1974: chap. 15).

30 In the *Dialogue of the Common Laws,* for example, Hobbes has the lawyer agree with the philosopher "that Statute Law taken away, there would not be left, either here, or any where, any Law at all that would conduce to the Peace of a

clusively demonstrates that Hobbes believed in a morality that applies in the state of nature and must therefore transcend mere human convention. It is possible that Hobbes repeatedly and unequivocally insists on endorsing such moral evaluations throughout his works even though they flatly contradict the moral theory he intends to defend. If we can find no other moral theory that can more consistently be attributed to him, we shall be forced to accept this conclusion. In the absence of such an extreme lack of alternatives, however, the fact that Hobbes so consistently persists in identifying moral standards in the state of nature must surely undermine the interpretation of Hobbes as a moral contractarian.

In addition to the fact that Hobbes believed in moral distinctions in the state of nature, one other important element of his philosophy successfully undermines the contractarian interpretation of his ethics. This is Hobbes's view, clearly present in all his major normative works though rarely attributed to him, that it is possible for sovereigns to do wrong to their subjects.[31] The sovereign, on Hobbes's account, does not take part in the covenant which establishes civil society. In this sense, the sovereign remains in a state of nature with respect to his subjects; no agreements limit the sovereign's behavior. If morality is purely the product of agreement, therefore, the sovereign will be incapable of doing wrong.

But Hobbes insists, in a variety of places, the sovereign can correctly be judged as having done wrong. In *De Cive*, for example, he argues that although the sovereign of a democracy, oligarchy, or monarchy cannot be guilty of injury (since by definition injury is the breach of contract and the sovereign does not take part in the social contract), "the people, the nobles, and the monarch may diverse ways transgress against the other laws of nature, as by cruelty, iniquity, contumely, and other like vices, which come not

Nation; yet Equity, and Reason, which Laws Divine and Eternal, which oblige all Men at all times, and in all places, would still remain, but be Obeyed by few" (*D:* 55–6).

31 It is so commonly denied that Hobbes endorses this view that he is frequently cited as its paradigmatic opponent even in works having almost nothing to do with him. Christopher D. Stone, for example, describes the view of the theorist who "follows Hobbes in holding that sovereigns are unfettered by any moral principles at all," in *Earth and Other Ethics: The Case for Moral Pluralism* (1987: 232). Ralph Ross, Herbert W. Schneider, and Theodore Waldman note this unfortunate neglect. Hobbes, they write, "is clear that although the sovereign, being the source of law, cannot by definition act unjustly, he can act immorally. . . . To overlook this aspect of Hobbes's teaching is to know him inadequately" (1974: 6–7).

under this strict and exact notion of *injury*" (*DC:* 7.14).[32] There are wrongs that are vices even for kings, and Hobbes does not hesitate to condemn them in the strongest moralistic language: "If the *monarch* make any decree against the *laws of nature*, he sins himself" (*DC:* 7.14).[33] The king is charged with maintaining the peace, Hobbes notes in the *Dialogue of the Common Laws*, and "if he do not his utmost endeavour to discharge himself thereof, he committeth a sin, which neither King nor Parliament can lawfully commit" (*D:* 63). In *Leviathan*, he argues that "All Punishments of Innocent subjects, be they great or little, are against the Law of Nature" and that a sovereign who inflicts such punishment is guilty of ingratitude and inequity (*L:* 359–60).[34] He also notes that it is unjust for a judge to refuse to hear evidence, and insists that "all Judges, Sovereign and subordinate, if they refuse to hear Proofe, refuse to do Justice: for though the Sentence be Just, yet the Judges that condemn without hearing the Proofes offered, are Unjust Judges" (*L:* 325).[35]

32 Similarly in the *Dialogue of the Common Laws:* "There may indeed in a Statute Law, made by Men be found Iniquity, but not Injustice" (*D:* 70; see also *EL* II: 9.1).

33 Dudley Jackson notes, for example, Hobbes's insistence that a tax on wealth as opposed to one on commodities is "against equity, and therefore against the duty of rulers" (*DC:* 13.11), and argues that Hobbes's theory of taxation thus shows the sovereign to have duties that must, at least in part, be understood as moral in character (1973: esp. 180–2). The moral character of Hobbes's criticism of unjust taxation is most pronounced in his discussion in the *Dialogue of the Common Laws:* "if Levying of Money be necessary, it is a Sin in the Parliament to Refuse, if unnecessary, it is a sin both in King and Parliament to Levy" (*D:* 63). On the question of whether a king may grant to Parliament the power to restrain his raising of taxes, Hobbes writes, "I am satisfied that the Kings that grant such Liberties are bound to make them good, so far as it may be done without sin: But if a King find that by such a Grant he be disabled to protect his subjects if he maintain his Grant, he sins" (*D:* 63).

34 The sovereign can be judged wrong not only for punishing the innocent, but also for pardoning the guilty: "If the King think in his conscience [that pardoning a murderer] be for the good of the Common-wealth, he sinneth not in it; but I hold not that the King may pardon him without sin, if any other Man be damnified by the Crime committed, unless he cause reparation to be made, as far as the party offending can do it" (*D:* 153). In the treatise *Of Liberty and Necessity*, Hobbes insists that "a man that shall command a thing openly, and plot secretly the hindrance of the same, if he punish him that he so commandeth, for not doing it, it is unjust" (*LN:* 249; it is true that Hobbes does not use the word "sovereign" here, but only a sovereign, according to his account, can command or punish).

35 The same goes, Hobbes writes in the note to the reader which prefaces his *Answer to Bramhall's "Catching of Leviathan,"* for those who would condemn

In *De Corpore Politico,* Hobbes insists that "divers actions done by the people [i.e., the sovereign in a democracy] may be unjust before God Almighty, as breaches of some of the laws of nature" (*EL* II: 2.3), and that acts of sovereign power that "tend to the hurt of the people in general [are] breaches of the law of nature, and of the divine law" (*EL* II: 9.1).[36] In his discussion of the laws against heresy in the appendix to the Latin edition of *Leviathan,* he unequivocally declares that "Any law is unjust which does not first threaten before it wounds, and, however discretionary the right of supreme powers may be in setting down the laws, still it is not within their discretion to exact penalties which have not previously been defined in the laws" ("*AL*": 372).[37]

It is also worth mentioning that Hobbes at times suggests that the sovereign of one nation can do wrong to the sovereign of

Hobbes's writings on the basis of Bramhall's remarks alone: "To judge and not examine is not just" (*EW* IV: 282).

36 Hobbes argues, for example, that since a growing population enhances the welfare of the community, "in them who have sovereign authority: not to forbid such copulations as are against the use of nature; not to forbid the promiscuous use of women; not to forbid one woman to have many husbands; not to forbid marriages within certain degrees of kindred and affinity: are against the law of nature," and that since personal liberty is essential to commodious living, it is "contrary to the law of nature" to restrict it in ways that are not necessary for the public good (*EL* II: 9.3, 9.4). It is also worth noting that in the same work Hobbes insists that in the state of nature which results when a commonwealth is dissolved by the death of a monarch, "if there be any man, who by the advantage of the reign of him that is dead, hath strength enough to hold the multitude in peace and obedience, he may lawfully, or rather is by the law of nature obliged so to do" (*EL* II: 2.9).

37 This claim is also implicit in Hobbes's treatment of such laws in his *Historical Narration Concerning Heresy.* Responding to the fact that "a book called *Leviathan*" has recently been "accused in Parliament . . . of heresy," Hobbes complains of the unfairness of the charge, on the grounds that at the time the book was written there were no laws "in force to restrain any man from preaching or writing any doctrine concerning religion that he pleased" (*EW* IV: 407). In an earlier manuscript on heresy, Hobbes adopts much the same approach, arguing that "there is no need of answer to any particular doctrine mentioned by my accusers" since a careful consideration of existing statute law demonstrates that "at this day there is noe Statute in force, nor any Law in England whereby to punish any man for any matter of Doctrine in Religion" (MH: 414). (As it turns out, Hobbes was wrong about this: "Despite Hobbes's certainty on this point, there was a statute, 5 Eliz., c. 23, still on the books and presumably still in force, by which the heretic, once excommunicated, could be imprisoned if after forty days he had not come to terms with his bishop and been released from that excommunication" [Willman 1970: 613].)

another, although they, too, remain in a state of nature with respect to each other. Thus, in *Leviathan,* Hobbes insists that "if a weaker Prince, make a disadvantageous peace with the stronger, for feare; he is bound to keep it; unlesse . . . there ariseth some new, and just cause of feare, to renew the war" (*L:* 198). A truce made between sovereigns is a covenant made in a state of nature, and Hobbes clearly maintains that it is binding.[38] Hobbes also implies in the *Dialogue of the Common Laws* that there are standards of justice that apply to international relations, arguing that one cannot expect lasting peace between two nations, "because there is no common power in this world to punish their injustice" (*D:* 57).[39] The fact that Hobbes endorses moral distinctions that govern the behavior of one nation toward another is often acknowledged in discussions limited to his views on international relations,[40] but the significance of this has not typically been addressed in works on his ethics as a whole: that such distinctions cannot be the mere product of sovereign fiat. It is clear, therefore, from the moral limits on what the sovereign may legitimately do both to his own subjects and to sovereigns and citizens of other nations, that Hobbes be-

38 This is also suggested by Hobbes's insistence in *De Cive* that "he who is freed from subjection, whether he be a servant, son, *or some colony,* doth promise all those external signs at least, whereby superiors used to be honoured by their inferiors," and that the law of nature requires this agreement be honored (*DC:* 9.8, emphasis altered). It is not often noticed that for Hobbes "absolutely binding contracts are possible in the international state of nature," but for a useful recent exception, see Johnson (1993: 89, 85–94).

39 When the Lawyer asks, near the end of the *Dialogue,* whether it is lawful for one sovereign to make war against another, the Philosopher replies, "It is Lawful, or not Lawful according to the intention of him that does it." War can be justified, but not all war. In particular, he insists that "Injuries receiv'd justifie a War defensive; but for reparable injuries, if Reparation be tendred, all invasion upon that Title is Iniquity" (*D:* 159).

40 The passage most frequently cited in this regard is from *Leviathan:* "the Law of Nations, and the Law of Nature, is the same thing. . . . And the same Law, that dictateth to men that have no Civil Government, what they ought to do, and what to avoyd in regard of one another, dictateth the same to Commonwealths, that is, to the Consciences of Soveraign Princes, and Soveraign Assemblies; there being no Court of Naturall Justice, but in the Conscience onely" (*L:* 394; the identification of the law of nations with the laws of nature is also made at the conclusion of *De Corpore Politico* [*EL* II: 10.10]). There are standards of justice that apply to the relations between sovereigns, even if they apply to the conscience only, and these standards cannot be the product of convention since no authority has been established above them. One writer who notes that on Hobbes's view "nations practice injustice toward each other," is Tommy L. Lott (1989: 93).

lieves in an ethics that transcends the power of the sovereign, and this provides an additional reason to reject the contractarian interpretation of Hobbes's moral theory.

Finally, it is worth recalling one of the many remarks that made Hobbes notorious among his contemporaries. Arguing that religious controversies must be settled by the sovereign and not by the people, Hobbes maintains that "religion be not philosophy, but rather in all states law" (*DH:* 14.4). Religious truths, that is, are not accessible to human reason, and must therefore be established by agreement. One might expect that if Hobbes were a contractarian about morality he would similarly insist that ethics is not philosophy, but law. Hobbes instead refers frequently to moral philosophy, or to the science of morals, and this too implies that there is more to morality on Hobbes's account than mere human convention.

3.2.3 There is sufficient textual evidence to warrant the conclusion that Hobbes believes in a morality that is independent of human artifice; however, it remains true that in many other passages he implies that this is not possible. Time and time again he explicitly appeals to nonconventional moral standards, yet other passages clearly imply that morality can have no place outside of convention. How, therefore, shall we interpret Hobbes? As already noted, there can be no doubt that at times Hobbes's texts contradict one another. How should we evaluate the conflicting views, both of which might reasonably be attributed to Hobbes? Hobbes himself provides the only sensible answer:

> When it happeneth that a man signifieth unto us two contradictory opinions whereof the one is clearly and directly signified, and the other either drawn from that by consequence, or not known to be contradictory to it; then (when he is not present to explicate himself better) we are to take the former of his opinions; for that is clearly signified to be his, and directly, whereas the other might proceed from error in the deduction, or ignorance of the repugnancy. (*EL* I: 13.9)

That the moral law is a natural law, that the natural law governs the state of nature, that various sorts of behavior by individuals in the state of nature or by sovereigns unhindered by contract are transgressions of the moral law, unjust, vicious, sinful – all these claims Hobbes clearly, directly, and repeatedly endorses. That these claims cannot be true is only implied, and only by some of Hobbes's more general statements about value. The most reasonable conclusion would thus seem to be that although Hobbes at times limits himself so that his ethics seem entirely contractarian, he himself ultimately rejects these limits in pursuit of an ethic that goes beyond mere human convention and embraces what he refers to as a "Morality of Naturall Reason" (*L:* 711).[41] A satisfactory account of Hobbes's moral theory must recognize the contractarian streak in his writings, but it must also explain how Hobbes tries to go beyond it. This the contractarian interpretation fails to do.

3.3 HOBBES AS RULE EGOIST

One recent writer who agrees that "there *is* morality in Hobbes's state of nature," and that morality on Hobbes's account "is not purely conventional," is Gregory Kavka (1986: 357, 353).[42] In his important book *Hobbesian Moral and Political Theory,* Kavka argues that Hobbes is a sort of rule consequentialist and, in particular, that he is a rule egoist. Kavka makes the extremely strong claim that "viewing Hobbes as a rule egoist is surely necessary to enable us to understand what he is up to in his moral philosophy" (1986: 383). This is a somewhat remarkable claim, given that Kavka can find no evidence of anyone's holding this interpretation before the 1970s,[43] and it therefore prompts two immediate questions: What is rule egoism, and what grounds are there for attributing it to Hobbes?

3.3.1 Rule egoism, according to Kavka, is identified by two distinguishing features. First, it is a species of rule consequentialism as opposed to act consequentialism. Rule egoism claims that types of actions, or rules requiring them, are the appropriate objects of moral evaluation, and that this evaluation should be carried out "in

41 Thus the position taken here is similar to that taken by Jean Hampton, who concludes that "Hobbes usually embraces a nonconventionalist position in both [physics and ethics], but occasionally, in despair, slips into a conventionalist position in both areas" (1986: 48n). The problem of accounting for Hobbes's apparently contractarian statements while endorsing a noncontractarian moral theory is briefly taken up again near the end of section 3.5.2.

42 The view that Hobbes endorses a morality independent of political convention has perhaps fewer genuine historical antecedents than does the contractarian account, but it is not a purely modern invention. The introduction to one nineteenth-century collection of Hobbes's writings, for example, rightly emphasizes that "Hobbes believed in a morality independent of and antecedent to the will of the sovereign, in an eternal and immutable morality which is binding upon the conscience of man" (Sneath 1898: 32).

43 Kavka identifies a two-part article by Stanley Moore, "Hobbes on Obligation, Moral and Political," *Journal of the History of Philosophy* 9 (January 1971), pp. 43–62; 10 (January 1972), pp. 29–41, as the first published account of Hobbes as a rule egoist (1986: 258n).

terms of the (actual or expected) outcomes of certain agents performing, or trying to perform, acts of that type as a rule" (1986: 358). Second, it is a species of egoistic, as opposed to utilitarian, consequentialism. Rule egoism, in other words, insists that the consequences to be considered are those that affect the agent, and not those that affect other interested parties or society as a whole. The rule egoist believes that morality consists of a set of prescriptive rules of conduct, and that these rules are "grounded or justified by" a rule-egoistic principle of the following sort: "Each agent should attempt always to follow that set of general rules of conduct whose acceptance (and sincere attempt to follow) by him on all occasions would produce the best (expected) outcomes for him" (1986: 358–9). Kavka claims that Hobbes's laws of nature constitute a set of rules "grounded or justified" in just this way.[44] The rule "always perform your covenants," for example, would be defended by showing that an agent who accepted and tried to follow it could expect the best results for himself. In this way, Kavka claims, Hobbes attempts to reconcile the demands of traditional morality with the appeals of prudence.

Kavka identifies several considerable virtues of rule egoism as a theory of morality (1986: 364–5). Since the theory is egoistic, its potential motivating force is readily apparent. The theory is thus eminently practical, since the question "why be moral?" can be answered entirely in terms of the interest of the agent. Since the theory is a type of rule consequentialism, it features the numerous advantages over act-consequentialist theories that have been noted in the literature. Although Kavka does not explicitly point to this as an advantage of the theory, the fact that rule egoism (at least as in the form in which Kavka attributes it to Hobbes) seeks to justify the traditional rules of morality ensures that it will fit nicely with at least some of our important moral intuitions. Rule egoism is, therefore, at the very least an intriguing and perhaps neglected form of moral theory. The question is whether there are sufficient grounds for attributing it to Hobbes.

Kavka's case for attributing rule egoism to Hobbes is brief. He begins by claiming that "It is obvious from Hobbes's definition of, descriptions of, and comments on the laws of nature that they are general prescriptive rules of conduct" (1986: 360). It is also clear,

44 Although Kavka adds in a footnote that the rule-egoistic principle "is not to be attributed to Hobbes in all its particulars," he does maintain "that a rule-egoistic grounding of some such sort is what he intends and that this is the most defensible form in which it can be put" (1986: 358n).

Kavka maintains, that "the main aim of his moral theory is to reveal the consequentialist grounding or justification of traditional morality and its requirements." As evidence, Kavka cites the following lengthy passage from *Leviathan* (1986: 360):

> all men agree on this, that Peace is Good, and therefore also the way, or means of Peace, which (as I have shewed before) are *Justice, Gratitude, Modesty, Equity, Mercy,* & the rest of the Laws of Nature, are good; that is to say, *Morall Vertues;* and their contrarie *Vices,* Evill. Now the science of Vertue and Vice, is Morall Philosophie; and therfore the true Doctrine of the Lawes of Nature, is the true Morall Philosophie. But the Writers of Morall Philosophie, though they acknowledge the same Vertues and Vices; Yet not seeing wherein consisted their Goodness; nor that they come to be praised, as the meanes of peaceable, sociable, and comfortable living; place them in a mediocrity of passions. (*L:* 216)

These few observations, Kavka claims, "would suffice to establish the general rule-egoistic interpretation of Hobbes's moral theory were it not for the prominent competing view – best represented by Warrender – that Hobbes's moral theory is a divine command theory" (1986: 360–1). Kavka dismisses the divine command account rather handily, and with that his case for the rule-egoistic interpretation of Hobbes comes to a close.

3.3.2 Setting the divine-command account aside until later,[45] we must ask whether the rule-egoistic interpretation is sufficiently established by Kavka's remarks. The interpretation attributes to Hobbes two distinct claims about the laws of nature: that they are prescriptive rules governing conduct, and that they are "grounded or justified" by the benefits sincere adherence to them brings to the agent. If both attributions are warranted, then Kavka's conclusion must be accepted as sound. The lengthy passage Kavka cites clearly shows that, for Hobbes, the laws of nature are good because of the contribution they make to maintaining peace. Since Hobbes argues that peace is a necessary condition for any person to secure his self-preservation, the passage shows that the laws of nature are good because of benefits they provide to the agent who follows them. But is it really "obvious," as Kavka maintains, that these laws of nature, understood as the means to peace, are general prescriptive rules of conduct?

In a sense the answer is clearly yes. Hobbes frequently refers to the laws of nature as rules of conduct and this has traditionally been understood to show that, as one recent defender of this inter-

45 See section 3.4.

pretation has put it, the laws of nature "require us to *behave* morally, but not to *be* moral" (Nunan 1989: 41). Hobbes, however, is also careful to remind us (though perhaps not so frequently as he should) that whereas each law of nature *refers* to conduct, strictly speaking it *governs* intentions only. In *De Cive,* for example, he argues that *"The laws of nature are immutable and eternal: . . .* For *pride, ingratitude, breach of contracts (or injury), inhumanity, contumely,* will never be lawful, nor the contrary virtues to these ever unlawful, as we take them for dispositions of the mind, that is, as they are considered in the court of conscience, where only they oblige and are laws" (*DC:* 3.29). This imagery is repeated in *Behemoth,* where Hobbes again insists that "moral duties" apply to "the inner court of conscience" (*B:* 6), and in *Leviathan,* where he argues that the laws of nature apply to commonwealths, "that is, to the Consciences of Soveraign Princes, and Soveraign Assemblies; there being no Court of Naturall Justice, but in the Conscience onely" (*L:* 394). In *Human Nature,* he specifies that since "the laws of nature concern the conscience, not he only breaketh them that doth any action contrary, but also he whose action is conformable to them, in case he think it contrary. For though the action chance to be right, yet in his judgment he despiseth the law" (*EL* I: 17.13). In *De Corpore Politico* he reiterates that "observation of the law of nature" requires only "the endeavour, and constant will to do that which is just" (*EL* II: 6.10). In *Leviathan,* he makes it clear that when they are understood apart from civil society, "the Lawes of Nature, which consist in Equity, Justice, Gratitude, and other morall Vertues on these depending . . . are not properly Lawes, but qualities that dispose men to peace, and to obedience" (*L:* 314) and that the moral laws are "habits of the mind" (*L:* 330).[46] It is regrettable that Hobbes often refers to these dispositions of the mind improperly as laws, and understandable that this improper usage has often been taken to prove that the laws of nature are meant to be understood as prescriptive rules of conduct. But Hobbes himself pointedly and unequivocally acknowledges that his use of the term "law" in this context is improper, and he explicitly insists that the virtues the laws of nature define are, in fact, qualities, habits, or dispositions of the mind. The fact that Hobbes believed that the "laws" of nature are good because they are the means to peace does not constitute sufficient evidence that he believed their goodness can be used

46 The description of the laws of nature as "habits of the mind" also appears in *Human Nature* (*EL* I: 16.4).

to "ground or justify" a set of prescriptive rules that only require that we behave morally but do not insist that we be, by habit or disposition, moral.

The very passage Kavka cites in defense of the rule-egoistic interpretation strongly suggests that Hobbes wished to avoid just this conclusion. Hobbes notes in that passage that the laws of nature are good "that is to say, *Morall Vertues,*" and he insists that "the science of Vertue and Vice, is Morall Philosophie" (*L:* 216). When Hobbes claims that justice, gratitude, modesty, and so forth, have been shown to be good, he makes a point of the fact that he is using these terms to refer to moral virtues. In the same chapter, he explains specifically what he means when he refers to, for example, justice as a virtue.

Hobbes begins his explanation by noting the difference between attributing justice to an action and attributing it to a person. An act is just when it conforms to reason, but a person is not called just simply for performing just acts. The performance of just acts merely renders a person guiltless. Rather, Hobbes insists, a person is called just when his or her "manners" are in conformity to reason. A just man, that is, "is he that taketh all the care he can, that his Actions may be all Just: and an Unjust man, is he that neglecteth it" (*L:* 206). The just man "does not lose that Title, by one, or a few unjust Actions, that proceed from sudden Passion, or mistake of Things, or Persons" (*L:* 206). The reason for this is clear: When we call a person just, according to Hobbes, we are describing his character, asserting that the person is generally disposed to be just. Such a person may, owing to lack of self-control or an error of judgment, commit isolated acts of injustice. Hobbes devotes a long paragraph to developing this important distinction, and concludes by specifying: "This Justice of the Manners, is that which is meant, where Justice is called a Vertue; and Injustice a Vice" (*L:* 207). When Hobbes is careful to note at the end of Chapter 15 that it is in the sense in which they are virtues that justice, gratitude, and so forth, have been shown to be good, therefore, he is reminding the reader that he is referring to the justice of manners and not to the justice of acts.[47] The only passage that Kavka provides to support his

47 Nor is this a revision of the position taken in his earlier works. In *De Corpore Politico,* Hobbes writes of "the observation of the law of nature, which is that for which a man is called just or righteous (in that sense in which justice is taken not for the absence of all guilt, but for the endeavour, and constant will to do that which is just)" (*EL* II: 6.10).

claim that Hobbes is trying to "ground or justify" a rule requiring only a certain type of action shows instead Hobbes ultimately defending a kind of character trait or disposition. The rule egoist is distinguished by an insistence that it is rules governing actions that are the appropriate object of moral evaluation and justification, but by focusing the reader's attention on moral virtues in the very passage that Kavka cites, Hobbes explicitly distances himself from this view. Justice of actions is no doubt important, but moral philosophy is the science of virtue, and ultimately concerned with the justice of manners.

Kavka seems at times to overlook the importance of distinguishing between the claim that Hobbes is justifying the goodness of certain rules of action and the claim that he is justifying the goodness of certain types of dispositions. At one point, for example, he refers to "the kinds of acts or dispositions prescribed in each of these laws [of nature]" as if justifying the goodness of a character trait were equivalent to justifying the goodness of a class of actions (1986: 342).[48] Rules and dispositions are two different things, and which one Hobbes's laws of nature refer to makes a crucial difference in evaluating Kavka's interpretation.[49] Only when they are understood as rules governing action can the laws of nature be used to support the claim that Hobbes was a rule egoist, and as already mentioned, Hobbes explicitly warns us not to understand them in this way.

Finally, it must be noted that Kavka truncates his citation in the middle of a sentence, and this incomplete reference masks a fur-

48 Moore, in defending his rule-egoist interpretation of Hobbes, does much the same thing. He notes Hobbes's distinction between a just act and a just man, but then insists that on Hobbes's account "the just man is a rule-egoist" (1971: 50). As we have already seen, and will see in more detail in what follows, a just person on Hobbes's account is more than merely a person whose acts are in accordance with a just rule.

49 Kavka also overlooks this distinction in an earlier article in which he initially sets forth his rule-egoist account. Kavka twice describes the laws of nature as requiring the practice of "the traditional moral virtues" (1983: 123, 126), but at the same time he treats the laws of nature as "rules" which determine "right and wrong conduct" (1983: 126), as if rules governing conduct and virtues of character are one and the same. When he does make the distinction clear, Kavka is consistent in his portrayal of Hobbes as interested in rules rather than dispositions. In another piece, which preceded his book, Kavka wrote that "Plato argues the prudential advantages of moral dispositions or ways of life, while Hobbes focuses on providing a prudential grounding for moral rules" (1985: 298).

ther point against his interpretation.[50] Kavka's passage ends with Hobbes complaining that the (Aristotelian) writers of moral philosophy, failing to understand what made the virtues good, placed them "in a mediocrity of passions." Hobbes goes on to say in the uncited remainder of the sentence that this is to view the virtues "as if not the Cause, but the Degree of daring, made Fortitude; or not the Cause, but the Quantity of a gift, made Liberality" (*L:* 216). The point of this thinly disguised attack on Aristotle seems to be: Aristotle believed the virtues are good *because* they are a mean between two extremes (hardly a satisfactory account of Aristotle, but this does seem to be Hobbes's view);[51] whether an act is an instance of liberality, on this account, depends on its quantity. But, Hobbes prefers to say, this is wrong; what makes an act liberal is its *cause,* the reason the giver has for giving.[52] If caused by a virtuous character that disposes one to be liberal, then it is an act of liberality in the sense in which liberality is a virtue. But if it is caused, for example, by a fear of punishment or by a desire to win admiration, then it is not an instance of the virtue of liberality.[53] As Hobbes says earlier in the chapter, the unrighteous man does not "lose his character, for such Actions, as he does, or forbeares to do, for feare: because his Will is not framed by the Justice, but by the apparant benefit of what he is to do" (*L:* 206–7). This position, moreover, is repeated in an important passage in *Behemoth,* which confirms that for Hobbes there are virtues that apply to people independently of civil society: "It is not the Much or Little that makes an action virtuous, but the cause; nor Much or Little that makes an action vicious, but its being unconformable to the laws in such men as are subject to the law, or its being unconformable to equity or charity in all men whatsoever" (*B:* 44).

50 I do *not* mean to suggest that Kavka intentionally omits the end of the final sentence because he recognizes that it is inimical to his interpretation. Rather, my point is that precisely because he does not consider the importance of Hobbes's definition of virtue, he does not realize that the end of the sentence he cites is relevant to the question of whether Hobbes is a rule egoist.

51 See section 5.1 for a more detailed treatment of Hobbes's understanding of, and attitude toward, Aristotle's ethics.

52 That this is what Hobbes has in mind here is perhaps made clearer in the corresponding passage in *Human Nature:* "[I]n gifts it is not the sum that maketh liberality, but the *reason*" (*EL* I: 17.14, emphasis added).

53 Not all writers have overlooked the significance of this passage. Strauss, for example, cites it as evidence that for Hobbes "the reason, the motive of an action or of a form of behaviour is the only criterion of its moral value" (1936: 54).

If Hobbes were a rule egoist, he would have to endorse the claim that a person is morally good to the extent that he or she always follows rules which prescribe certain sorts of acts as good. Hobbes, however, insists that always doing good acts is neither a necessary nor a sufficient condition for a person to be deemed morally good. It is not a necessary condition, because a person disposed to justice may nevertheless fail from time to time to perform justly. It is not a sufficient condition, because a person who always does the right thing, but does so because of the apparent benefit of doing so, is rendered not good but simply guiltless. The evidence Kavka provides in defense of the rule-egoist interpretation is therefore insufficient.

In addition to the paucity of convincing textual support for Kavka's interpretation, there is one other powerful reason to deny that Hobbes was a rule egoist. This reason arises from a problem with rule egoism itself. To show that rule egoism is a flawed theory does not demonstrate that Hobbes did not advocate it. But if the flaw is a serious one, and if it can be avoided by means of another plausible reading of the texts, then surely the latter reading is to be preferred.[54]

The rule egoist, according to Kavka, maintains that the fact that always attempting to follow the rule "Always do *x*" produces the best results for the agent can be used to "ground or justify" the rule "Always do *x*." It must eventually be asked, in what sense does trying to follow the rule (without necessarily succeeding) provide a justification for the rule itself? And, in particular, how can it justify the claim that one should adhere to the rule when such adherence would clearly prove disadvantageous to oneself? The theory, after all, is avowedly egoistic; in evaluating competing sets of rules, it allows consideration of only those consequences that affect the agent. The theory also takes general rules of conduct to be appropriate objects of moral evaluation. The problem is that the egoistic foundation of the theory seems to show only that it is good generally to do *x* or that it is good to try always to do *x* (rather than that it is good to succeed at always doing *x*), whereas the rules themselves, which the theory is supposed to justify, say that it is good always to do *x*. Rule egoism, in short, seems to endorse an unjustifiable form of rule worship.[55]

54 See the discussion of the Foole in section 4.3.1 for an account of how the flaw with rule egoism identified here can be overcome on the interpretation of Hobbes defended in this work.

55 The same problem presumably also arises for rule utilitarianism (see, e.g., Smart 1973: 9–12).

Kavka recognizes this potential problem for rule egoism, and acknowledges its force. For the egoist to follow a rule in a particular case when he knows that doing so will harm him just because he also knows that he benefits from following the rule in general, Kavka allows, might seem to be "like following a map that is generally accurate but [which] you have reason to believe will lead you astray in seeking the best route to your current destination" (1986: 378). If it is the long-term benefit to the agent of promise keeping that justifies the practice of keeping promises, for example, it would seem to justify only the rule "Keep your promises except in those cases in which breaking them is in your long-term interest," and not the rule "Always keep your promises." The problem is particularly acute in the case of Hobbes, because he insists that the same laws of nature apply to all individuals. It would therefore seem that he could provide an egoistic jusitification of the rule "Always keep your promises" only if it were in the interest of every individual in every situation to keep promises. He would also have to endorse a similar claim with respect to all the other laws of nature, if he were to provide a comprehensive defense of his moral theory.

This problem raised by the rule worship objection has two important implications for the reading of Hobbes as a rule egoist. The first is that it seems to show that Hobbes can defend his moral theory only by collapsing it into a defense of act egoism. If the rule "Always do *x*" can be justified only by showing that each act of doing *x* is in the agent's best interest, then it can only be justified by reducing it to the claim that one should always do what is in one's best interest. This poses a problem for at least part of Kavka's defense of rule egoism as a theory, since it deprives Hobbes's theory of the advantages often supposed to recommend rule consequentialism over act consequentialism. The second implication of the rule-worship problem seems to be that any defense of Hobbes's moral theory as a rule-egoistic theory is bound to be absurd. There will always be circumstances in which one would benefit by taking advantage of others and violating the laws of nature, but the rule-worship problem suggests that Hobbes can defend his theory only by denying this obvious truth. What does Kavka have to say about this potent difficulty?

Kavka's response runs as follows: "It will not be possible to defend Hobbes's moral theory if it is interpreted as requiring that it be most prudentially rational in every case, for every agent, in every possible (or even actual) social environment to follow the laws of nature and eschew offensive violations. But at least for the purposes of Hobbesian theory we need not so interpret it" (1986: 381). Kavka, it must be noted, explicitly remarks at the outset of his book that he is concerned to develop and defend a "Hobbesian" theory "suggested and inspired by Hobbes" that departs from Hobbes's views in a variety of ways that are "not trivial" (1986: 3). In the case of the rule-worship objection, he seems content to allow that the problem is insoluble for Hobbes's rule egoism, but that it can be satisfactorily addressed by his own modified Hobbesian rule egoism. In particular, Kavka argues that because his theory depends on what he calls predominant egoism rather than pure egoism, he can rely on the assumption that agents will typically "care very much about the well-being of certain others, and care to some extent about the well-being of people in general." From this he argues that for Hobbesian agents (though not, on Kavka's account, for Hobbes's) it will pay "to adopt a generally *conscientious attitude* toward moral rules" which means that one comes "to value one's own compliance with them at least partly for its own sake" (1986: 382). If Hobbesian theory can justify the claim that each agent has reason to value compliance with moral rules for its own sake, then it can apparently overcome the objection that it endorses an irrational form of rule worship. Kavka's view is that Hobbes*ian* theory can do this but that Hobbes's theory cannot.

We shall return to the question of whether Hobbes's theory can justify valuing compliance for its own sake in the sections that follow, but for now we must consider the relevance of the rule-worship objection to Kavka's claim that Hobbes was, in fact, a rule egoist. The relevance of the objection seems to be this: Kavka says the aim of his book is to introduce Hobbes into that "select group" of "great philosophers of the past" who "are taken seriously as expositors of fundamentally sound moral and political views" (1986: xii). He argues, as we have noted, that "viewing Hobbes as a rule egoist is surely necessary to enable us to understand what he is up to in his moral philosophy," but he also acknowledges that the rule-worship objection means it is "not possible" to defend that moral theory as attributed to Hobbes. The only way to understand Hobbes's theory is as an indefensible one. With friendly readers like Kavka, Hobbes hardly needs critics.

It is possible that Hobbes's moral theory is indefensible, and many if not most of his readers have so concluded. If Kavka is right that one must read Hobbes as a rule egoist to understand what he is doing, we have no choice but to conclude that Hobbes's theory as it stands is wrong. Even the most conservative principle of charitable interpretation, however, must insist that if we can find another way of understanding Hobbes that is consistent with the texts and does not burden him with so flawed a position, that interpretation is to be preferred. The severity of the rule-worship objection provides a reason for questioning the rule-egoistic interpretation that is independent of the absence of compelling textual evidence for it.

3.3.3 Kavka's rule-egoistic interpretation of Hobbes has several important merits. It recognizes that Hobbes does not view morality as a product of human convention, and it understands Hobbes's goal to be that of reconciling the demands of traditional morality with those of individual well-being. In doing so, it correctly points to Hobbes's concern with the effects of morality and immorality on moral agents, and leads to the nearly unavoidable conclusion that Hobbesian morality must in some way be concerned with consequences. But in arguing that it is prescriptive rules of conduct that Hobbes ultimately evaluates in terms of consequences, Kavka runs into two serious problems. It is insufficiently supported by Hobbes's texts, since it cannot be reconciled with his repeated and unequivocal warnings that the laws of nature must be understood as endorsing qualities or dispositions of the mind and not as rules prescribing the performance of certain classes of action. It also burdens Hobbes with a position that is, even by Kavka's account, indefensible. A satisfactory account of Hobbes's moral theory must surely incorporate the fundamental insights that lead Kavka to reject the contractarian interpretation. But it must just as surely attempt to avoid the difficulties arising from Kavka's exclusive emphasis on rules of conduct. Kavka proceeds on the assumption that the only alternative to rule egoism worth considering is the divine-command interpretation associated with Taylor and Warrender. If that view also proves unacceptable, we shall have to generate, from the considerations that lead us to reject these traditional views of Hobbes, an alternative worthier of acceptance.

3.4 HOBBES AS DIVINE-COMMAND THEORIST

In 1938, A. E. Taylor published an important article, "The Ethical Doctrine of Hobbes," defending three distinct, though related, claims about Hobbes's moral theory: (1) that it is logically independent of Hobbes's (allegedly) egoistic psychology, (2) that it is deontological in character, (3) that it is a form of divine-command theory. Taylor's article provoked an enormous amount of discussion, but it found few genuine supporters until Howard Warrender published his influential work on *The Political Philosophy of Hobbes* a full twenty years later. Warrender provided a detailed and impressive argument for claims 1 and 3, and the conjunction of these two positions (but most important, position 3) came to be known as the Taylor-Warrender thesis. That thesis, it is fair to say, has been almost universally rejected by Hobbes scholars in the past thirty years, for a variety of reasons only a few of which will be touched on here. Warrender's thorough study undoubtedly did much to bolster the argument that Taylor had only sketched in his paper, but its very success ultimately proved a disservice to Taylor. Although Taylor's name came to be appended to the thesis defended in Warrender's book, Warrender explicitly rejected Taylor's claim 2 that Hobbes's moral theory is deontological,[56] and largely lost in the rush to refute the "Taylor"-Warrender thesis has been the fact that claim 2 was the one Taylor considered central to his paper. As he emphasized in the article's concluding paragraph, after noting that his "serious concern" was not with Hobbes's personal beliefs about God, "The point I am really anxious to make is that Hobbes's *ethical* theory is commonly misrepresented and unintelligently criticized for want of sufficient recognition that it is, from first to last, a doctrine of *duty*, a strict deontology" (1965: 54). To complicate the picture even further, A. P. Martinich recently published an impressive study, *The Two Gods of Leviathan* (1992), which surpasses even Warrender's work in the strength of its case for 3, while denying 1,[57] and which will renew and enhance the discussion of the role of religion in Hobbes's moral and political thought. We are concerned here with Hobbes's moral theory, in particular, and the discussion of Hobbes's views on religion therefore raises two important questions which must be addressed: Are there adequate grounds for

56 Warrender acknowledges the debt his work owes to Taylor, but he is also careful to note their many differences. In the conclusion, he emphasizes that "the greatest discrepancy . . . between Professor Taylor's interpretation and that to which we have subscribed, arises from the attitude taken to what might be called the Kantian analogies in Hobbes's doctrine. . . . [W]e have regarded the drawing of analogies between the theories of Hobbes and Kant as generally misleading" (1957: 336–7). Warrender reiterates his disavowal of the deontological reading of Hobbes in (1987: 303–4).

57 Martinich explicitly rejects 1, concluding that "the claim that Hobbes's psychology of motivation is independent of his moral theory must . . . be discarded." He does not specifically consider 2, which is not a part of the Taylor-Warrender thesis but only of the Taylor thesis, but it is clear that the role for self-interest that he endorses is incompatible with 2 (1992: 135).

endorsing the Taylor-Warrender (and now Martinich) thesis (claim 3)? And if not, what effect does this have on the status of the Taylor thesis (claim 2)? I begin by considering the grounds Taylor and Martinich provide for reading Hobbes as a divine-command theorist, and conclude by attending to what is left of the Taylor thesis once God is removed from the picture.

3.4.1 Taylor begins by distinguishing between two questions Hobbes is concerned to answer: "the question why I *ought* to behave as a good citizen, and the question what inducement can be given me to do so if my knowledge of the obligation to do so is not in itself sufficiently effective" (1965: 36). The egoistic psychology typically attributed to Hobbes, Taylor notes, is relevant to answering the second of these questions. Since Hobbesian agents (on this view) necessarily act out of self-interest, the claim that being good will serve that interest will induce them to behave themselves. But, Taylor insists, Hobbes's egoism is irrelevant to answering the first question. It is important to Hobbes's system that each individual benefit from being a good citizen, but that is not the reason each citizen *ought* to be a good citizen. Instead, Taylor argues, Hobbes believes that I ought to be a good citizen because "I have, expressly or tacitly, pledged my word to be one, and to violate my word, to refuse to 'perform my covenant as made,' is *iniquity, malum in se.*" I should be good because it would be bad not to be, and thus Taylor characterizes Hobbes's position as "a very strict deontology, curiously suggestive, though with interesting differences, of some of the characteristic theses of Kant" (1965: 37).

The most striking evidence Taylor provides for this claim is Hobbes's distinction in *De Cive* between a just act and a just man (1965: 37–8; bracketed sentence omitted in Taylor's citation):

> When the words are applied to persons, *to be just* signifies as much as to be delighted in just dealing, to study how to do righteousness, or to endeavour in all things to do that which is just; and *to be unjust* is to neglect righteous dealing, or to think it is to be measured not according to my contract, but some present benefit. [So as the justice or injustice of the mind, the intention, or the man, is one thing, that of an action or omission another; and innumerable actions of a just man may be unjust, and of an unjust man, just.] But that man is to be accounted just, who doth just things because the law commands it, unjust things only by reason of his infirmity; and he is properly said to be unjust, who doth righteousness for fear of the punishment annexed unto the law, and unrighteousness by reason of the iniquity of his mind. (*DC:* 3.5)

Taylor also notes Hobbes's later statement that "although a man should order all his actions so much as belongs to external obedience just as the law commands, but not for the law's sake, but by reason of some punishment annexed to it, or out of vain glory; yet he is unjust" (*DC:* 4.21; cited in 1965: 38n). He could also have cited the very similar passage from *Leviathan,* noted earlier in discussing Kavka's interpretation,[58] distinguishing just acts from just men. Although Taylor also overlooks Hobbes's footnote in *De Cive* elaborating on the meaning of genuine obligation, it nonetheless provides an additional piece of evidence in his favor: "A man is obliged by his contracts, that is . . . he ought to perform for his promise sake" (*DC:* 14.2n). There seems to be a variety of unambiguous passages from Hobbes's most important works to support Taylor's fundamental claim that Hobbes believes a just person is one who does just things because the law commands it.

Taylor makes two more observations about Hobbes's conception of morality, both firmly supported by Hobbes's texts. The first is that moral obligation exists even in the state of nature. The laws of nature, Taylor notes, are described as "dictates, never as *consilia,* or pieces of advice" even when Hobbes is discussing the state of nature. The moral obligation to obey the natural law, Taylor therefore insists, "is antecedent to the existence of the legislator and the civil society" (1965: 40, 41). The second point Taylor focuses on is that within civil society, the sovereign "is just as much under a rigid law of moral obligation as his subjects. He is obliged to equity, the strict observance of the natural (or moral) law, which means, in effect, that he is bound to command and forbid always with a view to the good of the community" (1965: 45). Taylor warns against the temptation to dwell exclusively on the extensive rights Hobbes grants to the sovereign, and notes that Hobbes also devotes an entire chapter of *De Cive* (Chapter 13) to *"the Duties of those who bear Rule."* In that chapter, Taylor emphasizes, Hobbes does not refrain from describing a wide variety of sovereign activity as "iniquity" and "sin" (1965: 45). Taylor's comments touch on the considerations raised in section 3.2.2 against the contractarian interpretation of Hobbes's moral theory.

One final element of Taylor's interpretation must be noted before we can consider how he attempts to fit them all together. Having

58 The distinction is also drawn in *Human Nature,* in which Hobbes maintains that "an unjust man may have done justly not only one, but most of his actions" if he "abstaineth from injuries for fear of punishment" (*EL* I: 16.4).

argued that the just person is one who does just things because it is the law to do so, and having claimed that this applies to both individuals in the state of nature and sovereigns in civil society, Taylor stops to ask what Hobbes means by a law. Taylor turns again to *De Cive* for the answer, and notes Hobbes's distinction there between following counsel and obeying law. "*Law is the command of the person, whether man or court, whose precept contains in it the reason of obedience. . . . Law* belongs to him who hath power over those whom he adviseth; counsel to them who have no power. To follow what is prescribed by *law,* is *duty;* what by *counsel* is *freewill*" (*DC:* 14.1; cited in 1965: 46–7). Although Taylor avoids depending on *Leviathan* for support for his thesis, Hobbes makes similar remarks there: "Law in generall, is not Counsell, but Command; nor a Command of any man to any man; but only of him, whose Command is addressed to one formerly obliged to obey him" (*L:* 312). To follow a law is, therefore, to obey the command of one whose command legitimately obliges.

Although Martinich does not endorse Taylor's Kantian characterization of Hobbes's moral theory, the foundation of his argument for reading Hobbes as a divine-command theorist is much the same as Taylor's. Like Taylor, Martinich recognizes that for Hobbes moral obligations can exist in the state of nature. Martinich draws a conceptual distinction between the state of nature understood in isolation from the laws of nature, which he calls the "primary state of nature," and the state of nature understood in conjunction with the laws of nature, which he calls the "secondary state of nature" (1992: 76). His claim that moral obligations exist in the state of nature refers to the state of nature in its secondary sense. Like Taylor, Martinich cites Hobbes's definition of law as a kind of command, though he documents and discusses it in substantially more detail (1992: chap. 4).

From this largely common set of assumptions, Taylor and Martinich are led to a puzzle. Taylor casts the puzzle in terms of the sovereign's moral duty to his subjects: "If the fulfilling of the law of nature is a duty in the sovereign, it follows that the law of nature is a *command,* and a command the reason for obedience whereto is that it is the precept of a 'person' with the *right* to command. What 'person', then, is this, whose commands are binding on princes because they are *his* commands?" (1965: 49). Martinich identifies essentially the same problem, casting it in terms of the moral duties of individuals within the state of nature: "If justice and injustice require a law, and law requires a common power, as Hobbes claimed in his discussion of the primary state of nature, what law and what common power make justice and injustice possible in the secondary state of nature?" (1992: 79). This is a genuine problem, if Taylor and Martinich are right about Hobbes's use of the term "law" and about his claim that the laws of nature are moral laws. And both propose the same solution. Taylor describes his response as follows: "I can only make Hobbes's statements consistent with one another by supposing that he meant quite seriously what he so often says, that the 'natural law' is the command of God, and to be obeyed *because* it is God's command" (1965: 49). Martinich answers his own question by noting: "The only law in the state of nature is the law of nature. And the only common power in the state of nature is God. Consequently, justice and injustice exist in the (secondary) state of nature, because there is a law, established by a common power, namely, God" (1992: 79). For both Taylor and Martinich, then, the insistence that God plays an integral role in Hobbes's moral theory serves not as a starting point from which to develop an interpretation but, rather, as the only consistent way to conclude it. As Martinich puts it, "God is an essential component of the moral laws, according to Hobbes, because laws involve obligation and the only person with the irresistible power necessary to create obligation is God" (1992: 136). Taylor urges us to read Hobbes as a divine-command theorist because "in no other way can we make his explicit statements about the connection between the notions of a *duty*, a *command*, and a *law* coherent with each other. A certain kind of theism is absolutely necessary to make the theory work" (1965: 50).[59] The puzzle identified by Taylor and Martinich is real, and we must therefore ask whether their proposed solution to it is satisfactory, and, if not, whether a superior one can be found.

3.4.2 One argument often marshaled against the divine-command interpretation rests on the claim that Hobbes was an atheist. A number of his contemporaries believed, or at least

59 F. C. Hood's interpretation of Hobbes in many respects forms a more natural companion to Taylor's view than does Warrender's. Hood follows Taylor in emphasizing the distinction between just acts and just men and, in reading Hobbes's moral theory as a theory of moral duty, he argues that on "principles of nature, Hobbes does not, and cannot, account for the performance of moral duty," and concludes that "Scripture was the only source of Hobbes's moral convictions" (1964: 31, 4). Martinich spells out some of his differences with Hood in (1992: 13–14).

claimed, he was,[60] and if Hobbes did not believe in God,[61] it is at the very least dubious to attribute to him a moral theory whose acceptance must ultimately rest on such a belief. This objection is potentially powerful, but it is insufficiently supported. It is not clear that there are sound reasons to conclude that Hobbes was an atheist, and Martinich's book provides an extremely compelling case for concluding that he was not merely a vague and noncommittal theist but a sincere believer committed to a specific set of Christian doctrines. Until someone can convincingly overturn Martinich's argument, the claim that Hobbes was an atheist will remain an unacceptably weak point from which to reject the interpretation of him as endorsing a divine-command theory of morality.

Even if we accept that Hobbes was a devout Christian, however, it is possible that his expressed views about the nature of religious knowledge could undermine the divine-command interpretation of his moral theory. One thing Hobbes clearly believed, for example, was that any rational knowledge we might have about God (as opposed to knowledge obtained through revelation) is severely limited. The only quality we can literally predicate of God is His existence. We can say that God is infinite, or eternal, or holy, but in Hobbes's account this is "meant not to declare what he is, (for that were to circumscribe him within the limits of our Fancy,) but how much wee admire him, and how ready we would be to obey him" (*L:* 403). If there is a God at work in Hobbes's system of thought, it is one about whom we can rationally understand little if anything beyond the fact of His existence.[62]

Hobbes seems to doubt that we can even know God exists through reason alone. It is true that he at times notes we seem compelled to posit the existence of God when we try to trace chains of effects back to their original causes and are finally led to assent to the existence of a first cause. In *Leviathan,* for example, he writes that curiosity "draws a man from consideration of the effect, to seek the cause; and again, the cause of that cause; till of necessity

60 John Milward's *Diary* entry for October 17, 1666, reports that "It was moved in the House [of Commons] that certain atheistical books should be burned, among which Mr. Hobbes's *Leviathan* was one" (Robbins 1938: 25).

61 Though it is important to note that in the sixteenth and early seventeenth centuries, the terms "atheist" and "Deist" were used almost interchangeably; the charge by his contemporaries that Hobbes was an atheist could, therefore, strictly speaking, have been compatible with his belief in the existence of God. (See Wootton 1988: 704–5.)

62 On the implications of this position for Hobbes's critique of representational religious art, see Woodfield (1980).

he must come to this thought at last, that there is some cause, whereof there is no former cause, but is eternall; which is it men call God" (*L:* 167). But this passage need not be read as endorsing the soundness of such an inference; it can be understood as a claim about how curiosity leads people to believe in God.[63] As one student of Hobbes's theology has put it, the arguments Hobbes describes in such passages "are not 'arguments' in a theological sense, but only remarks about the feelings to which a student of natural causes of phenomena necessarily inclines" (Pacchi 1988: 180). Hobbes is more explicit elsewhere about his doubts as to the soundness of such an inference. In the critique of White's *De Mundo,* for example, he insists of those who "declare that they will show that God exists" that they "act unphilosophically" (*DME:* 26.2). In *De Corpore,* he specifically declares that the possibility of an infinite regress of causes that fails to terminate with a first cause cannot be ruled out by philosophy: "Though a man may from some effect proceed to the immediate cause thereof, and from that to a more remote cause, and so ascend continually by right ratiocination from cause to cause; yet he will not be able to proceed eternally, but wearied will at last give over, *without knowing whether it were possible for him to proceed to an end or not*" (*Co:* 26.1, emphasis added; see also Hobbes's response to Zeno's paradox, *Co:* 5.13). Hobbes plainly states, "I cannot therefore commend those that boast they have demonstrated, by reasons drawn from natural things, that the world had a beginning."[64] He concludes that ques-

63 The same can be said of Hobbes's account of this procedure in his fifth objection to Descartes: The person who traces such effects back to their causes, he writes, "is finally led to the supposition of some eternal cause which never began to exist and hence cannot have a cause prior to itself, and he concludes that something eternal must necessarily exist. [He then] gives the name or label 'God' to the thing that he believes in, or acknowledges to exist" ("O": 127). Note that although he refers to the person thinking of this as a necessary conclusion, Hobbes himself merely says that the existence of a first cause is a "supposition" which such a person eventually makes, and that God is something he now "believes in," not something whose existence he has now demonstrated.

64 Hobbes reaffirms his rejection of such arguments in his "Considerations Upon the Answer of Doctor Wallis to the Three Papers of Mr. Hobbes," which he composed at the age of eighty-four. In response to Wallis's challenge to reconsider his claim "that there is no argument in natural philosophy to prove that the world had a beginning," Hobbes argues that any such argument would also absurdly show that God, too, had a beginning, and he therefore dismisses such attempts to prove the existence of a first cause as "but the ambition of schoolboys" (*EW* VII: 445 [original in italics], 446).

tions about the beginning of the world, "are not to be determined by philosophers, but by those that are lawfully authorized to order the worship of God" (*Co:* 26.1). Hobbes seems to believe that reason alone cannot demonstrate to us that God exists,[65] and even in those passages that suggest he might think otherwise,[66] it remains clear that reason can tell us nothing further about God than his existence.

Taylor is right to say that this fact alone cannot warrant the conclusion that Hobbes is an atheist. To insist on the utter incomprehensibility of God by reason, he notes, was "the common stock-in-trade of orthodox Christian scholastics" (1965: 51). Martinich goes into an impressive amount of detail to show that "Hobbes's explanation of what can be said about God is a sophisticated and astute defense of traditionally approved talk about the Judeo-Christian God" (1992: 203). Although Hobbes's belief that knowledge of God through reason is strictly limited need not force us to read him as an atheist, it creates a difficulty for our reading him as a divine-command theorist. For people, as Hobbes insists in *Behemoth,* "can never by their own wisdom come to the knowledge of what God hath spoken and commanded to be observed, nor be obliged to obey the laws whose author they know not" (*B:* 46). If we know so little about God, how can we know what God wants us to do? According to Hobbes's theology, we cannot attribute any wants or desires to God at all (*L:* 402). Taylor's treatment of this potentially severe problem is unfortunately brief. He concedes that he does

65 K. C. Brown argues that Hobbes believed the existence of God can be known by reason through the Argument from Design and that this is "more fundamental" to Hobbes than the argument from the need for a first cause. But the few pieces of textual evidence in favor of attributing this argument to Hobbes which Brown deems "unequivocal" are susceptible to precisely the same sort of explanation offered above: that Hobbes is not endorsing the soundness of the argument, but merely observing its tendency to generate a belief in God among people. Thus Hobbes writes in *Leviathan* that "By the visible things in this world and their admirable order, a man may conceive there is a cause of them which men call God" (*L:* 167) and in *Decameron Physiologicum* that "It is very hard to believe that, to produce male and female, and all that belongs thereto, as also the several and curious organs of sense and memory, could be the work of anything that had not understanding" (*DP:* 176), but in neither case does he explicitly endorse the claim that reason validates the conclusion that God exists (1962: 341, 342).

66 In his *Answer to Bramhall's "Catching of Leviathan,"* for example, Hobbes does maintain "that right reason dictates, there is a God" and that atheism is "a sin of ignorance," but he says nothing to indicate how reason is supposed to verify God's existence (*EW* IV: 293).

"not know whether there is any way of reconciling the various passages" in which Hobbes justifies the claim that the natural law is the divine law, and he admits that he does not know how Hobbes would suppose that "persons unacquainted with the Scriptures [could] have discovered that the natural law *is* a command of God" (1965: 50). His response to the problem is to repeat that he can find no way to make Hobbes's various claims consistent other than to ground them in the claim that the natural law is the divine law.

Martinich's response to this problem is more specific: God's commands are promulgated to everyone because they are deducible by reason and "deducibility is the only natural method of promulgation available to all humans." Hobbes "takes it as beyond question that what is deducible by reason as the best means to self-preservation must be the command of God" (1992: 335). Hence, even though our knowledge of God through reason may be strictly limited, we can by reason discover what rules best promote our self-preservation, and these are God's commands. It is one thing, however, to say that we can know from reason the means to self-preservation and that these are God's commands and quite another to say that we can know from reason the means to self-preservation and know from reason *that* they are God's commands. Hobbes may take it as beyond question that what is deducible by reason as the best means to self-preservation must be the command of God, but he has provided no reason for us to do so. Unless this fact about the content of God's commands can be deduced by reason, we are left with the problem that we cannot by reason alone know what God commands. Such a deduction would seem a tall order.

Finally, it is worth noting one general problem with the divine-command account of Hobbes's theory of morality. Hobbes, as we noted, insists that ethics is a branch of natural philosophy, or science. It is so represented in the table of science he provides in *Leviathan* (*L:* 149), and he repeatedly refers to ethics as moral science or the science of morals. Yet Hobbes is equally insistent that whatever knowledge we have of God, it is not scientific or philosophical knowledge. "We ought not to dispute of God's nature," he declares in *The Questions Concerning Liberty, Necessity, and Chance.* "He is no fit subject of our philosophy" (*LNC:* 436). Theology appears nowhere in Hobbes's table of philosophy, and he clearly states at the outset of *De Corpore* that philosophy "excludes *Theology,* I mean the doctrine of God, eternal, ingenerable, incomprehensible" (*Co:* 1.8). According to the divine-command account,

Hobbes's ethics would ultimately become a branch of religion or theology,[67] and thus not of science or philosophy, and could therefore purchase consistency in one part of Hobbes's system only by abandoning it at another.

The objections considered here, as well as others raised in the literature, create serious doubts that Hobbes is best understood as a divine-command theorist. But uncovering difficulties with the divine-command interpretation is not enough. Both Taylor and Martinich claim that reading Hobbes in this way is made necessary because it is the only way to render consistent his various statements about law, command, and duty. The divine-command view merits support so long as it is seen as the only available, albeit problematic, solution to the puzzle Taylor and Martinich identified. The interpretation can be surpassed only by providing an alternative solution to the puzzle. This I now propose to do.

The existence of the puzzle, it is important to remember, depends crucially on the claim that when Hobbes calls the laws of nature "laws," he is doing so in the proper sense of the term as he has defined it. Martinich argues that for Hobbes "the laws of nature are literally laws," that "Hobbes thinks the laws of nature are, properly speaking, laws" (1992: 100, 135). "If Hobbes thought that a law of nature was not a genuine law," Martinich reasonably supposes, "then one would expect him to say that he is using the term figuratively. But he does not" (1992: 104).

But he does. "Law, properly is the word of him, that by right hath command over others," Hobbes says in *Leviathan* (*L:* 217). Yet

67 Or, perhaps, of history. As J. G. A. Pocock notes in his discussion of history and religion in Hobbes's thought, "If God cannot be known to us through the operation of his spirit upon ours, he can be known to us, and can work upon us, only through his words, and knowledge of these words is historical knowledge; they were given to us in past time, and both their content and the faith we repose in them have been transmitted through complex social processes taking place in time and involving awareness of their earlier stages" (1971: 183). God understood as a first cause may be present to all through reason, but God understood as a divine ruler is not present to us now and is revealed only through words from the past. Knowledge of God in this latter sense cannot be scientific or philosophical, but only historical, and knowledge of God in this sense must underwrite any divine-command theory of morality. (Pacchi's analysis supports the same conclusion; he distinguishes between "Hobbes's philosophical God," the "final, purely supposed term of a chain of material causes," and "the personal God of the Hebraic-Christian tradition" which can serve as a divine ruler, and argues that although the two are not incompatible, they are nonetheless distinct. The latter is a part of Hobbes's thinking, but not a part of his philosophy [1988: 184–7].)

"the Lawes of Nature, which consist in Equity, Justice, Gratitude, and other morall Vertues on these depending, in the condition of meer Nature (as I have said before in the end of the 15th Chapter,) *are not properly Lawes*, but qualities that dispose men to peace, and to obedience" (*L:* 314, emphasis added).[68] As we saw in section 3.3.2, although Hobbes often refers to the laws of nature as if they are rules commanding certain sorts of actions, he repeatedly steps back from this characterization to specify that they describe "dispositions of the mind," binding only in the "court of conscience" (*DC:* 3.29). The laws of nature are to be understood as "*Morall* Lawes; consisting in the Morall Vertues, as Justice, Equity, and all habits of the mind that conduce to Peace, and Charity" (*L:* 330). Yet virtues, dispositions, and habits of the mind are precisely what must remain, according to Hobbes's account, beyond the domain of command. A ruler (whether earthly or divine) may command us to perform a just act, but not to be a just person. Our inner thoughts necessarily remain beyond that sort of control. Since this is how Hobbes insists we are to understand the natural law as a moral law, the moral law cannot be a "law" in the proper sense of the term, cannot be a command.

Martinich urges that "it is a basic principle of interpretation that a sentence should not be given a metaphorical interpretation unless a literal interpretation is absurd" (1992: 380n6). But this dictum fails to support his position for two reasons. First, once it is clear that for Hobbes the moral laws refer to moral virtues, interpreting them literally as laws *is* absurd. It is to read them as commands which command that which cannot be commanded. Second, Hobbes also says that the laws of nature "are not properly Lawes, but qualities." It would be extremely odd (though not, perhaps, absurd) for Hobbes to intend a statement specifying that he was not using a term properly to be taken other than literally.

Understanding that for Hobbes the laws of nature refer to moral virtues is important because once his laws of nature are understood in this way, the puzzle identified by Taylor and Martinich can be resolved without inserting God into the picture. When Taylor asks us whose command it is, if not God's, that the sovereign ruling over civil society must be just, or when Martinich asks us whose command it is, if not God's, that people in the (secondary) state of

68 If it is asked why Hobbes uses the term "law of nature" in his writings at all if he does not intend to use the term "law" properly in doing so, the answer is presumably, as at least one writer has surmised, that "he has done so only to pay homage to tradition" (Bobbio 1993: 44).

nature be just, we can answer that it is nobody's command at all. This need not force Hobbes into inconsistency, because after defining law in general as a certain sort of command, he is careful to note that the natural law by itself is not a law in that sense. In addition to the fact that there are serious problems with the divine-command account of Hobbes's moral theory, therefore, the primary problem it is intended to solve can be more naturally and parsimoniously solved without it.

That Hobbes's writings can be rendered coherent without making theological concepts an "inextricable" (Martinich 1992: 1) and "absolutely necessary" (Taylor 1965: 50) part of his moral philosophy does not in itself prove that this is how Hobbes intended them to be read. Perhaps his moral theory can plausibly be made to rest on fewer assumptions than he himself realized. Martinich presses this point in response to Gauthier's claim that "theistic suppositions are logically superfluous" in Hobbes's system. "Perhaps they are," Martinich concedes, "but it is fallacious to conclude that Hobbes does not rely on them" (1992: 44). Martinich is surely right about this, but its significance in the present case is limited. The principal argument in favor of interpreting Hobbes as a divine-command theorist is an argument about what is and is not logically superfluous to Hobbes's argument. Both Taylor and Martinich claim that a theological foundation should be attributed to Hobbes's system because it is made necessary by his various claims about law, command, and morality. Once it is seen that this is not necessary, that Hobbes's moral theory can be understood to rest on claims independent of his theology, the case for the divine-command reading is seriously undermined. This is not to say that Hobbes should not be understood as a sincere Christian, or that he did not think it urgent that his moral and political views be compatible, and be seen to be compatible, with a specific set of Christian doctrines. It is to say that Hobbes should not be understood as making the truth of his moral theory depend on the truth of claims about God. Hobbes repeatedly insists that ethics is a branch of philosophy and that theology is no part of philosophy. This establishes a powerful presumption against reading his ethics as resting on his theology. The arguments thus far marshaled in favor of the divine-command interpretation, though at times ingenious, are not powerful enough to warrant overturning this presumption.

3.4.3 Having attempted to undermine the reasons for reading Hobbes as a divine-command theorist, we must be careful not to assume that rejection of the Taylor-Warrender (and Martinich) thesis justifies rejection of the Taylor thesis. What shall we say about it? Understood as the claim that there is a deontological dimension to Hobbes's moral theory overlooked by most of Hobbes's critics, both before Taylor and after him, the thesis is difficult to deny. Hobbes does make a point of distinguishing between just acts and just people, a distinction most of his commentators have been content to pass over as insignificant. The distinction clearly states that a just person performs just acts because they are just, not because of any beneficial consequences they may provide (or because of any harmful consequences omitting them might entail). At the very least, therefore, Taylor has justifiably brought to light an element of Hobbes's theory not adequately accounted for by the other interpretations (including Warrender's and Martinich's) thus far considered. Hobbes scholarship has suffered from the fact that Taylor's article has come to be tied so closely with Warrender's book and generally been dismissed with it.

There is an important difference between acknowledging that there is a significant deontological aspect to Hobbes's moral theory and claiming, as Taylor does, that the theory as a whole is a "very strict deontology." The difference is perhaps best clarified by returning to the two questions with which Taylor begins his analysis. Taylor insists that Hobbes distinguishes between the questions (1) What reason can be given to show that I ought to be just? and (2) How can I be induced to be just? Taylor claims that Hobbes's answer to 1 is that I ought to be just because the moral law commands it. Taylor has shown that Hobbes believed the just person acts justly because the moral law commands it, but this does not establish that Hobbes would answer question 1 by saying that I should be a just person because the moral law commands it. There may be a difference between the reasons the just person acts on and the reason that it is good to be the sort of person who acts on such reasons. Hobbes has claimed that the fact that a particular act is just is for the just person a reason to do it, but it is not a reason to do it for the unjust person (who may, nonetheless, do it because of self-interested reasons and thus remain guiltless). Hobbes, at least as far as Taylor has presented him, has not yet explained, however, why I ought to be a just person in the first place. If the answer is that I ought to be a just person because the moral law commands it, we may conclude that Hobbes's theory is a strict deontology. But it might also turn out that I ought to be a just person for some reason other than that the law commands it. If this is the case, we must conclude that Hobbes's theory is not, at its foundation, a strict deontology, but it nonetheless defends as the model of a just person, the person who is just because the moral law commands it. Taylor's account leaves this an open, indeed an unasked, question, and so we cannot yet say with any confidence whether we ought to accept or reject the Taylor thesis in its strongest form.

What we can confidently conclude about Taylor's position is: He has identified and focused on an element of Hobbes's moral theory that must be satisfactorily accounted for by any adequate interpretation of Hobbes. He is right to force Hobbes's readers to reflect on those neglected passages in which Hobbes insists that always performing just acts is neither necessary nor sufficient for being deemed a just person. He is also right, at least to a degree, to see in this position some interesting parallels with Kant. Taylor is wrong, however, to argue that we can only accommodate these passages in Hobbes by reading him as a divine-command theorist. Hobbes's explicit statements about God and about moral science undermine any attempt to read him in this way, and doing so will not provide the consistency Taylor seeks to rescue. Doing so is not necessary, in any event, since we can salvage Hobbes's doctrine more satisfactorily (and more consistently with the texts) by heeding his reminder that the laws of nature are not to be understood as laws in the proper sense of the term. Taylor seems to have understood, better than most of Hobbes's readers, the virtuous person Hobbes places at the center of his moral philosophy,[69] but he has not provided a satisfactory account of the foundation on which that philosophy rests.

3.5 HOBBES AS VIRTUE ETHICIST

Although the views prevalent in the literature on Hobbes's moral theory must ultimately be rejected, they provide a number of important insights any adequate interpretation of Hobbes must take into account. The claim that Hobbes had no moral theory at all, though unjustifiable in its strongest form, is valuable in pointing to certain limitations on the sort of moral theory Hobbes might legitimately be able to defend. The view of Hobbes as a moral contractarian is unable to account for Hobbes's belief in moral constraints on the sovereign in civil society and on individuals in the state of

69 Although as we shall see in the following section, his characterization of the just person is incomplete.

nature, yet it undeniably identifies a tendency in Hobbes's writings to characterize moral distinctions as the object of human agreement. Kavka's recent rule-egoist account errs by making rules of action the ultimate object of moral evaluation, but it correctly characterizes Hobbes's project as one of reconciling the demands of rational self-interest with those of traditional morality. Taylor's much maligned interpretation of Hobbes, while pressing Hobbes's affinities with Kant too far and relying on a theological foundation Hobbes adamantly refuses to provide, nonetheless recognizes an important deontological element in Hobbes's theory which many have failed to see. The various characterizations of Hobbes's writings as contractarian, consequentialist, egoistic, deontological, all merit a certain degree of assent, though none fully captures their content.

3.5.1 Having considered these various views and found them wanting, we must try to construct a more acceptable interpretation from the elements of Hobbes's thought we have thus far discussed. The contention of this section, and the conclusion of this chapter, is that when we do, we find that Hobbes is best understood as a sort of virtue ethicist.[70] For Hobbes, moral philosophy is the science of virtue and vice. The virtues, on his account, are certain praiseworthy character traits, dispositions, habits of the mind. Virtuous people are those who have cultivated these virtues, and as a result they lead lives recognizable as good by standards of reason each individual can accept. The virtuous person is not one who does the right thing because of the beneficial consequences of doing so, but we nonetheless recognize that it is good to be a virtuous person because of the beneficial consequences of living a virtuous life.[71] This section provides a sketch of Hobbes's moral theory understood in this way. The interpretation is more fully developed and

70 Like all labels, this one can be somewhat misleading since it means different things to different people. Chapter 5 offers a more extensive consideration of the ways in which Hobbes fits in with the virtue ethics literature.

71 James Lowde's biting attack on Hobbes, in his *Discourse Concerning the Nature of Man* (1694), perhaps comes closest to providing a genuine historical precursor to this sort of interpretation. He notes, as few of his contemporaries did, that for Hobbes the just man is one who has "a real and sincere desire" to do justice. He characterizes Hobbes's position as holding that "the reasons of Justice and other Moral Vertues, are . . . ultimately to be resolv'd into that natural support and advantage they bring to a Society and Commonwealth" (1694: 162, 161). The few modern commentators who have suggested that Hobbes's ethics should be understood in terms of his views of virtue are noted in the text below.

defended in the following chapter, where we consider how Hobbes attempts to ground his moral theory in his science of human nature.

Let us begin by remembering what Hobbes, throughout his writings, considers to be the subject matter of moral philosophy. In *De Corpore,* he writes that moral philosophy is concerned with "the motions of the mind" and that it "treats of men's dispositions and manners" (*Co:* 6.6, 1.9). In *Human Nature,* he identifies moral philosophy with the study of "the faculties, passions, and manners of men" (*EL* I: 13.3). In *Thomas White's De Mundo Examined,* he writes that one part of philosophy "concerns the passions, the manners and the aims or purposes of men, and is called ethics or moral philosophy" (*DME:* 24). In *Leviathan,* moral philosophy is described as "the science of Vertue and Vice," where those terms are explicitly defined as referring to human "manners" or "dispositions" rather than to human actions (*L:* 216, 206–7). This insistence that the moral virtues with which ethics is concerned must be understood as dispositions or habits can be found throughout Hobbes's works. Thus, in *Human Nature,* he says that "the habit of doing according to [the] laws of nature . . . is that we call VIRTUE; and the habit of doing the contrary, VICE" (*EL* I: 17.14). In *De Cive,* he argues that the natural law is called moral because it commands "good manners or habits, that is, virtues" (*DC:* 3.31). In *De Homine,* he notes that "Dispositions, when they are so strengthened by habit that they beget their actions with ease and with reason unresisting, are called *manners.* Moreover, manners, if they be good, are called *virtues,* if evil, *vices*" (*DH:* 13.9). When Hobbes comes to define the field of moral philosophy, he focuses consistently on human character, on how individuals are disposed to act, rather than on the actions they do, in fact, perform.[72] This is not to say that ethics, according to Hobbes, is indifferent to actions; it is to say that it makes character its central concern.

That Hobbes's moral philosophy is in this sense an ethics of character rather than of action is also confirmed by his claim, repeated throughout his works, that the natural law, which is the moral law, requires only the endeavor to comply. Thus, in *De Cive,* Hobbes writes that the virtues commanded by the laws of

72 This analysis is also confirmed by the table of science from *Leviathan* which has been referred to on several occasions. Ethics is identified there as being concerned with "Consequences from the *Passions* of Men," and the passions, as Hobbes explains earlier, are the "*Interiour Beginnings of Voluntary Motions*" that he also calls "endeavour" (*L:* 149, 118, 119).

nature are "dispositions of the mind" that must be "considered in the court of conscience, where only they oblige and are laws" (*DC:* 3.29), and he therefore concludes that the laws of nature are easily observed "because they require the endeavour only (but that must be true and constant); which whoso shall perform, we may rightly call him *just*" (*DC:* 3.30). This claim is repeated virtually verbatim in *Leviathan*, when Hobbes argues that the laws of nature "require nothing but endeavour; he that endeavoureth their performance, fulfilleth them; and he that fulfilleth the Law, is Just" (*L:* 215). The position is repeated many times in Hobbes's works when he argues that the natural law is identical (or at least compatible) with the divine law, since that argument often rests on the observation that "God accepts the will for the deed,[73] and that as well in good as in evil actions" (*DC:* 4.21).[74] This interpretation of Hobbes is supported by his much discussed claim that the laws of nature oblige *in foro interno* though not always *in foro externo.* Hobbes explains that by *in foro interno* he means that the laws "bind to a desire they should take place," and that "they oblige onely to a desire, and endeavour, I mean an unfeigned and constant endeavour" (*L:* 215). There is an abundance of textual evidence to support the claim that Hobbes's moral philosophy is ultimately concerned with what makes just people, rather than with what makes just actions.

Before investigating Hobbes's position any further, we must stop to consider more precisely what he thought a just person is and, in particular, what he means by justice itself. We have already noted one way in which the term "justice" has two different meanings for Hobbes; it means one thing when applied to actions and another when applied to people. But there is also a sense in which justice has two different meanings when applied to people, although Hobbes never explicitly acknowledges this. Hobbes consistently means by a just or unjust person one who has a kind of disposition

73 That Hobbes is inclined to think in such terms is reflected even in his personal correspondence. A letter written to Lord Scudamore from Paris closes by saying that even though Hobbes is living happily in France, "yet if you will be pleased to accept of the will for the deed I may still retayne the title of
Your Lordships most humble and
most obliged servant
THOMAS HOBBES" (LS: 160).

74 In the Sermon on the Mount for example, as Hobbes notes in Part IV of *Leviathan*, Jesus insists that "the inward Anger of a man against his brother, if it be without just cause, is Homicide" and that "he that had the Will to hurt his Brother, though the effect appear but in Reviling, or not at all, shall be cast into hell fire" (*L:* 656).

to do just or unjust acts, but he does not always mean the same thing by calling an act just or unjust.

Sometimes Hobbes gives the terms a narrow or technical meaning. Most famously in *Leviathan,* he declares that "the definition of INJUSTICE, is no other than *the not Performance of Covenant.* And whatsoever is not Unjust, is *Just*" (*L:* 202). In *De Cive,* he writes that "an injury, and an unjust action or omission, signify the same thing, and both are the same with breach of contract and trust" (*DC:* 3.3). Many writers have focused almost exclusively on this narrow definition of justice, and have interpreted Hobbes's ethics as a morality in which all right and wrong is ultimately reducible to promise keeping.

Hobbes often, however, uses the terms "justice" and "injustice" in a far broader sense. As we have already seen, he often calls just the person who endeavors to fulfill *all* the laws of nature. These laws command, among other things, that people be grateful, sociable, and forgiving, that they not be vengeful, hateful, or proud, and that they treat everyone as equals. Hobbes often calls adherence to the sum of the laws of nature "righteousness" (e.g., *DC:* 4.3), and he calls justice "a will to live righteously" (*DC:* 18.6n). Although he often uses the narrow sense of the term "justice" when focusing on just actions, he typically has the broader sense in mind when discussing the just person. Thus, when he says in *De Cive* that to be a just person is "to study how to do righteousness, or to endeavour in all things to do that which is just" he seems to equate doing justice with doing righteousness (*DC:* 3.5). When he explains in *De Corpore Politico* that by justice he means, "not absence of guilt, but the good intentions of the mind," he adds that this "is called righteousness by God, that taketh the will for the deed" (*EL* II: 6.10). The important passage from *Leviathan* cited earlier confirms this same identification even more explicitly: "A Just man . . . is he that taketh all the care he can, and his Actions may be all Just: and an Unjust man, is he that neglecteth it. And such men are more often in our Language stiled by the names of Righteous, and Unrighteous; then Just, and Unjust; *though the meaning be the same*" (*L:* 206, emphasis added). When Hobbes speaks of the just person, he is usually speaking of the righteous person. The just person, in this sense, goes far beyond the person who does not violate contracts. And it is the just person, in this sense, with whom Hobbes's moral theory is primarily concerned.

There is thus an important difference between the narrow and broad senses in which Hobbes uses the term "justice." This difference is not always given the careful attention it demands, and it is rarely if ever explained as anything other than carelessness on Hobbes's part. Yet there is an underlying unity to Hobbes's various senses of justice which should be kept in mind as we proceed. In his dedicatory letter to *De Cive*, Hobbes writes of "the very word *justice* (which signifies a steady will of giving every one his *own*)."[75] The focus on a steady will reflects Hobbes's view that justice applies most crucially to character or disposition, and less significantly to actions. More important, his definition of the word reveals the essential continuity between his narrow and broad senses of justice, for giving to each his own can be understood both narrowly and broadly. Narrowly, it can be taken to mean giving each what (rightfully) belongs to him; this reflects Hobbes's narrow conception of justice as the keeping of contracts and covenants. More broadly, giving to each his own can be understood as giving each the treatment due him, treating each person as it is appropriate to treat him. Since Hobbes argues that charity, forgiveness, and equity are due to each, this notion issues in Hobbes's broader conception of justice as righteousness.[76] There is an important connection between Hobbes's narrow and broad conceptions of justice, but the connection does not imply that justice in its broad sense can be derived from the narrow notion of keeping one's covenants.

Having noted the important distinction between these two senses of justice, having seen that the one cannot be reduced to the other, and having emphasized that in speaking of the just person Hobbes is typically concerned with justice in the broad sense, we can return to our main line of inquiry. Hobbes's moral theory is

75 The definition is repeated almost verbatim in the *Dialogue of the Common Laws:* "Justice is the constant will of giving to every man his own. . . . A just man is he that hath a constant will to live justly" (*D:* 72, see also *D:* 58). In *Leviathan,* Hobbes notes with approval that the Scholastics say "that *Justice is the constant Will of giving to every man his own*" (*L:* 202).

76 These two ways of viewing justice as giving to each his own are essentially the same as those found in Book I of Plato's *Republic.* In the early part of that Book (1974: 331a–332c), Cephalus and Polemarchus both endorse Simonides' claim that "it is just to give to each what is owed to him," but they differ over just what this means. Cephalus interprets this as meaning that justice is paying one's debts, closely paralleling Hobbes's narrow conception of justice. Polemarchus, on the other hand, reads it as meaning that one should give to each "what is proper to him," which is what lies beneath Hobbes's broader conception. Hobbes praises Plato as the best of the ancient philosophers (*SL:* 346; *L:* 686) and it is possible that Hobbes is borrowing from him here, not simply accepting the definition of the Scholastics, about whom he expresses a much lower opinion.

primarily concerned with just people, rather than with just actions. A just person is one whose will is "framed" by justice, and, as Taylor insists, this entails that he is disposed to follow the moral law "for the law's sake" (*DC:* 4.21). The just person endeavors to fulfill all the laws of nature, many of which identify virtues that go beyond promise keeping. He does so because it is right, and not because of any apparent benefit from doing so. But there is more for Hobbes to being a just person than this, and here we must make the first of two significant departures from the Taylor thesis. The just person does not only act justly for justice's sake; he also enjoys doing so. The just person is one who by nature is "delighted in just dealing" (*DC:* 3.5). He is honest not only because it is right to be, but because he "scorns to be beholding for the contentment of his life, to fraud, or breach of promise" (*L:* 207). To be fully virtuous, according to Hobbes's account, to have one's will "framed by justice," involves more than acting out of respect for the law; it involves taking pleasure in so doing.[77]

Hobbes, it must be admitted, is not always explicit about this. Often he merely speaks of the just person as one who is disposed toward justice, or whose will is framed by it, or who endeavors to do justice, without fully articulating what this involves. But that there must be a desiderative element to the just person's character is clear from Hobbes's analysis of will and endeavor. To endeavor to do justice is to desire to do it, and pleasure is the result of the satisfaction of desire (*L:* 119, 122). The just person must also be one who takes pleasure in doing justice, and when Hobbes articulates the content of the just person's character more fully, he is careful to specify that virtue does indeed involve both acting and feeling in a certain way. "When justice and injustice are attributed to men," as he insists in *Human Nature,* "they signify proneness, and affection, and inclination of nature, that is to say, passions of the mind apt to produce just and unjust actions" (*EL* I: 16.4). Although Hobbes is

77 It might be objected that Hobbes has in mind merely the vanity that comes from knowing that one is powerful enough to eschew injustice, so that he means taking pleasure in one's own status rather than in justice itself. It does seem possible to read this meaning into the passage cited from *Leviathan,* but the expression from *De Cive* is substantially less ambiguous: One is delighted in the just dealing itself, not in what it reveals about one's own power. In addition, it seems clear that the unjust person is one who enjoys doing injustice, and since Hobbes treats the two cases symmetrically, it seems again to follow that the just person enjoys the justice, not merely what his doing justice reveals about him (though he may, of course, take pleasure in that as well).

not always careful to distinguish these two components of the just person – that he does justice for its own sake and that he enjoys doing so – we must take this to be his considered view. The just person is one who is just (in the narrow sense), gracious, modest, equitable, merciful, and so forth, in the sense that he possesses these traits as passions of the mind, as habits of the mind, as moral virtues. He does justice "for its own sake" and is "delighted" in so doing.

I have already noted that there is one sense in which this interpretation of Hobbes departs from Taylor's: It makes enjoying doing the right thing part of what it is to be a just person. Having said this, we must ask why, for Hobbes, it is good to be a just person so understood. Since we have seen that a just person is one who possesses the moral virtues, the answer to this question must be found by considering what makes possessing the moral virtues good. Here we must again depart from Taylor, whose answer is that Hobbes endorses a "strict deontology," and take instead Kavka's view that Hobbes is ultimately concerned to reconcile traditional morality with the dictates of rational self-interest. The virtuous person whom Hobbes implores us to emulate is one who is guided by a respect and love for justice, but we are implored to emulate the virtuous person because doing so is good for us. This is the crucial point of the interpretation of Hobbes as a virtue ethicist, and it is therefore worth repeating some of the important passages that strongly support it.

One is a passage Kavka cites in defense of his own interpretation: "All men agree on this, that Peace is Good, and therefore also the way, or means of Peace, which (as I have shewed before) are *Justice, Gratitude, Modesty, Equity, Mercy,* & the rest of the Laws of Nature, are good; that is to say, *Morall Vertues*" (*L:* 216). Kavka, as we saw earlier, mistakenly takes this passage to mean that Hobbes is ultimately concerned to vindicate certain rules of behavior as good because of their contribution to peace. His mistake lies in making rules of conduct the ultimate object of Hobbes's evaluation, not in reading beneficial consequences as Hobbes's criterion for doing the evaluating. Hobbes is, indeed, saying that justice is good because it is the way to peace, but by justice he means the virtue of justice, the disposition to do just acts because they are just and to enjoy doing so. Similarly, in *De Homine,* he argues that "good dispositions are those which are suitable for entering into civil society; and good manners (that is, moral virtues) are those whereby what was entered upon can be best preserved" (*DH:* 13.9). In *De Cive,* he argues: "Reason declaring peace to be good, it follows by the same reason, that all the necessary means to peace be good also; and therefore that modesty, equity, trust, humanity, mercy (which we have demonstrated to be necessary to peace), are good manners or habits, that is, virtues" (*DC:* 3.31). The answer to the question of why it is good to be a just person is, therefore, that being a just person is necessary for attaining peace, which is something that all agree to be good. The strengths of both Taylor's and Kavka's views can thus be incorporated into an account that does not suffer from the weaknesses of either.

3.5.2 Despite differing markedly from the dominant traditions of Hobbes scholarship, this interpretation of Hobbes as a kind of virtue ethicist is not entirely without precedent.[78] Strauss's early study portrayed Hobbes as "a zealous reader, not to say a disciple of [Aristotle's] *Rhetoric,*" whose political philosophy exhibits "the progressive supplanting of aristocratic virtue by bourgeois virtue" (1936: 35, 126) and both the affinity with Aristotle and the emphasis on virtue are noted in several recent works on Hobbes. Bernard Gert, in the introduction to his edition of *De Homine* and *De Cive* and in a more recent article, maintains that "Hobbes, following Aristotle, regards morality as concerned with character traits or habits" and that for Hobbes "the laws of nature prohibit the practice of vice and prescribe the practice of virtue" (1978: 16; 1988: 27). Tom Sorell has suggested that "Hobbes is closer to Aristotle than he realizes," since for both "what are called the moral virtues are precisely the qualities or characteristics that are appropriate for leading the best sort of human life" (1986: 106, 107).[79] And Robert Ewin explicitly argues that "Hobbes was a virtues theorist" (1991: 5). These few scholarly accounts broadly anticipate the interpreta-

78 In addition to the works cited in this section, see also Skinner (1991). Skinner correctly identifies Hobbes's project as an attempt to "demonstrate that the laws of nature and the traditional moral virtues are one and the same," and he argues for the importance of understanding "Hobbes's concern to establish a science of virtue" as a response to an important skeptical challenge to the virtues rooted in the discipline of rhetoric (1991: 33, 3). Richard E. Flathman (1993), also points to the virtues as "qualities of character and disposition, with which Hobbes was more concerned than most of his commentators and critics have recognized," but on Flathman's account, Hobbes's "primary concern" remains with justice of actions rather than justice of manners, and the subject of virtue is more like a "supplement" to his doctrine of morality (1993: 55, 81, 82).

79 Sorell also emphasizes that Hobbes's laws of nature enjoin "good manners" rather than good actions in (1988: 76).

tion of Hobbes developed in the present work,[80] but there are a variety of important reasons for rejecting each as inadequate.

First, none of the previous attempts to read Hobbes as a kind of virtue ethicist provides a satisfactory account of the role Hobbes's science, of nature in general and of human nature in particular, plays in the foundation of his ethics. Gert offers no account at all of Hobbes's science, and instead attempts to ground Hobbes's defense of the laws of nature in the doctrine that reason has as "an end of its own" the preservation of the individual (1978: 13). As we saw in section 2.5.3, however, this account is incompatible with the science of human nature as Hobbes develops it. Strauss insists that the moral foundation of Hobbes's normative views are entirely independent of, and incompatible with, his views of science. Sorell and Ewin both acknowledge the importance of science to Hobbes's ethics, but both offer flawed accounts of what that importance is. Sorell, as noted in section 1.1, argues that natural and moral science are both sciences on Hobbes's account only because both employ deductive reasoning as a way of improving human life, and he insists that the scientific status of Hobbes's ethics is not meant to rest on having any content in common with natural science (1986: e.g., 12, 26). To say that physics and ethics are both sciences, therefore, is simply to say that, in a very general sense, both employ the same method. But as we have seen, Hobbes meant to say much more than this: to say that ethics and physics are both sciences is to say that ethics is a branch of physics, that its claims rest on claims about nature (e.g., *L:* 149).

Ewin's account cannot serve as an acceptable analysis of Hobbes's science of virtue either. Ewin insists that Hobbes's science is "concerned only with conceptual connections and not with merely empirical connections," that it seeks to produce only "necessary statements" and "logical truths," yet he acknowledges that "empirical

80 Mary G. Dietz's recent paper also merits attention in this context. Dietz urges that Hobbes be understood as "a theorist of civic virtue" concerned with analyzing the "dispositions necessary to citizenship," and she argues that on Hobbes's account peace is best secured not by having citizens submit to civil laws through fear but "by way of habits, virtues, and beliefs" (1990: 92, 99). Her interpretation thus embraces the vocabulary of virtue central to the account defended in this work but it nonetheless departs from it on a crucial point. Hobbes, on the view taken here, defends the value of the virtues on the grounds that cultivating the virtues contributes to the well-being of the individual who cultivates them. Dietz, on the other hand, attributes to Hobbes only the weaker claim that everyone benefits when the virtues are widespread (1990: e.g., 107).

assumptions do come into Hobbes's arguments" when Hobbes attempts to justify his ethics (1991: 7, 9, 45). Ewin is, no doubt, right in making the latter claim, but his account of Hobbes's scientific method cannot accommodate it. It relies too heavily on the nonempirical side of Hobbes's science examined in section 2.1.1, without accounting for the significant empirical dimension described in section 2.1.2 and accounted for in section 2.1.3. Thus, even those writers who have pointed to the importance of virtue in Hobbes's thought have not adequately recognized that Hobbes sought to defend not merely a theory, but ultimately a science, of virtue.

In addition, not all the writers who have seen Hobbes as a virtue theorist have provided a satisfactory account of what his virtue theory is. Sorell's brief remarks on the subject are largely limited to a two-page passage correctly claiming that Hobbes thought people should possess the virtues but not explaining what possessing a virtue meant for Hobbes (1986: 106–7). Strauss's discussion of virtue is substantially more extensive; yet although he draws on an impressive range of historical sources, he too fails to provide a clear account of what Hobbes takes possession of a virtue to imply. He correctly emphasizes the importance of good intentions, on Hobbes's account, but does not specify that such intentions must involve doing justice, and enjoying it, for its own sake. Ewin's more recent account is in part undermined by its affinity with the contractarian interpretation of Hobbes. Ewin allows that within civil society morality consists in cultivating and exhibiting the virtues, but he insists that this is so only within civil society. "Without the context of the rights that come with a sovereign or with a binding decision-procedure," he maintains, "there can be no other sort of morality; the virtues cannot flourish, or, indeed, be exhibited." Ewin does not exactly deny that one should possess the virtues in the state of nature. Rather, he insists that being virtuous in the state of nature "does not require that I do anything in particular. The virtue, the quality of character, does not emerge as any particular action and therefore cannot be tested by behavior." To Ewin, "the home of morality is civil society" (1991: 36, 128, 47). His interpretation ultimately blends elements of the virtue ethics interpretation offered here with elements of the contractarian interpretation considered in section 3.2. But as discussed at length in that section, there are compelling reasons to reject the view that for Hobbes morality is at home only in civil society and never requires any forms of behavior from people in the state of nature (or from the sovereign in civil society). Although Ewin thus comes closer to capturing the content of Hobbes's virtue ethics than most commentators, he nonetheless falls significantly short.

Finally, and by far most important, none of the writers who have linked Hobbes to the virtue tradition explains why, according to Hobbes's account, one must be virtuous in order to live well. All recognize that the actions recommended by the virtues promote peace and that those associated with the vices promote discord, but none offers an answer to the question, Why does Hobbes's theory insist that one should not simply do just acts but be a just person? Why should one be disposed to do just acts for their own sake and enjoy doing so?[81] This is a crucial question, perhaps *the* crucial question. It is essential both to making credible the interpretation of Hobbes as a virtue ethicist and to distinguishing this view from the interpretation of Hobbes as a rule egoist. In spelling out the value of the virtues, Sorell, at least, seems to lose sight of this distinction altogether: "What made certain patterns of action virtuous and others vicious, was that certain patterns of action promoted civil order or peace, while others disturbed it" (1986: 2–3). For Hobbes to be a virtue ethicist, however, it is not enough that he endorse certain "patterns of action" because of their beneficial consequences. That is the domain of the rule consequentialist. Rather, Hobbes must be understood as endorsing the goodness of certain traits of character. His theory judges people not simply on how they behave but on why they behave as they do. This raises the inevitable question, Why is this Hobbes's concern? The lack of a substantial answer to this question represents an unacceptable, gaping hole in the few published suggestions that Hobbes be understood as a virtue ethicist, a hole that the second half of the following chapter aims to fill. Having concluded that Hobbes is best understood as maintaining that one should be a virtuous person, we must next consider in some detail the argument that Hobbes makes in defense of this claim.

Before we turn to that task, however, two more points about the interpretation of Hobbes as a virtue ethicist merit notice. The first is that it parallels Hobbes's views on religion in an important way. In *De Homine*, Hobbes argues that we should perform those acts that

81 Strauss, for example, correctly notes that on Hobbes's account "the moral attitude, conscience, intention, is of more importance than the action," and that the moral virtues have "their ultimate foundation in fear of violent death" (1936: 23, 116). Nowhere does he explain how grounding ethics in the avoidance of death leads Hobbes to a concern not merely with just actions but with just intentions.

are signs of piety toward God because "these are pleasing to God, and by them alone can His favour be returned to us" (*DH:* 14.8). It is good to be pious because piety (and thus pleasing God) is a necessary condition for enjoying certain desirable consequences. But in the same chapter, Hobbes also insists that what is displeasing to God, what is the very antithesis of piety, is "the simulation of justice by those lacking in it. For those who do just works and give alms only for glory or for the acquiring of riches or for the avoidance of punishment are unjust, even though their works are very frequently just" (*DH:* 14.7). It is good to be pious because of the consequences of piety, but the pious person does not perform pious acts because of the good consequences that will follow.[82] Earlier we identified the incongruity between the divine-command account and Hobbes's theology as a point against that interpretation. Similarly, the close tie between Hobbes's theology and the virtue ethicist account must count as a point in its favor.

Second, we must return, albeit briefly, to the view of Hobbes as a moral contraction. We found in section 3.2.2 that there are insuperable difficulties posed by the claim that Hobbes is a moral contractarian, but we were forced by the prevalence of textual evidence to acknowledge that there is a contractarian tendency that recurs throughout his writings. We conceded that any adequate interpretation of Hobbes must prove capable of taking this tendency into account, and we must now stop to ask how the reading of Hobbes as a virtue ethicist can do this.

In a sense the answer is that it cannot. Hobbes, according to our interpretation, is committed to the view that "*The laws of nature are immutable and eternal:* what they forbid, can never be lawful; what they command, can never be unlawful." These laws of nature, for Hobbes, are "virtues of the mind . . . which cannot be abrogated by any custom or law whatsoever" (*DC:* 3.29). There is no way to

82 This sort of indirect consequentialism, it is worth mentioning, need not be limited to New Testament theology. The central prayer of Judaism, the Shema, seems to make much the same point. Its first paragraph (Deuteronomy 6:4–9) exhorts us to love God unconditionally, but its second (Deuteronomy 11:13–21) describes the beneficial consequences enjoyed by those who love God in this way ("thou shalt eat and be satisfied") and the terrible costs inflicted on those who do not ("there shall be no rain" so that "ye perish quickly"), and it concludes by urging that "*therefore* shall ye lay up these My words in your heart and in your soul" (emphasis added). As the explanatory note in one popular prayer book characterizes it, "the moral law is the counterpart of the natural law, since evil-doing inevitably brings disaster in its wake" (Silverman 1951: 214).

reconcile this claim with the view that what is moral is determined entirely by the command of the sovereign in civil society. There are passages in which Hobbes seems to espouse this extreme form of contractarianism, and when he does so the interpretation of Hobbes as a virtue ethicist can say no more than that he is contradicting himself. This is admittedly a less than ideal position to fall back on, but since the texts do at times seem undeniably inconsistent, it need not pose more of a problem for the virtue ethicist interpretation than for any other.

Any fully adequate account of Hobbes's understanding of morality must account for the existence of such contradictory statements, however, and Jean Hampton has offered a convincing explanation how Hobbes would be led to make such statements without abandoning his commitment to a noncontractarian moral theory: "It is not that Hobbes was skeptical about the existence of genuine moral knowledge, but rather that he was skeptical about the idea that large numbers of human beings could attain such knowledge." Hobbes settled for a political doctrine in which the sovereign determines what is to count as right and wrong in civil society, not because there are no natural moral standards (his doctrine of virtue shows that there are) but because access to these natural standards (which he defended) is often "difficult for us less-than-reliable, biased and glory-prone human reasoners" (1989: 57, 59; see also 1986: chap. 1).

Hampton's explanation is strengthened by an important passage in *De Cive* in which Hobbes discusses the need for the sovereign to settle controversies of opinion if civil discord is to be avoided: "All these things, namely, right, policy, and *natural-sciences,* are subjects concerning which Christ denies that it belongs to his office to give any precepts, or teach any thing beside this only; that in all controversies about them, every single subject should obey the laws and determinations of his city" (*DC:* 17.12, emphasis altered). As Richard Popkin has emphasized, this passage "makes clear that Hobbes was talking about scientific propositions as well as moral and religious ones being assigned their truth values by the political authorities" (1992a: 23; see also 1992a: 23–6; 1992b: 45–9). Although it is thus made clear that Hobbes believed that if, for example, controversy over the existence of the vacuum threatens to provoke civil unrest, then all subjects must accept the resolution of the controversy handed down by the sovereign, it is indisputable from his scientific writings that this is not because whether or not there is a vacuum depends on what the sovereign says. There are truths about nature that Hobbes purports to demonstrate even while agreeing to defer to the declarations of the sovereign should their judgments differ.[83] Hobbes insists that citizens defer to their sovereign on questions of morality, but this does not impugn the interpretation of Hobbes according to which he demonstrates moral claims that are true independent of the sovereign's commands.

The same sort of discussion is suggested by Hobbes's response, in *Of Liberty and Necessity*, to the objection that his defense of determinism, if accepted, would be taken by many as an excuse to do evil. "It is true that ill use might be made of it," he concedes, and he admits that for "the greatest part of mankind . . . the dispute of this question will rather hurt than help their piety"[84] (*LN:* 252, 256). Hobbes takes this fact as evidence not that his doctrine is false but that it may be inappropriate for untrained ears: "What use soever be made of truth," he insists, "yet truth is truth, and now the question is not, what is fit to be preached, but, what is true" (*LN:* 252).[85] There can thus be a difference between what is true and what is fit to be preached. If everyone attempts to follow his own theory of morals, conflict will ensue; what is fit to be preached, therefore, is that all must submit to the determination of the sovereign. This need not impugn the fact that in his own science of virtue, Hobbes endeavors to demonstrate what is true: that there are certain traits of character, habits of the mind, that it is good for each person to acquire.

It is important to notice that many of the passages in which Hobbes appears to advocate a kind of moral contractarianism de-

83 As Tom Sorell puts it in his discussion of this same passage, "What the passage is about is not truth exactly, but the settlement of controversy. . . . Hobbes's position is that if a controversy is to end the parties to it have to behave *as if* whatever the sovereign decides to be true is true" (1993: 131).

84 The full passage here nicely parallels the description in Hampton's suggestion: "if we consider the greatest part of mankind, not as they should be, but as they are, that is, as men, whom either the study of acquiring wealth, or preferment, or whom the appetite of sensual delights, or the impatience of meditating, or the rash embracing of wrong principles, have made unapt to discuss the truth of things" (*LN:* 256).

85 The essay was originally written as a lengthy letter to the Lord Marquis of Newcastle in answer to a treatise by the Bishop of Londonderry, and Hobbes thus adds that "if his Lordship had not desired this answer, I should not have written it, nor do I write it but in hopes your Lordship and his will keep it private." The work concludes with Hobbes saying, "I humbly beseech your Lordship to communicate it only to my Lord Bishop," and was eventually published only with a note "to the Sober and Discreet Reader" (*LN:* 256, 278, 231).

scribe a position significantly less extreme than the one thus far described. This more tempered contractarianism can be more directly reconciled with the claim that Hobbes is a virtue ethicist. In *De Corpore Politico*, for example, Hobbes writes that "the civil laws are to all subjects the measures of their actions, whereby to determine, whether they be right or wrong, profitable or unprofitable, virtuous or vicious" (*EL* II: 10.10). This sounds like the extreme view that what is right or wrong is determined entirely by the civil law, not by the moral law. But the passage immediately continues: "and by them [i.e., the civil laws] the use and definition of all names not agreed upon, and tending to controversy, shall be established. As for example, upon the occasion of some strange and deformed birth, it shall not be decided by Aristotle, or the philosophers, whether the same be a man or not, but by the laws." Hobbes's example here is most instructive. He insists that the law must decide for all what is to count as a man; he does not claim that the law must decide whether or not murdering a man is virtuous. The passage is therefore open to an interpretation holding that the moral virtues are natural and objective and beyond the power of the sovereign to repeal or amend, but that, to avoid controversy, the sovereign must provide standards to determine more completely what acts will count as exemplifying the virtues. A citizen cannot fully determine what acts are virtuous without referring to the standards established by the sovereign, but he can determine what the virtues are without relying on such standards. Interpreted in this way, Hobbes's tendency toward contractarianism poses no problem for the virtue ethicist interpretation of his moral theory.

This more moderate form of contractarianism is spelled out in even less ambiguous terms in an important passage in *De Cive*: "Theft, murder, adultery, and all injuries, are forbid by the laws of nature; but what is to be called *theft*, what *murder*, what *adultery*, what *injury* in a citizen, this is not to be determined by the natural, but by the civil law" (*DC*: 6.16).[86] Hobbes thus avers that the sover-

86 This tempered version of contractarianism is also confirmed by Hobbes's treatment of the "sacred laws" dictated by "natural reason" in, e.g., *De Cive*, Chapter 15. As Paul J. Johnson has pointed out, the relationship "between the natural and the positive law of verbal worship is identical with that between natural and positive political laws. . . . Natural reason can identify three classes of action which as such signify an intention of honoring; obedience, thanksgiving, and prayers. Here again [i.e., as in the case of modesty, honesty, equity, and so forth] what is to constitute such actions is generally a matter for civil decision" (1974: 117).

eign can do nothing to change the fact that murder is wrong, but he can determine what is to count as murder (presumably by determining what counts as a person, and what counts as justifiable killing).[87] Adultery is always wrong, to pick another of Hobbes's examples, but "that copulation which in one city is matrimony, in another will be judged adultery." Virtue demands that I fulfill my contractual obligations, but the civil law determines what counts as a legitimate contract.[88] There is thus a role for contractarianism in a complete account of Hobbes's thinking about morality, but it need not interfere with the interpretation put forth in this section.

In 1680, the executors of Hobbes's estate published a one-page document entitled "The Last Sayings or Dying Legacy of Mr. Thomas Hobbs of Malmesbury." An eclectic collection of pithy aphorisms and more fully developed affirmations of principle, it contains a variety of positions familiar from Hobbes's published writings, as well as a few parting shots at those who had persecuted him for them. ("No persons ought so justly to die for Religion," he pointedly notes in one, "as those that get their living by it.") One of the statements repeats Hobbes's view that "the Law of the Civil Magistrate, is the only obliging Rule of Just and Unjust." This might seem to confirm the contractarian reading of his position, but the document also records his insistence that "To measure Good or Evil by the Reward or Punishment assigned by the Laws of our own Countrey, is like little Children, who have no other measure of good or ill but from the correction of their Parents." Hobbes, as we have seen, sometimes seems to take a childish view of good and evil, but as this passage and many others suggest, we cannot take this to represent his mature view.

Writers such as Gauthier have been correct to point out the con-

87 In the *Dialogue of the Common Laws,* for example, Hobbes notes that "murder is distinguished from homicide by the statute laws [and thus by the sovereign], and not by any common-law without the statute" (*D:* 113).

88 This understanding also informs Hobbes's discussion of the statute against treason in the *Dialogue of the Common Laws.* "Not the statute only, but reason without a statute makes [treason] a crime. . . . all men, though of divers opinions, did condemn it by the name of treason, though they knew not what treason meant, but were forced to request the King to determine it" (*D:* 102). Some forms of behavior could be seen to be treasonous prior to any statute circumscribing it: The safety of the people depends on the safety of the king, so that "to design the Death of the then present King, was High Treason before the making of this Statute." Although some acts can clearly be seen by all to be treasonous, others are less clear and must be determined by statute: "the Killing of a Justice, or other Officer as is determin'd by the Statute, is not otherwise High Treason, but by the Statute" (*D:* 102, 103).

tractarian streak in Hobbes's writings and to criticize those who would ignore it. But in dwelling exclusively on such passages, they have failed to account for Hobbes's insistence that there are genuine moral constraints on the sovereign in civil society and on individuals in the state of nature. The account given here of Hobbes as a virtue ethicist can account for the contractarian tendencies in his writings without overlooking those fundamental features of his moral theory. It therefore fulfills the essential goals established at the outset of this chapter: It provides a coherent interpretation of Hobbes's moral theory, rooted firmly in Hobbes's texts and drawing on the significant insights of his major interpreters without suffering from their weaknesses. Hobbes's moral philosophy is thus best understood as one that culminates in a theory of moral virtue, and we shall next consider the argument he offers in its defense.

Chapter 4

From science to virtue

4.0 OVERVIEW

As we saw in Chapter 2, Hobbes's natural philosophy generates a descriptive account of human beings as complex, predominantly self-interested and death-averse bodies capable of experiencing a variety of sensations and desires, who consider good whatever happens to be the objects of those desires, and who have the potential to reason effectively about how best to attain those objects. As we saw in Chapter 3, Hobbes's moral philosophy is best understood as culminating in a normative account of human virtue which identifies an objectively valid moral law, and which celebrates as just the person who is disposed to follow that law, and to take pleasure in it, without regard to the beneficial consequences of doing so. Yet, as we saw in Chapter 1, Hobbes's frequent statements about the systematic nature of his thought clearly show that his moral philosophy is intended to be built on his natural philosophy, that his goal is to develop a moral science. How is this possible? The present chapter attempts to answer this question by tracing Hobbes's defense of his moral theory from its foundation in his view of human nature to its concluding vindication of the traditional moral virtues. The chapter begins with Hobbes's (in)famous claim that the absence of a central authority would result in a state of war, and then examines how he uses the resultant desirability of escaping from such a condition to ground his defense of the moral virtues. This completes the interpretive portion of this study and provides the foundation for the final chapter, an attempt to initiate the project of assessing the merits of Hobbesian virtue ethics.

4.1 THE STATE OF NATURE

If there is one position most closely identified with Hobbes, it is the claim in Chapter 13 of *Leviathan* that "during the time men live without a common Power to keep them all in awe, they are in that condition which is called Warre," a war which is one "of every man against every man," and in which life is "solitary, poore, nasty, brutish, and short" (*L:* 185, 188, 186).[1] This position has long been a familiar object of controversy. Only recently, however, have Hobbes's readers focused on what the argument in defense of it is.[2] Jean Hampton's important recent work on *Hobbes and the Social Contract Tradition,* in particular, presses the question of how Hobbes's argument can best be interpreted, and provides a useful typology for framing the search for an acceptable answer. Hobbes's claim that the state of nature would be a state of war serves as a foundation not only for his political theory but also for his science of virtue, so consideration of Hampton's question is indispensable to developing an adequate account of Hobbes's ethics. We need not arrive at a definitive account of Hobbes's argument, however, in order to proceed. We must find at least one way for Hobbes to be understood as grounding this conclusion in his science of human nature; if there proves to be more than one way for Hobbes to get from his picture of human nature to his conclusion about the misery of anarchy, so much the better for Hobbes's ethics.

4.1.1 Perhaps the most straightforward interpretation of the argument in Chapter 13 of *Leviathan* is what Hampton calls the rationality account of conflict, in which the causes of quarrel are "based solely on the rational pursuit of self-preservation by each person" (1986: 61). Individuals in the state of nature, because they are roughly equal in intelligence and strength, feel equally confident of their ability to obtain the objects of their desires. Hence, "if any two men desire the same thing, which nevertheless they cannot both enjoy, they become enemies" and "endeavour to destroy, or subdue one an other" (*L:* 184). This competition for scarce goods[3]

1 For evidence that Hobbes based his famous description of life in the state of nature in *Leviathan* on Thucydides' characterization of life among the earliest Greeks in Book I of his *History,* see Klosko and Rice (1985: 405–9).

2 Kavka suggests two explanations for this seemingly peculiar fact: that most writers have either embraced Hobbes's argument as "straightforward and correct" or have passed it by as "readily dismissible" (1986: 86). Gauthier has also noted that "Hobbes's explanation has seemed plausible to some, highly implausible to others, but few commentators, until recently, have paused to consider precisely what it is" (1988: 126).

3 Scarcity of goods seems implicit in the concern that two people will frequently both want the same thing. Each wants this particular object because there is no substitute available. In the absence of scarcity, though, Hobbes can still argue that such conflicts will occur by appealing to the desire for glory: Each may want

represents the first cause of conflict in the state of nature, but more important, it is the source of the "diffidence" or distrust which as a result pervades such a state. As Hobbes puts it, "if one plant, sow, build, or possesse a convenient Seat, others may probably be expected to come prepared with forces united, to dispossesse, and deprive him, not only of the fruit of his labour, but also of his life, or liberty" (*L:* 184). This mutual distrust is crucial to Hobbes's argument because it is the expectation that others are likely to attack that justifies his conclusion that "there is no way for any man to secure himselfe, so reasonable, as Anticipation; that is, by force, or wiles, to master the persons of all men he can, so long, till he see no other power great enough to endanger him" (*L:* 184). Preemptive attacks are reasonable on this account, because, despite the unpleasant costs of conflict, it is better to attack than to be attacked, and thus diffidence provides a second source of war. Hobbes also argues that glory provides a third source of quarrel in the state of nature, since there are some people who take pleasure in "contemplating their own power in the acts of conquest, which they pursue farther than their security requires" (*L:* 184–5), but the rationality account treats this as an unnecessary appendage to the core argument, a "harmless addition" provided to make the argument "more persuasive to the reader" (1986: 61). The heart of Hobbes's argument, on the rationality account, is that war characterizes the state of nature because, although each individual prefers peace to war, it nonetheless proves rational for each individual to engage in anticipatory violence, thereby ensuring that war, and not peace, will prevail.

As Hampton notes in her discussion, several modern commentators have seen in this somewhat paradoxical argument the structure exemplified in game theory by the prisoner's dilemma.[4] Consider, for example, the matrix represented below.[5]

		B	
		Not Attack	Attack
A	Not Attack	2,2	4,1
	Attack	1,4	3,3

a particular object, despite the availability of substitutes, in part because it is this particular object that is desired by the other. The role of glory in generating conflict in the state of nature is discussed in section 4.1.2.

4 John Rawls, for one, refers to "the prisoner's dilemma of which Hobbes's state of nature is the classical example" (1971: 269).

5 The figure is modeled after Hampton's Figure 2.1 (1986: 62).

A and B are Hobbesian individuals, endeavoring to satisfy their own desires and acting independently of each other with no common power over them. Each is wary of the other because no power prevents the other from attacking, and each realizes that the other is likely to be wary for the same reason. Faced with this seemingly ineradicable diffidence, each tries to discern the most reasonable course of action: to attack first, or to lie low. There are thus four possible states of affairs, and their preference orderings for each are represented in the corresponding quadrants of the matrix, with A's preference ordering on the left and B's on the right in each ordered pair, and with 1 representing the highest preference and 4 representing the lowest. A reasons roughly as follows: If I attack and B does not, I can master and plunder B, dramatically increasing my security; this would be the best possible outcome given the circumstances. If, on the other hand, B attacks and I do not, then my life will be in B's hands, and that would be the worst outcome. Of the two remaining possibilities, mutual nonaggression is preferable to mutual aggression, since it would at least allow me to maintain my present level of security and sustenance whereas I cannot reasonably expect a battle on equal terms to leave me as well off. B's situation is not relevantly different, so B's reasoning and preferences are symmetric with A's. This means, as the matrix clearly illustrates, that both A and B will conclude: No matter what the other does, I should attack. Attacking, to put things in the terminology of game theory, dominates not attacking. It is preferable when the other attacks (3 is preferable to 4), and it is preferable when the other does not attack (1 is preferable to 2). Thus, despite the fact that their both attacking puts them in the lower-right quadrant although *both* would prefer to be in the upper-left quadrant, both do the reasonable thing in attacking. As Hampton emphasizes, the prisoner's dilemma matrix "pictures the way in which the predominant cause of invasion is each person's *rational* pursuit of self-interest" (1986: 62).[6]

6 Andrew Alexandra (1992) has recently argued that Hobbes's state of nature should instead be understood in terms of the Assurance Game, in which the payoffs are understood as follows:

		B	
		Not Attack	Attack
A	Not Attack	1,1	4,2
	Attack	2,4	3,3

Despite the evidently straightforward nature of this account and the ample support for it in Hobbes's text, Hampton finds several difficulties she believes render it unacceptable. First, she argues, "accepting this account means abandoning the idea that there are valid hypothetical imperatives dictating cooperative action, and this amounts to jettisoning Chapters 14 and 15 of *Leviathan*" and, in particular, to abandoning Hobbes's response to the Foole (1986: 74–5). Hobbes avowedly denies the rationality of the Foole's claim that it is (sometimes) rational for him to violate his agreements after others have complied, yet the rationality account of conflict seems to endorse the claim that noncooperative strategies are always dominant. "Provided that the prisoner's dilemma (PD) matrix describes the game-theoretic situation underlying the choice whether or not to perform the actions dictated by [the laws of nature]," Hampton argues, "then if we are in the state of nature, no matter what our fellow human beings do, we are right not to cooperate with them. Reneging is always our dominant strategy" (1986: 75). This would mean, however, that we should renege on our agreements even when others have complied, and would thus force us to attribute to Hobbes the view he reserves only for Fooles.

Hampton's conclusion here clearly follows from her premise. If the PD matrix correctly describes the situation facing the Foole, then the Foole is right not to cooperate. The question, however, is whether her premise as clearly follows from the rationality account of conflict: Does that account's claim that it is rational to attack a potential enemy before he attacks first mean that it is also rational to betray the trust of a potential partner who has tangibly demonstrated a willingness to cooperate? Hampton does not pause to consider this question, but it poses a serious problem for her objection. She wants to say that the rationality account of conflict is unacceptable because it is necessarily incompatible with the claim that second-party compliance in the state of nature is rational. But

The third and fourth preferences for each remain the same as in the PD, but in this version, each prefers mutual nonaggression to unilateral attack. There is thus no dominant strategy (attacking is preferable if the other attacks; not attacking is preferable if the other does not attack), and two points of equilibrium (mutual cooperation and mutual aggression). There is no clear, convincing textual support for preferring this interpretation, but even if it is accepted one can still construct a kind of rationality account of conflict on Hobbes's behalf: Since there is no dominant strategy, and since each agent cannot know how the other will behave, reason might dictate that one act to avoid the one disastrous outcome, that of unilateral nonaggression, and this would lead each to prefer attacking to not attacking.

Hobbes's claim that the Foole is wrong need not entail that anticipatory violence is not rational. The Foole is wrong because he fails to see that breaking his covenant will prevent others from including him in defensive confederations. His reneging reveals to them that he thinks it reasonable "to deceive *those that help him*," and this revelation renders him unacceptable as a potential partner (*L:* 205, emphasis added). This feature of the Foole's uncooperative behavior does not, however, carry over to the case of two diffident people in the state of nature who have as yet no history of cooperation between them. The person in such a situation who, out of a reasonable fear, attacks the other first is *not* harming "those that help him" and is therefore not making himself unacceptable to those who would admit him to their alliance.[7] The cost of his attacking the other is not, therefore, comparable to the cost of the Foole's betraying his partner. Hobbes can, therefore, consistently maintain that in the state of nature both anticipatory violence and second-party compliance are rational. The PD matrix accurately reflects the situation of two distrustful people in the state of nature, but it does not reflect the position of the second party to a covenant. Hampton's first objection to the rationality account of conflict must therefore be rejected.

Not only does Hobbes claim in Chapter 15 that cooperation in the state of nature is rational, Hampton says in her second objection, but he also seems to be right in saying so; the rationality account is not just inconsistent with Hobbes's other statements, but false as well (1986: 75–6). People in a state of nature would not be in one-time PD situations, Hampton points out, but rather in multiplay situations. In deciding whether or not to cooperate, therefore, they would have to take into account not simply the immediate payoffs of their choices, but the long-term consequences as well. This means, if we follow Hampton's example of contract keeping as a form of cooperative behavior, that they would reason that reneging would have the long-term cost of precluding their making valuable agreements in the future, and they would therefore conclude that they should keep their contracts. "Not only does this iterated PD argument for the rationality of contract keeping seem correct," Hampton concludes, "it may even be right to say that it is a plausible interpretation and development of Hobbes's remarks in his answer to the fool." Rationality ultimately "counsels cooperation rather than conflict" (1986: 76).

7 This claim is more fully developed in section 4.1.2.

Hampton's second objection suffers from the same problem as her first. The question is not whether the iterated PD argument for covenant keeping is correct, but whether its correctness need impugn the plausibility of the rationality account of conflict. Again, Hampton passes over a potentially thorny problem for her position: "If Hobbes accepts the iterated PD argument," she claims, "he must accept the idea that reason dictates cooperation, and this means that conflict must be a function of people's irrationality, not their rationality" (1986: 76). But as my response to Hampton's first objection indicates, not all forms of cooperation are created equal. It remains open to Hobbes to agree that reason dictates that the Foole comply when he finds that others are complying first, but to deny that reason therefore dictates that he refrain from preemptive strikes against potential enemies who have failed to demonstrate a similar willingness to comply. Reason tells him that betraying a demonstratively cooperative partner has unacceptable long-term costs, but it also tells him that an anticipatory strike against someone else does not have such costs.[8] It may seem paradoxical to maintain that reason is a source of both cooperation and conflict in the state of nature, but this does not mean that it would be inaccurate to do so.

Finally, Hampton argues that the rationality account of conflict is unacceptable because it "would seem to make it impossible for people to escape from the state of nature" (1986: 78). The institution of the sovereign requires adherence to a social contract formed in the state of nature, and according to Hampton's argument, the rationality account of conflict denies that it is rational to adhere to such contracts. The problem with this objection should by now be clear. The Foole's reasoning may lead him to embrace the rationality account of conflict in the state of nature, but the defender of the rationality account need not embrace the reasoning of the Foole. The rationality account need not prove inconsistent with the formation of successful contracts in the state of nature, and need not therefore undermine Hobbes's strategy for escaping from it.[9] Hampton's objections to the rationality account of conflict thus prove insufficient, and the account should continue to be considered a viable one.

8 This claim is more fully developed in section 4.1.2.

9 Russell Hardin's argument against Hobbes's ability to use the social contract as a means of escaping the state of nature is thus undermined for the same reason, since it, too, rests on the erroneous claim that for Hobbes all contracts in the state of nature are void (1991: esp. 160–1).

4.1.2 A second argument for the claim that the state of nature is a state of war is less evident in Chapter 13, but it is clearly suggested by a variety of other passages in *Leviathan* and elsewhere in Hobbes's writings. According to this version, which Hampton dubs the passions account of conflict, war results not because people behave rationally but because their passions prevent them from doing so (1986: 63–8). Hobbes begins Part II of *Leviathan,* on Commonwealth, by noting that people wish to escape from "that miserable condition of Warre, which is necessarily consequent (as hath been shewn) to the naturall *Passions* of men" (*L:* 223, emphasis added). In the same chapter, explaining why the absence of a central authority leads humans, but not bees and ants, to quarrel, Hobbes relies not on the claim that humans, unlike such animals, rationally pursue their self-preservation but on such claims as that "men are continually in competition for Honour and Dignity, which these creatures are not" (*L:* 225), and that conflicts arise because unlike these creatures, "man, whose Joy consisteth in comparing himselfe with other men, can relish nothing but what is eminent" (*L:* 226).

According to this account of conflict, Hobbes's third argument in Chapter 13 to not peripheral but essential: We cannot begin with the assumption that all will rationally pursue their self-preservation, because the desire for glory will lead either "some" (in Chapter 13) or all (in the comparison with animals in Chapter 17) to acts of conquest "which they pursue farther than their security requires" (*L:* 185). At least some people will cause war by attacking others out of vanity, and others will cause war by preemptively attacking people out of a reasonable fear that others (either because of their vanity or because of their fear of others' vanity) will attack them first. The passion for glory and honor, therefore, provides Hobbes with a different sort of argument for the claim that the state of nature is a state of war. As Hampton puts it, "the irrational passions prevent some people from understanding the advantages of cooperation, and legitimate fear of these passions' disruptive effects causes the rest to behave uncooperatively in order to avoid getting hurt." In both cases, as Hampton emphasizes, "the irrational passions are held to be the cause, either directly or indirectly, of the warfare in the state of nature" (1986: 67).

Hampton poses for the passions account of conflict two problems in the form of a dilemma: If such irrational passions are deep-seated enough to generate a war of all against all, they will be powerful enough to prevent people from successfully instituting an absolute sovereign; if such passions are so weak that they cannot obstruct the social contract, they are too weak to generate a war of all against all. "The passions account of conflict must be rejected," Hampton therefore urges, "because it makes the sovereign's institution either unnecessary or else impossible" (1986: 74).

Let us grant Hampton's charge that an account in which the desire for glory consistently surpasses the desire for self-preservation will render the social contract impossible, and focus instead on the claim that without such prevalent passions, the absolute sovereign becomes unnecessary. Her argument runs as follows: If Hobbes's reply to the Foole is correct, there is a tremendous price for reneging on one's contracts, namely, the loss of a reputation as trustworthy, which will gravely impair one's future prospects for survival. In many covenants in which A agrees to comply first and B afterward, A will reason that the potential loss of credibility he will suffer by reneging outweighs the potential loss from being exploited if B were to renege unilaterally. Only in those rare instances in which A has promised to give away something precious will reason recommend that he preemptively renege. In many cases, therefore – those that Hampton calls low-risk contracts – people will comply with their agreements. Total conflict will not break out, and the state of nature will prove more Lockean than Hobbesian. This, Hampton argues, will deprive Hobbes of his justification for an absolute sovereign, rendering the passions account of conflict unacceptable.

One could take issue with Hampton's claim that what Locke called the "inconveniences" (1965: e.g., 397) of the state of nature could not suffice for Hobbes's political purposes, but there is a more fundamental problem that merits attention. Hampton's argument proceeds from the assumption that Hobbes's response to the Foole, if correct, establishes that every act of reneging on an agreement carries the substantial cost of diminishing the defector's reputation. More specifically, Hampton relies on the claim that even the first party to an agreement will be reluctant to renege, because of the costs involved. In low-risk contracts, she argues, "a rational person, even if he knows there is a good chance that his partner will renege, will always keep his part of the bargain, because no matter what his partner does, he stands to gain more if he keeps his promise than if he breaks it" (1986: 70).

Yet Hobbes's response to the Foole explicitly differentiates between first- and second-party compliance, and argues only that second-party compliance is rational: In the state of nature, "the question is not of promises mutuall, where there is no security of performance on either side," but only "where one of the parties has performed already" (*L:* 204). Furthermore, Hobbes is justified in drawing this distinction. The great cost he identifies for reneging is borne by only a second-party defector. As we noted earlier, the Foole's error lies in revealing his belief that "he thinks it reason to deceive *those that help him*" (*L:* 205, emphasis added). This renders him unfit for acceptance by defensive alliances. Members of such an alliance will not agree to help the Foole in exchange for his helping them, because they see that even when people help him first, the Foole turns around and betrays his helpers. But they will not draw a similar conclusion about a potential member of the alliance if he is a first-party defector. In that case, the candidate does not harm someone who has helped him; he merely acts on his reasonable suspicion that the other is going to exploit him. Such a person exhibits a healthy skepticism, given his knowledge that "there is a good chance that his partner will renege," and he therefore does nothing to make himself less appealing as a member in a defensive alliance.[10] A high level of conflict will therefore remain characteristic of the state of nature, because even though many people will accurately recognize the value of being second-party compliers, the rationality of first-party defection will minimize their opportunities to put their belief in second-party compliance into practice. Hampton's attempt to impugn the passions account by using it to reduce the state of nature from a state of Hobbesian misery to one of Lockean inconvenience thus seems to fail.

This suggested rebuttal to Hampton rests on the recognition that Hobbes distinguishes between first- and second-party compliance and that he recommends only the latter as rational in the state of nature. It remains open to Hampton to circumvent this objection by arguing that the rationality of second-party compliance entails the rationality of first-party compliance. Hampton does offer such an argument, and it must therefore be considered. Suppose, she says:

> Alice and Bill make a contract to exchange Alice's horse for Bill's cow. If Alice is to be the first to perform, she will reason . . . that it is rational for Bill to give her the cow if she keeps her part of the bargain by first turning

10 One might even argue that his first-party defection under such circumstances makes him a *more* desirable candidate for admission to a defensive confederation; his actions demonstrate that he is neither gullible nor easily swindled, and the members of such an alliance will surely wish to screen out individuals with poor judgment.

over the horse to him. But if this is so, then it is also advantageous for her to perform. Provided that Bill is rational, giving Bill the horse will allow Alice to reap the benefits of the bargain – Bill's cow. Hence, provided it is rational for the second party to perform, given the first party's performance, it is also rational for the first party to perform. (1986: 65)

Hampton's claim here would help to save her objection to the passions account of conflict. Alice, she argues, should comply first, "provided that Bill is rational," and this would seem to support the claim that widespread cooperation will characterize the state of nature after all, since it will turn out in many cases that Bill proves, in fact, to be rational. But Hampton's conclusion is premature. Assuming that Bill *is* rational is not enough to warrant the conclusion that Alice should comply; we must assume in addition that Alice *knows that Bill is rational.* This is precisely what the passions account permits us to deny. As long as Alice has reasonable doubts about Bill's rationality, she cannot confidently conclude that he will turn over the cow when she gives him the horse, and she must therefore conclude that reneging is preferable to complying (since, as I have argued, reneging first has no long-term costs). The significant population of irrational people posited by the passions account makes Alice's suspicion reasonable. If each person in the state of nature were rational *and were known by others to be rational,* Hampton's defense of the rationality of first-party compliance would succeed. Since this is not the case, Hobbes can continue to maintain that even a small minority of people dominated by their passions is sufficient to overturn the rationality of first-party compliance, and thus to generate a terrible state of war.

Both the rationality account and the passions account of conflict seem capable of surviving Hampton's criticisms. Since both can find adequate support in Hobbes's texts (though generally in different parts of them), the most likely conclusion seems to be that both reason and passion play an important role in generating Hobbes's war of all against all. Hampton, however, insists that we must choose between the two accounts because they are ultimately inconsistent. "Whereas the rationality account makes rationality a force disruptive of cooperation in the state of nature," she notes, "the passions account would have us think reason actually counsels cooperation" (1986: 68). But this dichotomy, as we have already seen, is too simple to reflect the subtleties of Hobbes's position. Rationality is indeed a disruptive force in the state of nature, because it counsels preemptive violence against people who have little to lose and much to gain by attacking first. It also recommends second-party compliance in the state of nature, because of the benefits of the good reputation such compliance provides. Whatever potential contributions this might make toward rendering the state of nature more peaceful, however, are obviated by the prevalence of passions that render first-party compliance unacceptably risky, and hence the opportunities for second-party compliance relatively rare. Rationality and irrationality both seem to contribute to the miserable state of war that results. This combination of sources of conflict should not surprise us, moreover, since Hobbes, as was shown in Chapter 2, sees in the human being a creature neither purely rational nor purely irrational, uniquely capable of both the most sublime accomplishments of intellect and the most grotesque heights of folly. Both accounts of conflict thus follow closely from Hobbes's science of human nature, and without a compelling reason to reject either or to choose between them, we do best to conclude that both sorts of accounts offer useful insights into Hobbes's analysis of the causes of conflict in the state of nature.

4.1.3 Hampton is motivated by her rejection of these two accounts to develop a third one on Hobbes's behalf, one she believes Hobbes "may even have been confusedly trying to present" himself (1986: 80; see 80–9). Although we may question whether Hobbes stands in need of such help, Hampton's account merits attention. In her version, the source of conflict in the state of nature lies neither in rationality nor in the passions, but in shortsightedness.

The shortsightedness account of conflict is straightforward and clear: Although the long-term benefits of complying with one's agreements outweigh the short-term advantages of reneging on them, many people will renege out of a shortsighted perspective, and others will renege out of fear of their partner's (possible) shortsightedness. Moreover, there is at least some relatively unequivocal textual evidence to indicate that Hobbes might have held such a view. In *De Cive,* for example, he complains of people's "irrational appetite, whereby they greedily prefer the present good (to which, by strict consequence, many unforeseen evils do adhere) before the future" (*DC:* 3.32). If shortsightedness is thereby equated with greed, the many passages in which greed is noted as a source of conflict might also be taken to lend support to this position. The shortsightedness account, though perhaps not as perspicuously evident in Hobbes's writings as a whole, is cogent and evident nonetheless.

Two problems face the shortsightedness account of conflict, but both can be satisfactorily addressed. One problem, which Hampton notes, is that Hobbes does not explicitly describe what leads people to take a shortsighted perspective. This lapse can be remedied in a number of ways, which need not impugn the strength of his position as a whole (1986: 82). Individuals may fail to discern the long-term differences their actions can make, for example, or they may discount the likelihood that they will ever have to face the long-term consequences of their behavior. It could hardly be obvious to everyone that their situation is that of a multiplay prisoner's dilemma.[11] The second problem with the shortsightedness account, which Hampton does not note, is that it implicitly treats first- and second-party renegers as equally shortsighted. Both sorts of people, on this account, perpetuate conflict because they fail to recognize the grave long-term implications of reneging. Yet as we saw in the previous section, the long-term consequences of defecting depend substantially on whether or not the other party has already complied; the first-party defector does not earn the reputation for treachery that will fall upon the second-party defector. The shortsightedness account of conflict should therefore be modified to recognize, as Hobbes does, that first-party defection is often rational even from a long-term perspective, whereas second-party defection is not. So modified, the shortsightedness account constitutes a valuable addition to, though not a replacement for, the other arguments already considered for Hobbes's claim that the state of nature is a state of war.

4.1.4 Finally, we must acknowledge a fourth account of conflict in Hobbes's writings that is not treated in Hampton's work: Conflict arises because people in the state of nature lack a common standard of good and bad, right and wrong. Thus Hobbes writes in

11 Another possibility is suggested by Mark C. Murphy, who offers additional textual evidence for attributing the shortsightedness account to Hobbes. Murphy argues that shortsightedness follows from Hobbes's account of the relationship between imagination and endeavor: An object of desire that is immediately present to the senses generates a stronger motion than does the imagination of enjoying such an object in the future. He cites in support of this view Hobbes's claim that "as all conceptions we have immediately by the sense, are delight, or pain, or appetite, or fear; so are also the imaginations after sense. But as they are weaker imaginations, so are they also weaker pleasures, or weaker pain" (*EL* I: 7.4). Thus, shortsightedness need not be viewed as a defect in the way in which one reasons from a given set of desires, but rather as a feature of human nature that influences the nature of the desires themselves (1993: 249).

De Cive that "all controversies are bred from hence, that the opinions of men differ concerning *meum* and *tuum, just* and *unjust* . . . *good* and *evil* . . . and the like" (*DC:* 6.9). He avers in the same work that when individuals disagree over what is good and evil "necessary it is there should be discord and strife. They are, therefore, so long in the state of war, as by reason of the diversity of the present appetites, they mete good and evil by diverse measures" (*DC:* 3.31). The same point is made in *De Corpore Politico,* when Hobbes argues that "all violence proceedeth from controversies that arise between men concerning *meum* and *teum,* right and wrong, good and bad, and the like" (*EL* II: 1.10). Even *Leviathan* contains strands of this argument: "So long a man is in the condition of meer Nature, (which is a condition of War,) as private Appetite is the measure of Good and Evill" (*L:* 216). The somewhat awkward construction of this sentence can obscure its meaning on a cursory reading, but its point remains nonetheless clear: Relying on private appetite as the measure of good and evil is the cause, and not the effect, of the state of nature's being a state of war.

Richard Tuck stresses this account of conflict in his recent discussion of Hobbes. Citing the passage from *De Cive* 3.31 noted above, he concludes that "It was conflict over what to *praise,* or morally to approve, which Hobbes thus isolated as the cause of discord [in the state of nature], rather than simple conflict over *wants.* What he was frightened of, it is reasonable to assume, were such things as the Wars of Religion, or other ideological wars; not (say) class wars, in which the clash of wants could more clearly be seen" (1989: 56).[12] Tuck overstates the case in insisting that Hobbes identifies conflict over what to praise as "the" cause of conflict in the state of nature. To say that such disagreement necessarily produces conflict does not erase the many passages that show that competition for limited resources has the same effect. It is not entirely clear how reasonable it is to assume, as Tuck does, that Hobbes has in mind religious or ideological conflicts, since it seems unlikely that the detailed doctrines requisite for such conflicts could develop or persist in a state with "no Arts; no Letters; no Society" (*L:* 186).[13] It

12 John Dewey also attributes to Hobbes the argument that "the state of war ensues . . . because what one man calls good another man finds evil" (1974: 26). Unlike Tuck, however, Dewey does not insist on this interpretation to the exclusion of the more familiar argument that conflict over wants causes such conflict.

13 As Robert P. Kraynak makes clear in his recent study of Hobbes's view of history, conflicts over ideology on Hobbes's account are "a new type of warfare

remains true, nonetheless, that Hobbes is greatly concerned with the power that beliefs about good and evil have to generate conflict. In explaining why the social animals such as bees and ants can live peacefully in the absence of authority, for example, he emphasizes that "they want that art of words, by which some men can represent to others, that which is good, in the likeness of Evill; and Evill, in the likenesse of Good . . . discontenting men, and troubling their Peace at their pleasure" (*L:* 226). Although it would be difficult to view this position as more than a supplement to the more familiar arguments already treated, it should be recognized as an important supplement and one not all Hobbes's readers have been prone to notice.[14]

There are thus a variety of grounds on which Hobbes can reasonably rest his claim that the state of nature is a state of war, grounds that rest on his understanding of human nature. Recent scholarship on Hobbes, prompted largely by Hampton's work, has included efforts to develop a more definitive account of his position than has been available. In the absence of a compelling need to choose from among them, we remain content to accept all these arguments as elements of Hobbes's analysis of the causes of war.[15] Our central concern remains Hobbes's ethics, and having seen that

that primitive men were spared by their ignorance." The "wars among intellectuals over opinions and doctrines" are entirely a product of civilization, and it is therefore difficult to see how they could occur in the state of nature which, even when viewed as a purely theoretical construct, must be understood as existing outside of civilization (1990: 16). François Tricaud expresses similar doubts in his survey of "Hobbes's Conception of the State of Nature from 1640 to 1651: Evolution and Ambiguities," allowing that this sort of account of conflict has a role to play for Hobbes, but noting that it is "difficult to believe that the fundamental cause of Hobbes's primordial war is so purely doctrinal" (1988: 114).

14 This account also figures prominently in S. A. Lloyd's recent study (1992: e.g., 260–4).

15 That the more reasonable course is simply to attribute all these arguments to Hobbes rather than try to identify one as definitive is also suggested by the fact that rationality, glory-seeking, shortsightedness, and disagreement over what is just all play a role in Hobbes's explanation of the causes of the English Civil War in *Behemoth*. Rational calculation is to blame in those who joined the war because they "had able bodies, but saw no means how honestly to get their bread" (*B:* 4); glory is often blamed in the text, since "the desire of most men to bear rule" creates further instability (*B:* 193); the role of shortsightedness is exemplified by those who betrayed the king because they "never look upon anything but their present profit" (*B:* 142); and the role of disagreement over value judgments is emphasized by the claim that it was "want of the science of justice, that brought them into these troubles" (*B:* 159).

there is at least some way for Hobbes to justify his fundamental claim that the misery of anarchy follows from his science of human nature, we now turn to his attempt to defend his moral theory by building on it.

4.2 THE LAWS OF NATURE

Hobbes maintains, as we saw in section 2.5, that death is the "chiefest of natural evils" (*DC:* 1.7). To live, and thus to secure the possibility of living well, one must first avoid this evil. As we have just seen, no one can reasonably expect to avoid this evil for long in the state of nature, in which the most salient feature of human life is that it is brutally short. It therefore follows that such a state of affairs is inimicable not only to the well-being of society as a whole but also to the well-being of every individual who inhabits it. As Hobbes puts the point in *De Cive,* no one "esteems a war of all against all, which necessarily adheres to such a state, to be good for him" (*DC:* 1.13). All people, therefore, according to Hobbes, can agree that war is bad, or put the other way around, "all men agree on this, that Peace is Good" (*L:* 216).

The claim that it is good for every individual to escape from, or avoid falling into, the anarchic war of all against all is a simple but pivotal corollary to Hobbes's analysis of the state of nature. It is simple because it straightforwardly follows from Hobbes's claim that death prevents each person from living well and his conclusion that in the state of nature no one is powerful enough to maintain security satisfactorily. It is pivotal because it serves to bridge the gap between the subjectivism and egoism that threaten to undermine his attempt to develop a substantive moral theory and the moral virtues that theory ultimately teaches us to praise. Because, for each individual, self-preservation is a necessary precondition for living well, there is no guarantee that there is anything all can agree to call good. The implication is that since my self-preservation is good for me and yours is good for you, the traditional project of searching for something all people by reason can agree to call good may be doomed from the start. Hobbes's conclusion about the terrible consequences of anarchy allows this possibility to remain open. Since peace is necessary to secure each person's self-preservation, peace is something all can agree to call good.

This simple agreement that peace is good is important because it secures the additional agreement that "therefore also the way, or means of Peace . . . are good" (*L:* 216). As Hobbes puts the principle underlying this conclusion in an important passage in *Human Nature,* "He that foreseeth the whole way to his preservation (which is the end that every one by nature aimeth at) must also call it good, and the contrary evil. And this is that good and evil, which not every man in passion calleth so, but all men by reason" (*EL* I: 17.14). The passions, as we saw in section 2.4.3, may thus interfere with an individual's reasoning, preventing him from perceiving what is in his long-term interest. The emotions are called "perturbations of the mind" precisely because "they militate against the real good and in favor of the apparent and most immediate good, which turns out frequently to be evil when everything associated with it hath been considered" (*DH:* 12.1). Reason, nonetheless, makes possible this distinction between the real good and the apparent good, and there is, despite the worry that Hobbes's subjectivism creates, a good that all can agree to call good by reason, namely, the way to peace. The way to peace, as Hobbes claims to demonstrate, lies in adherence to the laws of nature.

The enumeration of the laws of nature varies to some degree among Hobbes's writings. *De Corpore Politico,* for example, identifies as laws of nature "That men allow commerce and traffic indifferently to one another" (*EL* II: 3.13) and "That no man obtrude or press his advice or counsel to any man, that declareth himself unwilling to hear the same" (*EL* II: 4.8), laws not reiterated elsewhere. Laws of nature that appear consistently in Hobbes's writings sometimes appear in different arrangements, and are given varying degrees of emphasis. Thus, although Hobbes allows in *Leviathan* that drunkenness "may . . . be reckoned amongst those things which the Law of Nature hath forbidden," he immediately adds that such things "are not necessary to be mentioned, nor are pertinent enough to this place" (*L:* 214). When the same subject is treated at more length in *De Cive,* however, he emphasizes that "there is no difference between a man who performs not his duty [i.e., by violating the other laws of nature], and him who does such things willingly as make it impossible for him to do it [i.e., by violating the law against drunkenness]" (*DC:* 3.25). Even Hobbes's explication of the golden rule, his paradigmatic shorthand for the laws of nature, varies within and between texts. Some commentators have tended to identify Hobbes with a negative formulation of the rule; in Chapter 3 of *De Cive,* for example, he summarizes the rule as, "do not that to others, you would not have done to yourself" (*DC:* 3.26). But in the next chapter, he seems just as comfortable with the more familiar positive version, "all things whatsoever ye would that men should do unto you, do you even so to them" (*DC:* 4.23), and he turns to each with roughly equal frequency throughout his writings.

Despite variations in presentation, however, the core of Hobbes's doctrine of the laws of nature remain generally consistent throughout. Since the laws of nature aim at promoting the self-preservation of the agent who follows them, and since such self-preservation is gravely threatened in a state of war, the first or fundamental law of nature is "That every man, ought to endeavour Peace, as farre as he has hope of obtaining it; and when he cannot obtain it, that he may seek, and use, all helps, and advantages of Warre" (*L:* 190).[16] Since peace can be obtained only by abandoning the state of nature, and since this can be accomplished only when the individuals within it agree to relinquish the right to everything (a right that is characteristic of that state), a second law follows from the first dictating that each be willing, when others are as well, "as farre-forth, as for Peace, and defence of himselfe he shall think it necessary, to lay down this right to all things; and be contented with so much liberty against other men, as he would allow other men against himself" (*L:* 190). Since such mutual agreements would be "but Empty words" if they were not carried out, vain promises incapable of eradicating the war of all against all, there follows a third law of nature, "That men performe their Covenants made" (*L:* 201). Hobbes identifies compliance with this third law as justice, though as we saw in section 3.5 he often uses "justice" more broadly to refer to obedience to all the laws of nature.

If one passes over the remaining laws of nature described in Chapter 15 of *Leviathan,* as commentators have frequently been content to do (despite the fact that it is the longest chapter in Part I of that work), one is likely to come away with the view that morality, for Hobbes, is entirely a matter of keeping one's word.[17] But as

16 This law and those subsequently quoted are in italics in the original. The same law is presented in *De Cive* as commanding "that peace is to be sought after, where it may be found; and where not, there to provide ourselves for helps of war" (*DC:* 2.2). The fundamental law of nature is not explicitly formulated in *De Corpore Politico,* but Hobbes does preface his enumeration there by noting that there can be "no other precepts of *natural law,* than those which declare unto us the ways of peace, where the same may be obtained, and of defence where it may not" (*EL* II: 2.2).

17 A typical treatment of Hobbes asserts that "there is no need to comment in detail on any of the other laws of nature listed in this chapter [i.e., on any but

the "other laws" enumerated there clearly reveal, there is a great deal more to Hobbesian morality than this. Laws of nature prescribe, among other things, that people be grateful, sociable, forgiving, and not vengeful, hateful, or proud.[18] Hobbes's justifications for these additional laws vary in length and detail, but they are all at bottom variations on the same theme: An agent who violates a given law makes it less likely that others will be able or willing to coexist peacefully with him. As Kavka puts this point in a useful summary, the laws of nature as a whole rest on the supposition "that people are often inclined to fight when their efforts at peace are ignored or rebuffed, when they are cheated, when they are denied respect and equal rights, when they receive less than equal or fair shares of material goods, and when there is no opportunity to achieve impartial hearings and fair settlements of their disputes" (1986: 343–4).[19] Consideration of these "other" laws of nature is significant, in at least this one respect: It shows Hobbes to be capturing a much fuller range of traditional morality than is often thought.

A second advantage to considering these additional laws is that it helps prevent a common and important misunderstanding of their nature. Kavka, for example, argues that every law of nature has a two-part structure: a main clause imposing a particular moral requirement on each agent, and a qualifying clause releasing the agent from that requirement if others fail to satisfy it (or if they fail to satisfy the requirements of other laws of nature). Kavka argues, "A simple approximation of the logical form of each of Hobbes's laws of nature is 'Do *X*, provided others are doing so as well.'" He therefore disputes Hobbes's contention that the laws of nature are summarized by the golden rule. It is not, Kavka argues, that you should do unto others as you *wish* they would do unto you but, rather, you should "do unto others as they do unto you" (1986: 344, 347). Kavka calls this less glittering reformulation the Copper Rule, and it threatens to take some of the shine off Hobbes's moral theory.

This analysis of the laws of nature may seem to be vindicated by

the first law in Chapter 15]" (Raphael 1977: 56). Annette C. Baier has noted this unfortunate neglect of Hobbes's "other laws" (1987: 159 and corresponding endnotes), but hers seems to be a decidedly minority viewpoint.

18 The fourth through ninth laws, respectively (*L*: 209–11).

19 As Kavka goes on to say, "Experience suggests that these are accurate suppositions" (1986: 344).

an exclusive focus on the first three, but it is conclusively overturned by remembering that they are but the first of many. The seventh law of nature, for example (following the order in *Leviathan*), forbids cruelty in retribution for evils incurred: "We are forbidden to inflict punishment with any other designe, than for correction of the offender, or direction of others" (*L:* 210). The justification for this law is straightforward: "To hurt without reason, tendeth to the introduction of Warre; which is against the Law of Nature." Its scope is unqualified. There is no suggestion that I am permitted to seek revenge cruelly against my enemy if he has done so to me (or has violated some other law of nature). The law commands me to look "not at the greatnesse of the evill past, but the greatnesse of the good to follow," and further antagonizing my enemy does not serve that good. In *De Cive,* Hobbes explicitly states that "there are certain natural laws, whose exercise ceaseth not even in the time of war itself. For I cannot understand what . . . cruelty, that is, revenge which respects not the future good, can advance toward peace, or the preservation of any man" (*DC:* 3.27n).

Hobbes concedes in the same passage that it is not the case that "men are obliged to the exercise of *all* these laws in that state of men wherein they are not practised by others" (*DC:* 3.27, emphasis added). But this is decidedly not to say that they are obliged to obey none of them in such a state. The law against drunkenness is another clear counterexample to Kavka's claim. Drunkenness is forbidden by the law of nature because it can "destroy and weaken the reasoning faculty" of the agent who disobeys it; this is just as detrimental to the agent's prospects for peace with others (if not more so) when those others have violated the prohibition (*DC:* 3.25). The law of nature that commands "compleasance" (the fifth in *Leviathan*), that "every man strive to accommodate himselfe to the rest," provides further evidence for this view (*L:* 209). A person who persists in being stubborn and antisocial diminishes his prospects for peace, and Hobbes does not argue that such behavior becomes beneficial to the agent because it is indulged in by others. Although some of the laws of nature make their commands conditional on the compliance of others, this is a feature of their content; others make unconditional commands. A two-part structure is not essential to the form of natural law, which is thus more golden than Kavka would have us believe. Hobbes's defense of the laws of nature, taken as a whole, avers that reason leads each person to acknowledge the traditional demands of morality to be good. This, in a sense, completes Hobbes's argument from the nature of human beings to the goodness of morality.

But what about virtue? The argument developed to this point aims to show that morality is good by showing it to be instrumentally good. It is good for me to act honestly, gratefully, sociably, equitably, and so forth, because acting in these ways increases my prospects for living in peace, which in turn increases my prospects for living long and happily. But as we saw in Chapter 3, Hobbes insists that his moral theory demands more than this. The laws of nature require us not simply to do just acts but to be just people, and therefore a person who performs the acts described by the laws of nature but does so for the reward he expects to reap is not just (in Hobbes's broader sense of the term) but merely guiltless. The just, or righteous, person, in Hobbes's theory, is disposed to do the right thing, and to enjoy doing so, because it is the right thing to do. To be just is "to be delighted in just dealing." "That man is to be accounted just, who doth just things because the law commands it," and who keeps his promise "for his promise sake" (*DC:* 3.5, 14.2n). How can we get from the claim that it is good to follow the laws of nature for the benefits they provide to the claim that it is good to be disposed to follow them for their own sake? How do we explain Hobbes's insistence that "the Lawes of Nature, which consist in Equity, Justice, Gratitude, and other morall Vertues on these depending . . . are not properly Lawes, but qualities that dispose men to peace, and to obedience" (*L:* 314)? It is this final step that the interpretation of Hobbes as a virtue ethicist requires Hobbes to make, and on this final step both its credibility as an interpretation of Hobbes and its plausibility as a moral theory ultimately rest.[20]

20 With this last step, as noted in section 3.5, this account of how Hobbes defends his virtue ethics goes most significantly beyond those of Gert and Ewin. Gert asserts, correctly I think, that "Hobbes's argument for being just has considerably more force when one realizes that it is an argument for being a just person rather than an argument for performing a particular just action" (1988: 28). But he provides no clear account of why Hobbes thinks that there are stronger reasons for being just than merely for doing just actions. Ewin argues, also correctly I think, that "having the virtue of justice is in my interest because it makes possible life in a community with others and keeps us from the Hobbesian natural condition" (1991: 178), but he does not explain in sufficient detail how virtue makes this possible. Traces of what I call the argument from revealed disposition and the argument from habituation can be detected in Ewin's account (see, e.g., 1991: 117 and 157, respectively), but he does not set

Given the importance of this last step, it is unfortunate that Hobbes so often seems content to view its justification as self-evident. In *Human Nature,* for example, he argues that "the fulfilling of all these laws [of nature] is good in reason; and the breaking of them evil. And so also the habit, or disposition, or intention to fulfil them good; and the neglect of them evil." This explains, he says, why "the habit of doing according to these and other laws of nature is that we call VIRTUE; and the habit of doing the contrary, VICE" (*EL* I: 17.14).

But merely juxtaposing the claim that fulfilling the law is good with the claim that intending to fulfill it is good does not explain how the one follows from the other. Nor, perhaps more important, does it make clear why we should associate virtue and vice with people's dispositions (which may, after all, fail to issue in law-abiding actions) rather than with their actions, and why we should maintain, as Hobbes does, that moral philosophy is "the science of Vertue and Vice" (*L:* 216), concerned with people's character and not merely their actions. Although Hobbes does not always seem to recognize the need for justification of this position, two distinct and important arguments for it nonetheless emerge from his writings. They do not emerge immediately and all in one place, which may explain why they have been neglected for so long, but they do emerge. We must now turn to these two arguments.

4.3 THE ARGUMENT FROM REVEALED DISPOSITION

One argument runs roughly as follows: It is important to have a good disposition because one's disposition is revealed to others through one's behavior, and one is ultimately judged not so much by one's acts, as by one's character. The "best signes of Passions present" in a person, Hobbes argues, "are either in the countenance, motions of the body, actions, and ends, or aimes, which we otherwise know the man to have" (*L:* 129).[21] The righteous person

them out clearly and explicitly, and he offers virtually no textual evidence to justify attributing them to Hobbes (traces of the argument from habituation can also be seen in Flathman: "Virtues . . . help us to resist temptations to self-defeating actions" [1993: 79]. Flathman, too, fails to develop this in sufficient detail). Doing so in some detail is the task of the following two sections.

21 Hobbes's view that people's inner passions are revealed to others through their behavior is not often recognized, but it is present as early as his translation of Thucydides. One of the virtues of good historians, he writes in the preface, lies in their ability to thoroughly ground "subtle conjectures at the secret aims and inward cogitations of such as fall under their pen" in evidence that is compel-

"does not lose that Title, by one, or a few unjust Actions, that proceed from sudden Passion, or mistake of Things, or Persons: nor does an Unrighteous man, lose his character, for such Actions, as he does, or forbeares to do, for feare" (*L:* 206–7). The righteous person is distinguished from others by the disposition she reveals through her behavior, and she can reasonably expect to enjoy the peaceful cooperation of others. The war that characterizes the state of nature, Hobbes is careful to explain, "consisteth not in actuall fighting; but in the known disposition thereto" (*L:* 186),[22] and the argument from revealed disposition makes explicit the remedy this description suggests: War can be escaped only by those who make it known that they have developed a different disposition.

Before looking through Hobbes's writings for evidence of his intention to advance this argument, it is worth noting that evaluating individual acts as good or bad remains undeniably important. To insist that we follow Hobbes in ultimately focusing moral evaluation on just people rather than on just acts is not to say that just acts thereby lose all significance. But their importance comes to depend primarily on their usefulness in gaining insight into the character of the agent who performs them. As the lawyer puts the point in Hobbes's *Dialogue of the Common Laws,* "How can a man be indicted of avarice, envy, hypocrisy, or other vicious habit, till it be declared by some action which a witness may take notice of?" (*D:* 57). Actions are important as declarations of one's virtue or vice, but it is the virtue or vice they reveal, the disposition to embrace or betray the law of nature, that is ultimately at issue for Hobbes's ethics.[23]

ling to the reader (*EW* VII: viii). As David Johnston has noted, the quality that makes Thucydides a great historian on Hobbes's account is precisely "his extraordinary shrewdness as an interpreter of the thoughts and motives of other men" and his "acuity as an observer and analyst of the human character" (1986: 5). It should be noted, however, that Hobbes's statement in the Epistle Dedicatory that "No man better discerned of men" refers to the late father of William Cavendish (to whom the work is dedicated) and not, as Johnston misleadingly suggests, to Thucydides.

22 The definition of war in *Human Nature* is more explicit in maintaining that the "will and intention of contending by force" can be "sufficiently declared" not only by words, but by actions (*EL* I: 14.11).

23 It is true that according to this account people should care about the disposition of others because this assists them in foreseeing what actions those others may perform. This is perfectly consistent with the idea that the ethics they should therefore adopt urges them to focus their ultimate moral evaluations on the dispositions themselves.

4.3.1 One important passage suggesting Hobbes's endorsement of the argument from revealed disposition is his response to the Foole, a figure we have had occasion to consider before. The Foole maintains that reason may sometimes recommend injustice, in the narrow sense of covenant violation, in those cases in which the violater stands to benefit from reneging. Yet if such behavior is endorsed by reason, the Foole argues, "it is not against Justice: or else Justice is not to be approved for good." The Foole's position strikes at the heart of Hobbes's attempt to reconcile morality with human well-being; "from such reasoning as this," Hobbes worries, "successfull wickednesse hath obtained the name of Vertue" (*L:* 203).

As we have seen, Hobbes insists that "this specious reasoning is nevertheless false," and that even in the state of nature the Foole ought to comply with his covenants when his partner has complied first (*L:* 204). As we have also noted, the thrust of Hobbes's argument is that the Foole's defecting in such circumstances has unacceptable long-term costs that outweigh any possible short-term gains he may earn: He loses, or risks losing, the assistance of others necessary for his continued survival. We must now take a more careful look at how Hobbes articulates this reply:

> He which declares he thinks it reason to deceive those that help him, can in reason expect no other means of safety, than what can be had from his own single Power. He therefore that breaketh his Covenant, and consequently declareth that he thinks he may with reason do so, cannot be received into any Society, that unite themselves for Peace and Defence, but by the errour of them that receive him; nor when he is received, be retayned in it, without seeing the danger of their errour; which errours a man cannot reasonably reckon upon as the means of his security. (*L:* 204–5)

The central component of Hobbes's argument is perhaps best understood as containing two premises and a conclusion:

P1: If you reveal a disposition to betray those who have helped you, then you cannot expect others to help you survive.
P2: If you break your covenant (when the first party has already complied), then you reveal such a disposition.
C: If you break your covenant (when the first party has already complied), then you cannot expect others to help you survive.

Add to this the claim that in the state of nature no one "can hope by his own strength, or wit, to defend himselfe from destruction, without the help of Confederates" (*L:* 204), and the conclusion is that the Foole who reneges on his cooperating partner can expect only to perish.

This argument is clearly valid. Assuming that the Foole accepts its premises and does not really wish to ensure his own destruction, it appears that he ought to change his attitude toward justice. But how, specifically, should he change? What new attitude toward justice ought he to embrace? The argument seems to allow for two distinct possibilities: Since what ultimately gets the Foole into trouble is that his behavior reveals an unacceptable disposition to betray those who have cooperated with him (it "declares" that he thinks his behavior is reasonable), the lesson could be either that he should modify his behavior to conceal this unjust disposition or that he should modify his disposition so when it is revealed through his behavior, it will not be considered unacceptable by his potential allies.

The more straightforward interpretation of Hobbes's encounter with the Foole perhaps leans toward the former reading. The claim the Foole originally makes seems to be that it is sometimes rational to perform unjust acts, not that it is rational to be disposed to perform them. The Foole explicitly holds back from endorsing a general disposition toward covenant breaking, since he acknowledges that keeping covenants is sometimes in one's own interest. Hobbes's reply to the Foole also seems to frame the issue in terms of the rationality of acts and not of dispositions. When the Foole's partner has already complied with the covenant, Hobbes says, "there is the question whether it be against reason, that is, against the benefit of the other, to performe, or not" (*L:* 204). He does not say that the question is whether it is against reason for the other to be disposed to perform. According to this account Hobbes's disagreement with the Foole, therefore, is over whether or not one should refrain from performing unjust acts. The Foole maintains that such acts are sometimes rational because they are sometimes in one's interest, and Hobbes maintains that this is false. According to this interpretation, Hobbes raises the issue of the Foole's character or disposition in establishing the unacceptable consequences of the Foole's unjust acts, but he does not do so to pass judgment on the Foole's character or to recommend that his disposition must ultimately be criticized. Hobbes's consideration of the Foole thus does little to further the development of his moral theory, understood as a theory of moral virtue.

This is a sensible reading of Hobbes's treatment of the Foole, but it is not the only sensible reading. Several additional considerations suggest that Hobbes may be calling into question the Foole's disposition.[24] First, we must note carefully what the Foole means by his claim that there is no such thing as justice: "That every mans conservation, and contentment, being committed to his own care, there could be no reason, why every man might not do what he thought conduced thereunto: and therefore also to make, or not make; keep, or not keep Covenants, was not against Reason, when it conduced to ones benefit" (*L:* 203). Hobbes emphasizes that the Foole has said this "in his heart," not merely with his tongue, and this does seem to suggest a disposition of a certain kind.[25] In deciding whether or not to fulfill a covenant, the Foole considers in each case whether or not doing so conduces to his benefit. This is precisely what it is to be an unjust person: "*To be unjust* is to neglect righteous dealing, or to think it is to be measured not according to my contract, but some present benefit" (*DC:* 3.5). The Foole's will, therefore, is that of the unjust person; it "is not framed by the Justice, but by the apparant benefit of what he is to do" (*L:* 206).[26] To deny the existence of justice is to frame one's will always by the apparent benefits of one's actions, and Hobbes can reasonably be understood as pointing to this as the Foole's mistake.

It is worth remembering that the important passage distinguishing justice of actions from justice of manners follows almost immediately after the reply to the Foole. Hobbes insists here that "Justice of the Manners, is that which is meant, where Justice is called a Vertue; and Injustice a Vice" (*L:* 207). This insistence would trivialize the reply to the Foole if Hobbes did not mean to attack his manners. What would be the point of arguing that it is foolish to be unjust if one excluded from this claim the only sense in which one

24 For a third, and more Rawlsian, reading of Hobbes's reply to the Foole, see Zaitchik (1982).

25 Hobbes's choice of words here might be taken as providing support for this interpretation in another way. His description of the Foole clearly alludes to *Psalm* 14 ("The fool has said in his heart, / 'There is no God.' / Their deeds are corrupt and vile, / not one of them does right."), and we know from many of Hobbes's exegetical statements that he typically takes Biblical passages about good and evil to refer to people's dispositions rather than to their acts. (That Hobbes knows of the passage is made clear from his reference to it in his *Answer to Bramhall's "Catching of Leviathan," EW* IV: 293.)

26 This picture of the unjust person is also suggested by Hobbes's description of the "wicked man" in the preface to *De Cive* as "a man of a childish disposition," since he describes children there as peevishly insisting that all their desires be satisfied (*DC:* preface).

took injustice to be a vice? Hobbes makes clear his concern that by the Foole's reasoning "successfull wickedness hath obtained the name of Vertue" (*L:* 203). His pointed use of the language of virtue can only be understood if he means that the Foole's manners, and not merely his actions, have been mistaken for just when they are in fact unjust.

A final consideration in favor of this view of the text is that it equips Hobbes with what is, at least in one important respect, a substantially more cogent reply to the Foole. If Hobbes means to reveal to the Foole the advantage of just acts only and not of just manners, it is difficult to imagine how he will evade the charge of rule worship.[27] Even if the Foole comes to understand the long-term costs resulting from the loss of credibility, it seems likely that if he maintains his disposition to renege whenever it appears to be in his interest to do so, he will continue to find cases (though substantially fewer) in which he will renege. To insist that the Foole keep his covenants, even when reneging is in his long-term interest, because doing so is generally in his interest does seem to constitute an irrational form of rule worship. But not to insist that the Foole comply in such cases would be to capitulate to his defense of successful wickedness.

If Hobbes is arguing against the Foole's disposition, however, he may prove capable of escaping from this unhappy dilemma. For if the Foole's choice is between framing his will by justice and framing it by the apparent benefits of his actions, the defense of justice may proceed without succumbing to the folly of rule worship. The Foole's disposition must be rejected because even though it may allow him to exploit a few opportunities for gain that the just person cannot exploit, it exposes him to the unacceptable risk of being found out. The just person's disposition is preferable because it eliminates this risk. When we ask why the just person is not practicing an irrational form of rule worship when she refuses to exploit a clear opportunity to renege with impunity, we have a satisfactory answer: She is acting from a disposition justified in terms of its ability to maximize her prospects for security. Were she to alter her disposition to take advantage of short-term benefits, she would render herself the sort of person who would in the long run be exposed and killed.

These various considerations may be insufficient grounds for concluding that in holding up to criticism the figure of the Foole,

27 See section 3.3.2.

Hobbes must be understood as espousing what I have called the argument from revealed disposition. But they do show, at the very least, that the treatment of the Foole is compatible with and suggestive of that argument, that it is consistent with the claim that it is good to be disposed to do the right thing because having such a disposition will help one to secure the needed cooperation of others. This is not an insignificant fact; given that Hobbes does not always treat the problem of justifying good dispositions as explicitly as we would like, it may prove necessary for us to construct the argument on his behalf. The reply to the Foole can, therefore, supply us with some guidance.

4.3.2 If the Foole is all the evidence we have to go on, however, the skeptic may be justified in asking how much of Hobbes will remain in the argument that results. If we limit our considerations to the first three laws of nature, as so many of Hobbes's readers have done, we may well conclude that little more can be said on behalf of this first attempt to supply Hobbes with an argument from the goodness of good acts to the goodness of good dispositions.[28] If we go beyond them, however, we find that the reply to the Foole is neither the only nor the most compelling evidence for attributing this position to Hobbes.

Most significantly, we must consider Hobbes's undeservedly neglected fifth law, concerning sociability, or "compleasance," "that every man strive to accommodate himselfe to the rest." Hobbes's defense of this law is crucial to grounding the argument from revealed disposition in his writings, and is therefore worth quoting at some length:

> There is in mens aptnesse to Society; a diversity of Nature, rising from their diversity of Affections; not unlike to that we see in stones brought together for building of an Edifice. For as that stone which by the asperity, and irregularity of Figure, takes more room from others, than it selfe fills; and for the hardnesse, cannot be easily made plain, and thereby hindereth the building, is by the builders cast away as unprofitable, and troublesome: so also, a man that by asperity of Nature, will strive to retain those things which to himselfe are superfluous, and to others necessary; and for the stubbornness of his Passions, cannot be corrected, is to be left, or cast out of Society, as combersome thereunto. (*L:* 209)

28 Though some additional support might be found in the first law of nature, since the command to "seek peace," as one writer has put it, "does not so much enjoin one to perform a particular act designated as peace-producing as it enjoins one to change his attitude" (Waldman 1974: 76).

The general strategy in Hobbes's argument here parallels that exploited in his response to the Foole. A specific sort of behavior is shown to be contrary to the laws of nature because the agent who indulges in it will be excluded or expelled from society and left to suffer the consequences. Here, unequivocally, Hobbes's focus in proving this point rests entirely on the agent's disposition. The person who must struggle alone without the protection of society is not the one who commits a few isolated antisocial acts, who occasionally retains as luxuries goods needed by others, but the one who habitually strives to commit such acts, whose behavior issues from an antisocial disposition that is part of his nature. Hobbes specifically resists the claim that people who commit antisocial acts will suffer. His argument is that antisocial people will suffer.

This focus on dispositions is brought out clearly by the simile likening people to stones.[29] Hobbes does not draw the parallel by saying that every irregular stone must be cast aside as unfit for combining into a more secure edifice. If the stone can be reshaped without too much difficulty, it can still be used, and only those that are both of inappropriate shape and too hard to be usefully recut are therefore rejected. Similarly, not all people who needlessly hoard those goods required by others are unfit for society; only those who behave in this way out of a firm disposition to so behave are considered unfit. The argument is simple: People will tolerate antisocial acts, but they will not tolerate antisocial people.[30] That it

29 It is a simile, not a metaphor. Hobbes is frequently chastised for denouncing the use of figurative language in philosophy and then indulging in it at length himself. It is therefore worth noting in his defense that he is careful to distinguish similes, which simply note that one thing is in some respect similar to another, from metaphors, which misleadingly present one thing as if it literally were the other. "In Demonstration, in Councell, and all rigourous search of Truth, Judgement does all; except sometimes the understanding have need to be opened by some apt similitude; and then there is so much use of Fancy. But for Metaphors, they are in this case utterly excluded. For seeing they openly professe deceipt; to admit them into councell, or Reasoning, were manifest folly" (*L:* 136–7). In *De Corpore,* he writes that "every *metaphor* is by profession *equivocal,*" but is careful not to say the same of similes (*Co:* 2.12). The distinction between metaphor and simile is often overlooked even in those few works which seek to focus on Hobbes's literary style (Charles Cantalupo, for example, mistakenly refers to the passage comparing people to stones as a metaphor [1991: 103]), but the distinction is important to Hobbes, whose many illustrations are typically presented as similes rather than metaphors. Thus, although his edict is no doubt a bit severe, he cannot justly be accused of systematically ignoring it.

30 Hobbes draws this same sort of distinction in *Behemoth* by having *B* object to one of the propositions delivered by Parliament to the King: "What a spiteful

is the disposition and not merely the act that constitutes the vice associated with the fifth law of nature is also reflected in the terms Hobbes chooses to describe those who disobey it. Hobbes calls such people *"Stubborn, Insociable, Froward, Intractable"* (*L:* 210), again emphasizing that to trespass against the law involves not simply performing unsocial acts, but doing so repeatedly and as a matter of habit or disposition.

Finally, this interpretation is confirmed by his treatment of the same natural law in *De Cive*. In that work it appears as the fourth law rather than the fifth and is worded somewhat differently, commanding "that every man render himself useful unto others" and identifying those who violate it as "*useless* and troublesome." The expression "render himself useful" might in itself seem somewhat ambiguous, meaning either "make himself a useful person" or "do useful actions." But that Hobbes means the former, and is again focusing on the agent's disposition, is made clear by his use of the same image he uses in *Leviathan*. There is in human beings, he writes, "a diversity of dispositions to enter into society, arising from the diversity of their affections, not unlike that which is found in stones." And just as

> a stone, which in regard of its sharp and angular form takes up more room from other stones than it fills up itself, neither because of the hardness of its matter cannot well be pressed together, or easily cut, and would hinder the building from being fitly compacted, is cast away, as not fit for use; so a man, for the harshness of his disposition in retaining superfluities for himself, and detaining of necessaries from others, and being incorrigible by reason of the stubbornness of his affections, is commonly said to be useless and troublesome unto others. (*DC:* 3.9)

By the fault of such a man "there will arise a war," and such a person "therefore acts against the fundamental law of nature." It follows, Hobbes concludes, "that it is a precept of nature, that every man accommodate himself to others."

article was this! All the rest [of the articles] proceeded from ambition, which many times well-natured men are subject to; but this proceeded from an inhuman and devilish cruelty" (*B:* 107). Bad acts may be tolerated when they are consistent with the agent's being good-natured, but not when they are seen to proceed from a bad nature. The same distinction appears in his discussion of punishment in, e.g., *Leviathan*. The crimes which merit "the severest Punishments" include "those that spring from contempt of Justice," whereas with "Crimes of Infirmity; such as are those which proceed from great provocation, from great fear, great need, or from ignorance . . . there is place many times for Lenity, without prejudice to the Common-wealth; and Lenity when there is such place for it, is required by the Law of Nature" (*L:* 389–90).

The uniform emphasis on disposition is if anything more striking here than in *Leviathan*. The simile of the stones is again invoked to emphasize that the person shunned from society is not merely the one who acts in a particular way but the one who acts out of a deep-seated disposition to do so. The "diversity of Nature, rising from their diversity of Affections" that Hobbes focuses on in *Leviathan* is treated here more explicitly as "a diversity of dispositions to enter into society, arising from the diversity of their affections." Not merely the "asperity of Nature" of the antisocial person, but also the "harshness of his disposition," is cited as a source of his viciousness. Hobbes's often neglected law commanding us to accommodate ourselves to others thus provides powerful evidence for attributing to him the argument from revealed disposition.[31]

4.3.3 Although Hobbes's defense of the virtue of sociability offers the strongest case for attributing to him the argument from revealed disposition, and the encounter with the Foole offers the most familiar grounds (although the interpretation of the encounter offered here is less familiar), a few additional passages merit consideration as well. One concerns what is, in *Leviathan*, the fourth law of nature, "That a man which receiveth Benefit from another of meer Grace, Endeavour that he which giveth it, have no reasonable cause to repent him of his good will" (*L:* 209). Hobbes justifies this law commanding gratitude by arguing that the object of gift giving is some good to the giver, and that "if men see they shall be frustrated [in that end], there will be no beginning of benevolence, or trust; nor consequently of mutuall help; nor of reconciliation of one man to another; and therefore they are to remain still in the condition of *War;* which is contrary to the first and Fundamentall Law of Nature, which commandeth men to *Seek Peace.*"

As in the two laws of nature discussed above, the outline of Hobbes's argument here is that failure to comply with the law will

31 The image of humans who must be reshaped to be made fit for society also reappears later in *Leviathan*, when Hobbes writes of those who desire "to conforme themselves into one firme and lasting edifice" but who, "for want, both of the art of making fit Lawes, to square their actions by, and also of humility, and patience, to suffer the rude and combersome points of their presente greatness to be taken off, . . . cannot without the help of a very able Architect, be compiled, into any other than a crasie building, such as hardly lasting out their own time, must assuredly fall upon the heads of their posterity" (*L:* 363). As David Johnston has correctly noted, Hobbes's description here reflects his insistence that in order to enter into peaceful society, people must not simply change their behavior, but must have the "rude and combersome points" alluded to "eliminated from their characters" (1986: 188).

render the agent unacceptable for mutual cooperation and thus unable to secure peace (and thus security) for himself. There are again suggestions that it is the agent's disposition, rather than merely his actions, that ultimately renders him unacceptable. Most obviously, the law, in specifying the behavior it requires, explicitly refers to the agent's endeavor. To comply with the law is to *try* to make the giver pleased with his giving.

But more important, the argument in defense of this law seems to make sense only if the agent's disposition is being evaluated. Hobbes insists that people will not give if they "see" that their giving will go unrewarded, and he puts the point in the same terms in his treatment of the law (enumerated there as the third) in *De Cive:* "He should act without reason, that would confer a benefit where he sees it would be lost" (*DC:* 3.8). The giver must make this judgment about the potential recipient of his gift *before* he decides to give it, however; the crux of Hobbes's argument is that the lack of such trust will prevent him from giving in the first place when the recipient is perceived not to be grateful. What the giver is seeing cannot be the recipient's ungrateful actions in response to this particular gift, since the gift has not yet been given to him. The only thing the giver can see, and that can thus deter him from giving, therefore, is that the potential recipient is not the sort of person who endeavors to repay favors. The giver withholds his graces, to return to the distinction we have followed Hobbes in emphasizing, not from people who perform ungrateful acts, but from ungrateful people. Hobbes's argument in defense of the virtue of gratitude thus provides additional support for the view that it is good for one to have a good disposition, because others will recognize this fact and reward one for it.[32]

Evidence for this view can also be found, although in a somewhat less complete form, in Hobbes's unfortunately brief defense of the sixth law of nature (in the order of *Leviathan*) "that upon caution of the Future time, a man ought to pardon the offences past of them that repenting, desire it" (*L:* 210). Hobbes says here that pardon "is

32 It might be objected here, and elsewhere in this discussion of the laws of nature, that Hobbes's argument shows that it is good to have a good disposition in the sense of habitually acting in the right way, but not in the stronger sense of acting in the right way for its own sake and taking delight in so doing. This shows at most that there may be a problem with Hobbes's defense of his theory of virtue, not that there is a problem with attributing the theory to him in the first place. Hobbes's discussions of the laws of nature justify reading them as being ultimately concerned with dispositions, and Hobbes's discussions of dispositions justify reading them as involving doing the right thing for its own sake, as a matter of character, and taking pleasure in so doing.

nothing but granting of Peace" and, consequently, pardon "not granted to them that give caution of the Future time, is signe of an aversion to Peace; and therefore contrary to the Law of Nature." Refusal to pardon a genuinely penitent person for past aggressions reveals a disposition incompatible with peace. As Hobbes puts it in his equally brief treatment of the subject in *De Cive*, "to him that will not pardon the penitent and that gives future caution, peace itself it seems is not pleasing: which is contrary to the natural law" (*DC:* 3.10).

Hobbes once again makes it clear that the disposition revealed by the violator of the law of nature (in this case his aversion toward peace) renders his behavior unacceptable. He is not explicitly clear, however, as to *why* this aversion to peace is unacceptable. The most straightforward answer to this question might at first seem to be that such an aversion is unacceptable because the first, or fundamental, law of nature commands "That every man, ought to endeavour Peace, as farre as he has hope of obtaining it" (*L:* 190). On this reading, Hobbes's defense of the law commanding pardon would do little to advance the status of the argument from revealed disposition. But when the sixth law of nature is read in the context of the longer list of which it is a part, a more plausible reading emerges. The law commanding pardon comes immediately after the laws prescribing gratitude and sociability. Hobbes justifies each of these in considerably more detail; each is made to rest on a two-part argument: To violate the law in question is to possess an uncooperative disposition, and the revelation of such a disposition will render the agent unable to obtain cooperation from others. Given the already repetitive nature of the text at this point, it seems possible that Hobbes intends his much briefer defense of the sixth law to be understood as a shorthand version of the argument he has just reiterated. Hobbes tells us that the refusal to grant pardon to another is a "signe" of the agent's aversion to peace, and we are meant to fill in the remainder of the argument ourselves: The agent who provides such a sign of his disposition thereby antagonizes a potentially cooperative person and thus wastes the opportunity for peaceful coexistence (and security) presented to him. Considered by itself, therefore, the sixth law of nature offers, at best, ambiguous support for the argument from revealed disposition, but considered as one law among others, it provides significant support.

A few rather unexpected sources of support for the attribution of this argument to Hobbes also merit mention in conclusion. One is

Hobbes's theory of laughter. As David Heyd notes in his comprehensive article on the subject, "Hobbes clearly states that laughter itself is not a passion but only 'the signe' or the bodily manifestation of a certain passion," namely "the feeling of superiority, pride, and self-assertion." The ninth law of nature forbids pride, commanding instead that "every man acknowledge other for his Equall by Nature" (*L:* 211), and laughter provides a tangible sign when that acknowledgment is absent. Thus it is not surprising that, as Heyd notes, Hobbes "is highly critical of those who laugh excessively at others" (1982: 286, 291). To do so is to reveal that one does not view others as equals, and since men "will not enter into conditions of Peace, but upon Equall termes, such equalitie must be admitted" (*L:* 211). It is good not to be proud, because the proud person's character is manifested in excessive laughter, which renders him unsuitable for entering into peaceful association with others. Or, as Hobbes puts the point with characteristic directness in *Human Nature,* "men take it heinously to be laughed at" (*EL* I: 9.13).[33]

A second source which confirms our interpretation and which shows how early Hobbes was thinking along these lines, is a letter to Charles Cavendish dated August 22, 1638, in which Hobbes gently rebukes his young charge for his reported misbehavior in Paris. "I must humbly beseech you to avoyd all offensive speech," Hobbes writes. For "he which useth harsh language whether downright or obliquely, shall be sure to have many haters, and he that hath so, it will be a wonder if he have not many just occasions of Duell" (LC: 94).[34] The person who uses offensive words cannot reasonably expect others to cooperate with him, and Hobbes goes on to say, "The words of a gentleman should be perspicuous and justifiable and such as show greatness of couradge, not of spleene" (LC: 94). Hobbes's immediate worry here is young Cavendish's behavior, yet even at this very early date Hobbes's concern with

33 Hobbes also suggests that blushing can be viewed as a physical manifestation of an undesirable character trait (*EL* I: 9.3). Joel Kidder's analysis of the ninth law of nature suggests further support for the argument from revealed disposition. "The real sin" it identifies, he insists, is "the absence of that recognition [of others' equality] itself," and what it condemns most strongly is "behaviour which shows recognition itself to be lacking" (1983: 145).

34 Compare this with Hobbes's defense of the eighth law of nature in *Leviathan* over a decade later: "Because all signes of hatred, or contempt, provoke to fight . . . we may in the eighth place, for a Law of Nature, set down this Precept, *That no man by deed, word, countenance, or gesture, declare Hatred, or Contempt of another*" (*L:* 210–11).

human action leads inexorably to a concern with human disposition. He gives his pupil advice not merely about his acts but about his character: "If a man could value himself moderately, and at the rate that other men hold him currant," he advises, "I think it were not possible for that man either out of passion or in passion to be offensive" (LC: 95). The argument clearly suggested in this early letter is: It is bad to act offensively, because to do so reveals a disposition that inhibits one's ability to interact peacefully with others. The best way for a person to ensure that he not reveal an offensive disposition is to avoid being an offensive person. This is the argument from revealed disposition in one of its many forms.

A third passage that deserves notice in connection with the argument from revealed disposition is Hobbes's dedicatory letter prefacing the *Leviathan*. In praising Francis Godolphin's departed brother Sidney, Hobbes writes "There is not any vertue that disposeth a man, either to the service of God, or to the service of his Country, to Civill Society, or private Friendship, that did not manifestly appear in his conversation, not as acquired by necessity, or affected upon occasion, but inhaerent, and shining in a generous constitution of his nature. Therefore in honour and gratitude to him, and with devotion to your selfe, I humbly Dedicate unto you this my discourse of Common-wealth" (*L:* 75). Nearly every element of the argument from revealed disposition appears in this simple dedication: that virtues are dispositions, that they render people acceptable for private or public forms of cooperation (serving God presumably represents a divine variation on this argument), that they are made manifest in one's behavior (by "conversation," Hobbes means, as he typically does, interaction with others), and that those whose virtues are a genuine part of character, not merely "affected upon occasion," are the ones who are rewarded, in this case with honor and gratitude.[35]

Finally, it is worth noting that Hobbes seems to rely on the divine variation on the argument from revealed disposition in defending his own character. In his *Considerations Upon the Reputation, Loyalty, Manners, and Religion of Thomas Hobbes of Malmesbury,* Hobbes responds sharply to the seemingly ubiquitous attacks on his pro-

35 Hobbes makes a similar point in the Epistle Dedicatory to his translation of Thucydides. In explaining why he is dedicating the work to William Cavendish in memory of his father, Hobbes explains that "he was one in whom might plainly be perceived, that *honour* and *honesty* are but the same thing in the different degrees of persons. To him therefore, and to the memory of his worth, be consecrated this, though unworthy, offering" (*EW* VIII: v).

fessed belief in Christianity.[36] How, he demands of his adversaries, "will you prove that the obedience, which springs from scorn of injustice, is less acceptable to God, than that which proceeds from fear of punishment, or hope of benefit. Gravity and heaviness of countenance are not so good marks of assurance of God's favour, as cheerful, charitable, and upright behaviour towards men, which are better signs of religion than the zealous maintaining of controverted doctrines" (*EW* IV: 433). In *Leviathan,* he goes even farther, attacking those who would cite as evidence of their faith a covenant made with God: "This pretence of Covenant with God," he fumes, "is so evident a lye, even in the pretenders own consciences, that it is not onely an act of an unjust, but also of a vile, and unmanly disposition" (*L:* 230). The genuinely religious person can be distinguished from the imposter because the disposition of each is made evident through his behavior. The truly religious person, as we saw in section 3.5, is the one who does the right thing because it is the right thing to do. God is displeased by "those who do just works and give alms only for glory or for the acquiring of riches or for the avoidance of punishment" (*DH:* 14.7). Hobbes claims to be a good Christian, the sort of person whose will is framed by a "scorn of injustice" and not by the apparent benefits of his actions, and he claims that this assessment is confirmed by his behavior.[37] In arguing that his just treatment of others testifies to the sincerity of his Christianity, he is arguing that his good behavior reveals his good disposition. The point in this case is to establish that God will cooperate with Hobbes, rather than that other people will, but the argument remains largely the same: It is important for one to have a good disposition because that disposition is revealed in one's actions, and one is then judged and rewarded accordingly.

The argument from revealed disposition thus provides one way of arguing from the claim that the means to peace are good to the claim that having a just disposition, being a just person, is good. There is an impressive variety of evidence to warrant attributing

36 As noted in section 3.4.2, Martinich's recent book makes an extremely strong case for the view that Hobbes was a devout Christian (1992). Although some of the details of Hobbes's faith may remain open to dispute, it seems right to say, as another writer has put it, that Hobbes would be disturbed that his modern reputation has "robbed [him] of his Christian Piety" (Schneider 1974: 101).

37 Hobbes reiterates this argument in the Epistle Dedicatory to *Seven Philosophical Problems,* replying to the charge that he is an atheist with the claim that "there is no sign of it in my life" (*SPP:* 5).

this argument to Hobbes, and if this section has at times become cluttered with direct quotations, it is because the argument has not been sufficiently recognized in the secondary literature.

4.4 THE ARGUMENT FROM HABITUATION

Another argument in Hobbes's writings is intended to justify the goodness of good dispositions. Unlike the argument from revealed disposition, it does not rely on the claim that one's character is, or is likely to be, made known to others through one's behavior. Instead, it begins with Hobbes's initial conclusion that one must do good acts in order to obtain cooperation from others, and then asks how it is possible for a Hobbesian individual to get herself to do such acts consistently. The recognition that regularly doing just acts is in the Foole's long-term interest, for example, may not by itself guarantee that he will do so; as we saw in section 2.3.3, Hobbesian agents always act by attempting to fulfill their desires, and although the Foole learns that keeping his promises is in his long-term interest, this may prove insufficient to generate in him a desire to do so. If he does not have such a desire, it is difficult to see how he will be able consistently to perform those just acts necessary for his long-term well-being.

The argument from habituation seeks to address this problem. It runs roughly as follows: A person can be assured of doing good acts with enough frequency to elicit cooperation from others only when doing such acts becomes a matter of habit. Since doing good acts with such frequency is good and since only by making them habitual can this be done, it follows that it is good to make the doing of such acts habitual. In the argument's crucial second step, Hobbes insists that making good acts habitual involves coming to value and enjoy doing them for their own sake. Since it is good to make such behavior habitual, and since this involves treating them as good for their own sake, it follows that it is good to be the sort of person who values doing good acts for their own sake. It is good, therefore, not simply to be a person who does just acts, but to be a just person.[38]

38 Thus Hobbes's argument here comes close to Mill's utilitarian justification of virtue. Like Hobbes, Mill argues that a person can be made virtuous only "by making the person *desire* virtue," and he concludes that "the influence of the pleasurable and painful associations which prompt to virtue is not sufficiently to be depended on for unerring constancy of action until it has acquired the support of habit. Both in feeling and in conduct, habit is the only thing which

This argument from habituation, it is worth reiterating, does not rely on the claim that others will perceive that the agent is acting from such a disposition. Even though they might reward him for regularly doing just acts without being a just person, it proves necessary for him to be a just person to ensure that he will do the just acts regularly in the first place. The argument from habituation thus provides a second and independent means of concluding Hobbes's argument in defense of moral virtue. We must once again be mindful that Hobbes does not provide us with this argument fully and all in one place, but there is sufficient textual evidence in his writings to warrant attributing it to him nonetheless.

4.4.1 The foundation of the argument from habituation is developed in an important passage in *De Corpore* (*Co:* 22.20). In discussing the "easy" sort of motion that a body attains by "the weakening of such endeavours as divert its motion," Hobbes argues that this gradual weakening "cannot be done but by the long continuance of action, or by actions often repeated; and therefore custom begets that facility, which is commonly and rightly called *habit*."[39] This feature of motion is not limited to animate bodies – Hobbes invokes the example of the stretched crossbow whose tendency to return to its original position can be diminished only by habit[40] –

imparts certainty; and it is because of the importance to others of being able to rely absolutely on one's feelings and conduct, and to oneself of being able to rely on one's own, that the will to do right ought to be cultivated into this habitual independence" (1974: 294–5). Mill, however, is ultimately concerned to justify an agent's virtuous character in terms of its contribution to total happiness, whereas Hobbes's project is to demonstrate its contribution to the well-being of the agent.

39 Hobbes makes much the same point in an important though neglected passage in *Human Nature:* "It is the nature almost of every corporeal thing, being often moved in one and the same manner, to receive continually a greater and greater easiness and aptitude to the same motion; insomuch as in time the same becometh so habitual, that to beget it, there needs no more than to begin it" (*EL* I: 5.14).

40 Hobbes makes the same point in his *Seven Philosophical Problems*, arguing that "bows long bent lose their appetite to restitution, long custom becoming nature" (*SPP:* 34–5). In the *Decameron Physiologicum*, he explicitly likens habit in the inanimate bow to habit in people, saying that "though [i.e., if] the bow had sense, and appetite to boot, the cause will be still the same" (*DP:* 136). The bent bow initially has an endeavor to return to its original position, on Hobbes's account, and this endeavor can be overcome only by its gradually becoming accustomed, or habituated, to its new position. Hobbes exploits the same vocabulary in other parts of his natural philosophy as well, claiming, for example, that "the loadstone hath been given its virtue by a long habitude in the mine" (*SPP:* 58).

but it is more familiar in the case of people. A beginning musician, to take Hobbes's other example, cannot move effortlessly from one note on her instrument to the next. Since at each step she encounters distracting temptations to make a wrong move, she must continually make a deliberate effort to strike the appropriate note. Only after much repetition and practice, "by doing this often, and by compounding many interrupted motions or endeavours into one equal endeavour," can she make her hand "go readily on from stroke to stroke in that order and way which was at the first designed." If she does not make striking the appropriate notes habitual, she cannot diminish her propensity to err.[41]

The treatment of habit in *De Corpore* suggests the following analysis of, for example, the Foole: The Foole is a novice in the art of promise keeping. If he has been convinced by Hobbes's argument, he now understands that even in the state of nature it is in his long-term interest to keep his promises consistently (provided, as always, that the other party has complied first). Still, he is the sort of person who is often tempted to violate his agreements when he clearly perceives that some immediate advantage can be gained by doing so. As we saw in section 2.4.3, human beings are passionate as well as rational animals, and the passions are called "*perturbations* of the mind" (*DH:* 12.1) because they impede consideration of the long-term good by disproportionately dwelling on the short-term. How can the Foole best fight this temptation and behave in the sort of way that will most strongly encourage others to cooperate with him? The answer Hobbes's text suggests is: Practice. Each time the Foole forces himself to keep his promise, he helps to reduce his propensity to break promises, gradually weakening the endeavors within him that tend toward injustice. The more he does this, the more likely he is to keep his agreements in the future. The more this occurs, the more likely he is to find confederates who will assist him in his endeavor to stay alive. The lesson that the beginning musician must learn about habituation can sensibly be extended to the nascent moralist. This offers perhaps the

41 Hobbes expresses the same attitude toward the capacity to reason properly in Part I of *De Corpore:* The precepts of logic, he says, are not "so necessary as practice for the attaining of true ratiocination . . . no otherwise than little children learn to go, not by precepts, but by exercising their feet" (*Co:* 4.13). He notes in his work *Of Liberty and Necessity,* "Even the setting of a man's foot, in the posture for *walking,* and the action of ordinary *eating,* was once *deliberated* of how and when it should be done, and . . . afterward it became *easy* and *habitual,* so as to be done without *forethought*" (*LN:* 245).

clearest illustration that ethics, for Hobbes, ultimately proves to be a branch of physics. His account of habit and disposition applies to material bodies in general, and because the inner workings of humans are understood to be a special case of material bodies in motion, they can legitimately be subsumed under this general account.[42]

Nor is the extension of such considerations to the realm of morals a merely speculative version of Hobbes. In *De Homine,* he returns to the subject of habituation with more explicitly moral concerns in mind. Religious dogma, for example, Hobbes treats as a habit of the mind, one particularly difficult to break.[43] Those who succumb to such a habit, Hobbes warns, come to "hate and revile dissenters" and "the disposition of these men is not suited to peace and society" (*DH:* 13.3). Religious dogma serves as one instantiation of the argument from habituation: It is bad to have such a habit because one who has it is led to behave in ways unsuitable for members of a peacefully cooperative society.

In the same work, Hobbes writes more broadly that "Dispositions, when they are so strengthened by habit that they beget their actions with ease and with reason unresisting, are called *manners.* Moreover, manners, if they be good, are called *virtues,* if evil, *vices*" (*DH:* 13.8). And "good dispositions are those which are suitable for entering into civil society; and good manners (that is, moral virtues) are those whereby what was entered upon can be best preserved" (*DH:* 13.9). Here we have Hobbes's most general statement of the first part of the argument from habituation. A good disposition or manner allows the agent to enter into, or remain in, society and thus escape the evil of unassisted life in the state of nature. It does so by rendering the appropriate actions, in an echo of Hobbes's discussion in *De Corpore,* easy and unresisted. The person who does not cultivate such a character cannot count on producing the appropriate acts of honesty, generosity, pardon, sociability, and

42 The only writer who thus far seems to have noticed the significance of Hobbes's discussion of habit in physical objects for his moral philosophy is Brian Stoffel. Stoffel correctly notes that Hobbes's account of dispositions "goes for all physical objects and is quite insensitive to the distinction between animate and inanimate bodies," and he presents this as evidence that Hobbes's ethics rests on his psychology, which in turn rests on his "physical theory" (1987: 134, 123). Stoffel offers no account, however, of Hobbes's ethical theory.

43 More generally, he argues in *De Corpore Politico,* "opinions which are gotten by education, and in length of time are made habitual, cannot be taken away by force, and upon the sudden: they must therefore be taken away also, by time and education" (*EL* II: 9.8).

so forth with ease, and so cannot count on the benefits that consistently performing such actions ultimately provides. Like the musician who refuses to practice before an important concert, the person who does not develop a virtuous character risks succumbing to the many distractions that can more easily defeat the undisciplined performer.

But what about the second half of the argument? The discussion to this point establishes only that it is good to make a habit of doing just acts, not that it is good to do them, and to enjoy doing them, for the sake of being just. It now becomes necessary to consider Hobbes's analysis of habituation in more detail. "Those things that offend when new," Hobbes says in explaining how habituation can change a person's disposition, "(that is, those things that man's nature initially resists) more often than not whet that same nature when repeated; and those things that at first are merely endured soon compel love . . . And so those accustomed to wine from youth by no means easily break the habit; and those imbued with no matter what opinions from boyhood retain them even in old age" (*DH:* 13.3). To habituate oneself to drinking wine is to change one's disposition from an aversion toward wine into a desire for it. This suggests that the person who habituates himself to doing just acts must come to do them because he so desires. Even if he initially wants to do just acts merely for the sake of the benefit they provide, and even if he has a natural resistance to accepting such constraints on his behavior, in habituating himself to doing the just acts, he comes to desire to do the acts and to desire doing them for their own sake.[44]

This interpretation of Hobbes's position is confirmed by another set of passages in *De Homine.* "Even if first experiences of something be sometimes displeasing, especially when new or rare, by habit they are rendered not displeasing, and afterwards pleasing; that much can habit change the nature of single men" (*DH:* 11.3). Hobbes again emphasizes that the process of habituation involves coming to desire something originally not found desirable. The significance of Hobbes's position is here made even more explicit. On the following page, he unequivocally explains the distinction reflected in his terminology: "The thing that, when desired, is

44 Bishop Butler, ironically one of Hobbes's sharpest critics, makes essentially this point: "When virtue has become habitual, when the temper of it is acquired, what was before confinement ceases to be so, by becoming choice and delight" (cited in Hutchinson 1986: 106).

called good, is, if desired for its own sake, called pleasing; and if for some other thing, it is called useful. For the good that we desire for its own sake we do not *use,* since *usefulness* is applied to means and instruments, while *enjoyment* applies to something proposed as an end" (*DH:* 11.5).[45] Habituation, according to Hobbes, renders the object of habit "pleasing" to the agent, and this, he clearly specifies, means that the agent comes to desire it, and to desire it "for its own sake" and "as an end." The very nature of habituation provides the final link in the argument; since it is good to habituate oneself to doing just acts, and since this involves making the doing of such acts pleasing in Hobbes's sense of the term, it is good to be disposed to do just acts and to desire to do them for their own sake. It is good, that is, to be a just person.

4.4.2 Attributing the argument from habituation to Hobbes has thus far been justified by identifying the defense of its various components made explicit in his texts, and the somewhat extensive use of quotation has been warranted, since this argument, like the argument from revealed disposition, has not been adequately represented in the enormous secondary literature on Hobbes. This direct approach may usefully be supplemented by a less direct one. His concern with the importance of instilling good dispositions in people if they are reliably to do good actions is also reflected in others of his doctrines.

One position that merits consideration in this context is Hobbes's theory of punishment. The seventh law of nature (in *Leviathan*) specifies that in seeking retribution for evils incurred, "Men look not at the greatnesse of the evill past, but the greatnesse of the good to follow" (*L:* 210). Cruelty is the name given to the vice that opposes this law, for cruelty is "to hurt without reason" and this "tendeth to the introduction of Warre; which is against the Law of Nature." According to this law, therefore, "we are forbidden to inflict punishment with any other designe, than for correction of the offender, or direction of others." Hobbes thus rejects retribution based on revenge as a justification for punishment, and this rejection rests, as at least one modern writer has emphasized, on "a moral judgment" (Catteneo 1965: 288).

Although Hobbes therefore insists that punishment can be justi-

45 See also (*L:* 121), where Hobbes distinguishes between "Good in Effect, as the end desired, which is called *Jucundum, Delightfull;* and Good as the Means, which is called *Utile, Profitable.*"

fied only by the advantages it can provide in the future,[46] this does not render his a simple theory of deterrence. The goal of punishment is not merely to prevent the offender from doing evil, but to "correct" him, not merely to provide a disincentive to deter others from doing bad acts, but to help them to "become better" people (*DC:* 3.11). The definition of punishment Hobbes eventually offers in *Leviathan* emphasizes this specific feature of his theory, that harm must be inflicted "to the end that the will of men may thereby the better be disposed to obedience" (*L:* 353). To make people more likely to behave appropriately in the future, as the purpose of the institution of punishment requires, it is necessary not just to alter the consequences of their actions but to change their dispositions; they must become habituated to doing good acts.

Hobbes's position is perhaps best expressed in this attack on Bramhall:

> It seems [Bramhall] taketh punishment for a kind of revenge, and can never therefore agree with me, that take it for nothing else but for a correction, or for an example, which hath for end the *framing* and *necessitating of the will* to virtue; and that he is no good man, that upon any provocation useth his power, though a power lawfully obtained, to afflict another man without this end, to reform the will of him or others. (*LNC:* 177)

This passage is significant in several respects. For one, it provides further evidence of the consistency with which Hobbes maintains, throughout his writings, that morality imposes limits on what the sovereign can do. The lawfulness of the sovereign's power to punish does not shield his use of that power from moral criticism, a position clearly reiterated in the chapter on punishment in *Leviathan,* when his power to punish is described as complete "excepting the limits set him by naturall Law" (*L:* 354). More important, Hobbes's description of the goal of punishment as "framing" the will to virtue clearly echoes his account of the unrighteous man in *Leviathan* as one whose "Will is not framed by the Justice, but by the apparant benefit of what he is to do" (*L:* 207).[47] The argument from habituation we have attributed to Hobbes maintains that

46 For the claim that there is nonetheless a retributivist dimension to Hobbes's theory of punishment, see Norrie (1984). On the special problems created by his defense of the death penalty, see Heyd (1991).

47 As does his similar account in the work *Of Liberty and Necessity:* "The intention of the *law,*" he there argues, "is not to grieve the *delinquent,* for that which is past, and not to be undone; but to make him and others *just,*" and "to punish those that do voluntary hurt, and none else," he writes, "frameth and maketh men's *wills* such as men would have them" (*LN:* 253, 254).

one's will must be framed by justice to ensure that one will perform just acts consistently. This interpretation is reinforced by Hobbes's theory of punishment, which maintains that the will of others must be framed by justice to ensure that they will perform just acts consistently.

A second element of Hobbes's writings that merits attention is his frequent, and frequently blistering, attacks on the state of the English universities. Hobbes rarely passes over an opportunity to inveigh against the curriculum of the Scholastics, and the very frequency of his fulminations may prevent them from being recognized as forming a distinct component of Hobbes's thought. Yet Hobbes's contempt for the universities represents a considered position on the role of education in a peaceful society, providing additional support for the view that Hobbes should be read as endorsing the argument from habituation.

The "Instruction of the people," Hobbes writes in *Leviathan,* "dependeth wholly, on the right teaching of Youth in the Universities," which are "the fountains of civil and moral doctrine" (*L:* 384, 728). In the absence of a consistent policy of teaching the true doctrines of society (presumably his own),[48] Hobbes declares that "'tis no wonder if [those educated in the universities] retain a relish of that subtile liquor, wherewith they were first seasoned, against the Civill Authority" (*L:* 385). Hobbes's description of seditious doctrines as a kind of liquor again suggests the view that, "those imbued with no matter what opinions from boyhood" are like "those accustomed to wine from youth [who] by no means easily break the habit" (*DH:* 13.3).[49] This focus on the effect of education not simply on students' future acts but on their future dispositions

48 To the question of whether Hobbes is presuming to "undertake to teach the Universities," he cagily replies that "it is not fit, nor needfull for me to say either I, or No: for any man that sees what I am doing, may easily perceive what I think" (*L:* 384, 385). In *Behemoth,* he claims that the "rules of *just* and *unjust*" have been "sufficiently demonstrated" and that "notwithstanding the obscurity of their author, have shined, not only in this, but also in foreign countries, to men of good education." Although the few have thus been enlightened, Hobbes complains, "the light of that doctrine has been hitherto covered and kept under here by a cloud of adversaries, which no private man's reputation can break through, without the authority of the *Universities*" (*B:* 39–40).

49 The power of indoctrination applies to good doctrines as well as bad. As Hobbes writes in a letter to the Duchess of Newcastle, "subtile Cheating or Filch" is something that "a high and noble mind endued with Virtue from its Infancy can never come to the knowledge of" (LDN: 105).

is more explicitly confirmed by others of Hobbes's statements. In *De Homine*, for example, he maintains that authorities can change people's dispositions, and he specifies that authorities are those "whose precept or example is followed, because one hath been led thereto by a belief in their wisdom" (*DH:* 13.1).[50] The universities and the clergy are Hobbes's most obvious targets here. He insists that "from them, if good, the dispositions of youths are well formed, and deformed, if deformed" (*DH:* 13.7). In *Behemoth*, he writes that "men may be brought to a love of obedience by preachers and gentlemen that imbibe good principles in their youth at the Universities," and that the role of the universities is "the bringing up of young men to virtue" (*B:* 59, 147).[51] In the chapter "Of Manners," which concludes the *Six Lessons to the Professors of the Mathematics*, he defends the doctrine of his *Leviathan* by urging that "it hath framed the minds of a thousand gentlemen to a conscientious obedience to present government, which otherwise would have wavered in that point" (*SL:* 336).[52] Hobbes's philosophy of education maintains that in order to ensure that young people grow up to behave well, it is necessary not simply to control their actions, but to alter their dispositions; not simply to teach them obedience, but to frame their minds to it; not simply to make them obey, but to make them love obedience.[53] This lends support to the interpreta-

50 That Hobbes held this view of the relationship between disposition and reputation from an early stage is clearly revealed in the "Life and History of Thucydides" with which he prefaces his translation of the *Peloponnesian War*. Hobbes attributes Thucydides' accomplishment largely to "the disposition of his mind" toward impartial observation, and he answers the question of "How he was disposed to a work of this nature" by referring to the (probably apocryphal) story that as "a young man he heard Herodotus the historiographer reciting his history in public" and "felt so great a sting of emulation, that it drew tears from him" (*EW* VIII: xvii).

51 Hobbes's concern for the universities is strikingly familiar: "I have often heard the complaints of parents, that their children were debauched there to drunkenness, wantonness, gaming, and other vices consequent to these" (*B:* 147).

52 Note again the echo of the just man whose will is "framed" by justice.

53 One of the few works that explicitly takes into account this feature of Hobbes's views on education is S. A. Lloyd's recent study. On Hobbes's account, as Lloyd rightly emphasizes, the role of education is to "educate people in their moral and civil duty, and to *instill* in them a *disposition* to do what they ought to do," a disposition which involves "the desire to do their duty and to give it a priority over other considerations" (1992: 162–3). Lloyd convincingly applies this insight to the task of reinterpreting Hobbes's political philosophy: The role of the sovereign is not merely to alter the payoffs of antisocial behavior, as is often supposed, but to create social people. The insight can also be used to

tion that, for Hobbes, an individual must come to be disposed to do the right thing in order consistently to do the right thing.

Finally, let us take note of a fact that few writers on Hobbes's moral views have paused to consider: Near the end of his extremely long and eventful life, Thomas Hobbes undertook – and completed – the Herculean task of translating the entire texts of both the *Iliad* and the *Odyssey* from Greek into English. Both works had been translated fully and directly into English by John Ogilby only a few years before, so Hobbes did not have available to him the motivation he describes in the preface to his earlier translation from the Greek of Thucydides' *History.* Thucydides' work, at the time of Hobbes's contribution, had been translated into English from a French translation of a Latin translation of a poor copy of the original Greek, and a less corrupt Greek source had since become available from which Hobbes worked directly (*EW* VIII: ix).[54] Why, in the absence of similar circumstances, did Hobbes produce yet another translation of Homer?[55]

The writers who have thought to raise this question at all have tended to accept at face value the explanation Hobbes provides at the end of his preface to the reader. He had written it "because I had nothing else to do," and he had published it "because I thought it might take off my adversaries from showing their folly upon my more serious writings, and set them upon my verses to show their wisdom" (*EW* X: x).[56] Hobbes's words undoubtedly contain an element of truth, but they are surely offered in a jovial, if somewhat cantankerous, spirit. That Hobbes considered his other

reinterpret his moral philosophy: To best earn the trust of others, one must not merely shun antisocial behavior, but embrace a sociable disposition.

54 As Richard Schlatter has pointed out, the English translator was sometimes careless in his reading of the French text from which he was working. Schlatter, moreover, judges Hobbes's translation to be "sufficiently accurate for any reader who wants to know, in English, what Thucydides said. A review of the emendations made by the modern classicists who have edited Hobbes's translation demonstrates that nothing essential requires correcting" (1975: xiv, xvii).

55 It is also worth noting in this context that Hobbes's *Briefe of the Art of Rhetorique* (1637) constituted the first (though incomplete) English translation of Aristotle's *Rhetoric.*

56 The advertisement prefacing the Molesworth edition, for example, says that the work "may be fairly looked upon, as the translator has told us in his preface, as the amusement of his old age" (*EW* X). The biographical section of the Hobbes entry in *The Encyclopedia of Philosophy* concludes with the sentence: "At 86, for want of something better to do, he published a verse translation of the *Iliad* and the *Odyssey*" (Peters 1967: 32).

contributions "more serious," it must be emphasized, does not mean that he considered this, his last major project, as not serious. His comments on the nature of heroic poetry earlier in his preface and elsewhere indicate that the value he perceived in this last work again reflects his commitment to the principles underlying the argument from habituation.

The "end and design" of the poet, Hobbes writes in the preface to his translations, are both the profit and the delight of the reader. By "profit," Hobbes specifies, he intends "accession of prudence, justice, and fortitude, by the example of such great and noble persons as [the poet] introduceth speaking, or describeth acting. For all men love to behold, though not to practise virtue" (*EW* X: iii).[57] In those who do not love to practice virtue, the poet seeks to "raise admiration" (*EW* X: iv) for the virtues, including justice, and Hobbes goes on to analyze the various qualities required for doing so, and to assess them as they are exemplified in the great epic poets of antiquity. Almost the entire text of the preface treats the subject of heroic poetry as a serious matter,[58] as a significant way of benefiting people by helping to dispose them toward virtue. To the extent that this suggests one leads people to behave virtuously by leading them to love virtue, it reaffirms our attribution to Hobbes of the argument from habituation.

This picture of the role and importance of epic poetry is rendered

57 D. G. James argues for the importance of the sentence that immediately follows: "So that at last the work of an heroic poet is no more but to furnish an ingenuous reader, when his leisure abounds, with the diversion of an honest and delightful story, whether true or feigned." This, James claims, "gives away the game," showing that we are to "read Homer for the reason that Hobbes translated him – because he 'had nothing else to do,'" and Hobbes's talk of virtue here is mere "pretence" (1949: 53). This overlooks, however, what is for Hobbes an important distinction between saying that a poem should be read as a diversion and that it should be written as one. From the point of view of the reader, according to Hobbes, a poem should be approached primarily as a source of delight. If the reader is looking for moral education, he should look to the writings of the philosophers. But from the point of view of the writer, the reader's benefit is of primary concern and his entertainment secondary: "The design is not only to profit, but also to delight the reader" (*EW* X: iii). These two views are consistent, moreover, since it is precisely because the reader is led to enjoy the accounts of virtuous character that the author can use them to bring him to admire them. So there seems no good reason to treat Hobbes's remarks about the relationship between poetry and virtue here (and in the passages cited later) as pretense.

58 That Hobbes took poetry seriously should come as no surprise; *Leviathan* is dedicated to a poet.

even more clearly in Hobbes's earlier exchange with William Davenant. In 1650, Davenant composed a lengthy preface to his epic poem *Gondibert*, dedicating the work to "his much honour'd friend Mr Hobs" in gratitude to Hobbes for reading the work while it was still in progress (1970: 1).[59] That Davenant expresses an affinity with Hobbes in this preface is significant because of what he says about the relationship between poetry and virtue. "Poets are of all Moralists the most useful," Davenant writes, because through poetry "morality is sweetned and made more amiable" (1970: 64). People do not readily yield to duty "unless they are first conquer'd by Vertue . . . and the Conquests of Vertue be never easy, but where her forces are commanded by Poets" (1970: 61). The goal of Davenant's poem is to "present the beauty of Vertue" to worthy readers in the hope that they will be "reform'd and made Angelicall" by it (1970: 60). In identifying Hobbes as his philosophical guide (1970: 36–7), he provides further evidence that Hobbes shares this view of the importance of poetry.

That Hobbes is in agreement with Davenant on the subject of poetry and virtue is confirmed by his "Answer to the Preface to *Gondibert*," where he says the task of the poets "is, by imitating human life, in delightful and measured lines, to avert men from vice, and incline them to virtuous and honourable actions" (*EW* IV: 443).[60] The significance of this, he explains, is that where "the precepts of true philosophy . . . fail, as they have hitherto failed in the doctrine of moral virtue, there the architect Fancy must take the philosopher's part upon herself" (*EW* IV: 450).[61] Hobbes esteems

59 That Hobbes took such poetry seriously is further evidenced by the fact that he is thanked not simply for having read *Gondibert* in advance, but for having given it "daily examination as it was writing" and offering corrections and guidance along the way (1970: 36).

60 In one of the few sustained studies of the two writers, Lee S. Baier locates their philosophical agreement elsewhere, arguing that "the visions of Davenant and Hobbes involve the same basic principle of moral subjectivism" (1965: 143). This analysis, however, overlooks the confidence in the existence of objective moral truths implicit in both writings. Much closer to the mark is Cornell Dowlin's assessment that what unites Hobbes's "Answer" with Davenant's "Preface" is the conviction that "Moral improvement is the goal of poetry" (1934: 17).

61 Hobbes's claim that philosophy has failed can be somewhat misleading. Charles Hinnant, for example, writes of this passage that "Here Hobbes expresses a doubt about the capacity of philosophers to arrive at moral truth" (1976: 26). Hobbes does not, however, concede that philosophy has failed to explain the truth about the value of moral virtue; he claims to have done this himself. He admits only that it has thus far failed to inspire a love of virtue, for which he allows that poetry may prove a more effective means.

Homer to be the finest of the epic poets in this regard, and thus the view that heroic poetry can help to turn people's hearts to virtue renders his project of making Homer accessible to the general public far from trivial.[62]

Keeping in mind Hobbes's long-held view of poetry's power to inculcate virtue in those not disposed to it, one has only to open a copy of Ogilby's *Iliad* to see why Hobbes must have found it wanting: The pages are so overrun with lengthy, esoteric footnotes, often lapsing into entire paragraphs of Greek and Latin, that Homer's words are nearly lost in the fray. One hundred seventy-one footnotes are devoted to the first book of the poem alone, whereas Hobbes's version omits annotation altogether.[63] In addition, Ogilby's text is too long for popular consumption. Hobbes's version of Homer, although it covers all twenty-four books, is nonetheless abridged, with peripheral scenes often pared down or omitted entirely, rendering the overall lesson more readily discernible to the casual reader. Finally, although Ogilby's verse is arguably more pleasing, Hobbes's is more clearly designed to ensure that the reader understands the morals to be drawn from the various stories. After the articles of peace are broken by the Trojans, for example, Ogilby's translation of the *Iliad* describes Agamemnon's response as follows (1660a: 99):

> The *Trojans* for a bloody fight prepare:
> Nor were the valiant *Grecians* lesser keen,
> Nor sleeping hadst thou Agamemnon seen
> Nor trifling time, nor trembling in a fright,
> But hasting to the Glory-gaining fight.

Hobbes's narrative, by contrast, interrupts the action of the story to advise the reader that Agamemnon's acts are to be understood not simply as good acts but as the tangible manifestation of his virtuous character:

> Meanwhile the Trojans arm'd were coming in.
> And then the Greeks were forc'd to arm again.
> *And Agamemnon's virtue now was seen.*

62 Hobbes expresses a similar regard for epic poetry in a letter to Edward Howard, in which he praises Howard's *British Princess* for its "admirable and Heroick actions, set forth in noble and perspicuous language, such as becomes the dignity of the persons you introduce" (LEH).

63 It should in fairness be noted, however, that Ogilby's *Odysses* is less heavily annotated.

He did not at their coming sleep nor start,
But speedily prepared for the fight. (*EW* X: emphasis added)

A similar difference characterizes the two accounts of Ulysses' misfortune at the hands of the Cicons in the *Odyssey.* A number of Ulysses' men were killed when, while plundering the natives of the island, they greedily refused to heed his order to return to the ship before more hostile forces arrived. Ogilby's version of Ulysses' narrative simply says, "Then I bid hast aboard, they not obey'd" (1660b: 114). But Hobbes again insists on pedagogical embellishment: "I did command them all to go aboard; / But they, *fools as they were,* would not obey" (*EW* X: 383, emphasis added).[64] The message of Hobbes's Homer is unmistakable: The events portrayed in the stories are not simply good and bad actions but actions that issue from good and bad characters. If you have a good character, you will do the acts necessary for living well; if you have a bad character, you will not.

Translating both of Homer's works (into rhyming iambic pentameter verse, no less) is in itself an epic task, and Hobbes performs it tolerably well. Pope's remark that Hobbes's poetry was "too mean for criticism" is often repeated, but it is also often taken out of context. Pope noted that this was equally true of the Ogilby translation, and he cited Hobbes in particular for having successfully "given us a correct Explanation of the Sense in general" while at the same time condensing or omitting many details in the original (1967: 22, 21).[65] This is no small accomplishment, even in Pope's terms, yet on most interpretations of Hobbes's ethics it must

64 In one of the few scholarly treatments of Hobbes's translations of Homer, G. B. Riddehough also notes that "Hobbes does not scruple to supply an explanatory phrase not in the original at all, or to put in a pungent epithet gratuitously" and notes as an example (which further supports the view taken here) that Hobbes "makes Eumaeus call his Phoenician kidnapper 'the rat'" in Book 15 of the *Odyssey.* Riddehough invokes such tactics as evidence of Hobbes's "failure as a translator," but they are better understood, in light of Hobbes's theory of moral virtue, as an indication of his intent not merely to translate, but to popularize (1958: 59). This reading is further supported by the fact that Hobbes employs the same strategies in his condensed translation of Aristotle's *Rhetoric,* which was devised not as a scholarly translation but as an exercise book for his pupil, the young William Cavendish. Details and illustrations presented by Aristotle are often omitted to render the overall lesson simpler, and advice not contained in the original is at times inserted (for a useful discussion of the additions and omissions in Hobbes's translation of Aristotle, see Harwood 1986: 13–23).

65 Pope does complain, however, that of the details of the poems, Hobbes "often omits the most beautiful" (1967: 21).

seem entirely out of character for him to have devoted so much time and energy to it.[66] What value could Hobbes the moral contractarian, for example, have found in stories that lead readers to incline themselves toward what he calls "virtues of nature" (*EW* X: iv)? Thus the tacit acceptance of Hobbes's glib explanation of his project persists.

If we view Hobbes as a virtue ethicist, however, the final volume of his collected works takes its rightful place firmly alongside the rest. It becomes clear that Hobbes sought to popularize Homer for much the same reason he sought to popularize himself: He believed that reading good books could make good people.[67] His translations and praise of Homer ultimately support on several levels our attribution to Hobbes of the argument from habituation. The translations seem designed to highlight it directly, leading the reader to the conclusion that the heroes of the story must have a good character in order for them reliably to do good acts. His comments on the value of such poems, both in the preface and elsewhere, add to this view indirectly, since they suggest that the reader, too, profits not simply from being led to do good acts but from inclining his will toward virtue. That Hobbes labored to produce the translations in the first place reinforces the interpretation that gives the argument from habituation its purpose: His moral theory takes seriously its claim that the just person is the one whose will is framed by justice, and that Hobbes is best understood as a virtue ethicist.

In one of the few book-length studies of Hobbes written by a specialist in English literature, Charles Hinnant notes Hobbes's comment that the end of poetry is "to adorn virtue, and procure her lovers" (*EW* IV: 447). Hinnant acknowledges that Hobbes's remark "does seem to imply the existence of virtue as an objective entity," but he insists that "we should not put too much emphasis

66 It must also seem difficult to understand why of the "very few Bookes" that Hobbes owned, only Homer and Virgil were "commonly on his Table" (Aubrey 1957: 154).

67 This belief, which accounts for Hobbes's last major work, also accounts for his first. He says in the preface to his translation of Thucydides that Thucydides "so clearly set before men's eyes the ways and events of good and evil counsels, that the narration itself doth secretly instruct the reader, and more effectually than can possibly be done by precept" (*EW* VIII: xxii). As at least one recent commentator has noted, for Hobbes a "good history is a history that teaches moral and civic virtue" (Lloyd 1992: 191).

on this comment" (1977: 132).[68] This is an unfortunate, though not uncommon, mistake;[69] Hobbes takes seriously his views on the relationship between poetry and virtue, and in trying to understand his conception of morality, we benefit from doing so as well.

A variety of considerations suggest, directly and indirectly, that Hobbes has provided an argument in defense of the goodness of moral virtue distinct from the argument from revealed disposition. In this second argument, Hobbes dispenses with the claim that one's disposition is revealed to others through one's actions and, instead, develops the position that one can only ensure that one will perform good acts with sufficient consistency by coming to be disposed to perform them and enjoy performing them for their own sake.

The crucial role of disposition in Hobbes's moral theory has not often been appreciated, despite the fact that "disposition" is, as at least one modern writer has noted, a "favorite word of Hobbes" (Ross 1974: 45). Our task thus far has been to develop a fuller understanding of Hobbes's moral philosophy than has to this point been available. I have tried to show that it is best understood as a science of moral virtue, one that builds on his fundamental claims about human nature and concludes, through two independent but complementary arguments, with the claim that it is good to have a

68 The term "entity" is somewhat misleading here, but the point nonetheless remains that for Hobbes, the moral virtues are, as another writer has more aptly put it, "objectively good qualities" (Kemp 1970: 19).

69 Clarence DeWitt Thorpe, for example, does the same thing. Like Hinnant, he notes Hobbes's comment that the aim of the poet is "to avert men from vice and incline them to virtuous and honourable actions" (*EW* IV: 433), and he recognizes that poetry, in Hobbes's view, should portray "great persons as models of virtue." Although he thus acknowledges both that "moral teaching" is the "ultimate objective" of poetry for Hobbes and that such teaching must focus on the goodness of virtuous persons, Thorpe, like Hinnant, does not seriously consider the implication of this: that Hobbes's moral theory must therefore be concerned with moral virtue and not simply with good actions (1940: 158, 289). Similarly, Sascha Talmor acknowledges that Hobbes's general philosophy, including his views on ethics, informs his remarks on poetry, and recognizes that for Hobbes the task of the poet is "to teach moral virtue," but he does not see in this the implication that Hobbes's views on ethics must include concern for moral virtue (1984: 3, 8). Even Raia Prokhovnik, who insists that Hobbes's interest in literary matters is important to understanding his political philosophy and who recognizes that for Hobbes poetry is "a work of artifice that is concerned with moral virtue," fails to put the two together and conclude that moral virtue plays an important role in Hobbes's normative thought (1991: 56, 95).

just disposition, to be a just person. We began, in Chapter 1, with Hobbes's embrace of the language of virtue: "I teach justice and I cultivate it." I have tried to understand, and to do justice to, the theory that emerges from this embrace, attending to both the letter and the spirit of Hobbes's texts.

This interpretation of Hobbes as a virtue ethicist differs substantially from those prevalent in the current literature and should, for that reason, be of interest to those who seek to understand his writings. The virtue theory the interpretation attributes to Hobbes differs from those prevalent in the current literature on virtue. It seems worth asking in conclusion whether Hobbes's moral theory should be of interest to those who are interested in virtue. This question is addressed in the next chapter.

Chapter 5

Hobbes and the revival of virtue ethics

5.0 OVERVIEW

Works on virtue ethics written as recently as the 1970s invariably begin by bemoaning the modern neglect of the subject and by issuing a plaintive appeal on its behalf.[1] Works on the same subject published more recently tend instead to open with a comment on the virtual renaissance that has taken place in the field. Believers and critics alike now agree that we are in the midst of a genuine revival of virtue ethics,[2] but there has thus far been little consensus on what this revival involves or even on who its principal representatives are. Much of the work done so far has been of a negative or preliminary sort, identifying problems modern moral philosophy has encountered because of its neglect of virtue, or offering various (and often mostly suggestive) sketches of what a modern virtue ethic might eventually look like. There are, in addition, fundamental differences over such basic questions as whether or not the virtues are essentially theological in nature, and whether they are best understood from a social or individual perspective.

If there is one thing the members of this modern virtue movement agree on, however, it is that the writings of Hobbes have little to contribute to their cause. Indeed, Hobbes appears in contemporary writings on virtue, if at all, in the role of the villain. As one recent advocate has put it, to shift the focus of ethics away from its

1 The "plea for virtue" with which Lawrence C. Becker begins his critique is typical (1975: 110).

2 Thus the cover of a recent special issue of *The Times Literary Supplement* focusing on current work in philosophy reserves its largest type for the announcement of two reviews under the title "The Revival of Virtue," the first of which opens with the sentence: "The virtues are fighting back" (Midgley 1993: 3). Gregory E. Pence offers a useful critical survey of the "efflorescence of works on virtues" to the mid-1980s in (1984).

present preoccupations and toward questions about virtue is to shift it "away from Hobbes and toward Aristotle" (Pincoffs 1986: 21). This state of affairs is an unfortunate one, stemming largely from the widespread misunderstanding of what Hobbes's moral theory is. I can therefore best conclude the present study by clarifying the sense in which Hobbes's concerns are not so far from Aristotle's, and by then asking whether Hobbesian moral philosophy, properly understood, might thus have something to contribute to the revival of virtue ethics.

5.1 HOBBES AND ARISTOTLE

Recent writers in the virtue tradition have typically been inspired by Aristotle's analysis of the just person, and the suggestion that there are significant parallels between his picture of virtue and that of Hobbes runs strongly against not only the recent literature on virtue but also the dominant currents of Hobbes scholarship.[3] It is likely to seem somewhat suspect, if not perverse, in light of Hobbes's well-known and frequently articulated aversion to the ancients in general and to Aristotle in particular. Hobbes enthusiastically embraces Cicero's observation that "there is nothing so absurd, that the old Philosophers have not some of them maintained" (in fact, he embraces it twice; *L:* 113, 687), and he adds that "scarce any thing can be more absurdly said in naturall Philosophy, than that which now is called *Aristotles Metaphysiques;* nor more repugnant to Government, than much of that hee hath said in his *Politiques;* nor more ignorantly, than a great part of his *Ethiques*" (*L:* 687). Hobbes elsewhere complains of the "babbling philosophy of Aristotle and other Greeks" (*B:* 95), and even his praise for Plato as the "best of the ancient philosophers" (*SL:* 346) must be understood, in the context of Aristotle's domination of seventeenth-century thought, as constituting a clearly understood slight to Aristotle.[4] Hobbes's attitude toward Aristotle is almost unrelentingly

3 Hobbes's contemporaries also agreed that the ethics of Aristotle and of Hobbes lay at opposite extremes. As one anonymous critic put it (1680), though in somewhat strained verse:

> The *Morals* of the *Stagirite*
> Are *Stars* which to th' Dark World gave Light
> But *Hobbes* by his would turn our Day to Night.

4 Hobbes also calls Plato the "best Philosopher of the Greeks" in *Leviathan,* noting with understandable approval the fact that Plato "forbad entrance into his

negative,[5] and this fact must be addressed before moving on to the parallels between the two philosophers, so those parallels will not be dismissed as evidence that our interpretation of Hobbes as a virtue ethicist was mistaken to begin with.

5.1.1 How can we account for Hobbes's contempt for the greatest virtue ethicist of antiquity, without at the same time attributing to him a contempt for virtue ethics? One possibility is suggested by a view frequently expressed by Hobbes's contemporaries: Hobbes was motivated by a desire for fame, and this placed him in a natural competition with Aristotle. Hobbes worked in the hope of making himself "all the world over as great as Aristotle is in Oxford"; he wanted to "jostle Aristotle out of the Universities [and] to make Malmesbury as famous as Stagira"; he dreamed that "Aristotelity may be changed into Hobbeity, & instead of the Stagyrite, the world may adore the great Malmesburian Phylosopher."[6] Hobbes's angry attacks on Aristotle were thus motivated more by his envy of Aristotle's reputation than by disagreement with Aristotle's doctrines. A more cynical version of this explanation might hold that Hobbes attacked Aristotle with such fervor precisely because, at least with respect to his ethics, his views were uncomfortably close to some of Aristotle's.[7]

We need not attribute such motives to Hobbes, however, to reconcile his disdain for Aristotle with his own advocacy of an ethics of virtue. In the first place, although Hobbes includes Aristotle's moral theory within the scope of his condemnations, it is clear he is much more concerned with Aristotle's *Politics* than with his *Ethics*.[8]

Schoole, to all that were not already in some measure Geometricians" (*L:* 686; see also *D:* 124).

5 Not entirely negative. Aubrey recalls Hobbes remarking that "Aristotle was the worst Teacher that ever was, the worst Politician and Ethick – a Countrey-fellow that could live in the World would be as good: but his *Rhetorique* [of which Hobbes produced an abridged translation] and *Discourse of Animals* was rare" (1957: 158).

6 John Whitehall, Alexander Rosse, and Seth Ward, cited in Bowle (1951: 183, 69, 75).

7 Hobbes would not have been alone in embracing such tactics. In examining Hobbes's exclusion from the Royal Society, Noel Malcolm argues convincingly that "the more disreputable Hobbes became, the more necessary it was for the other scientists to dissociate themselves from him by attacking him, precisely because he was in some ways embarrassingly close to their own position" (1988: 57–8).

8 In *Behemoth*, for example, Hobbes says that Aristotle's *Politics* has caused us "much hurt," whereas his *Ethics*, by contrast, has merely failed to do us "any good" (*B:* 43, 44). The passage quoted from *Leviathan* condemns the *Politics* as

Hobbes associates Aristotle's normative views, above all else, with the doctrine of natural inequality: "I know that *Aristotle* in the first booke of his Politiques, for a foundation of his doctrine, maketh men by Nature, some more worthy to commande . . . others to Serve . . . as if Master and Servant were not introduced by consent of men, but by difference of Wit" (*L:* 211). Hobbes, much to his credit, finds this position both dangerous and absurd,[9] but there is nothing in his doing so that would impugn his defense of a virtue ethics. Furthermore, although Hobbes includes Aristotle's normative theory within the scope of his attacks, he is far more frequently concerned with Aristotle's physical and metaphysical views. He can hardly make it through the first chapter of *Leviathan* without complaining about the "frequency of insignificant speech" that pollutes the discussions of sense perception "grounded upon certain Texts of *Aristotle*" (*L:* 87, 86), and Aristotle's influence is apparent even when his name is absent, in the many bitter attacks on the empty "canting of Schoolemen" (*L:* 115) that follow. It is quite plausible that whatever merits Hobbes might have been willing to acknowledge in Aristotle's virtue ethics were overshadowed by his hostility toward Aristotle's system as a whole.

In addition, although Hobbes does not hesitate to attack Aristotle by name, he often seems much less concerned with what Aristotle himself believed than with how his words have been manipulated and abused by his followers, in particular by the Catholic Church. This attitude is often implicit in Hobbes's writings and is perhaps made most explicit in his treatment of Aristotle in *Behemoth*. In that work, Hobbes attacks the "school-divines; who, striving to make good many points of faith incomprehensible, and calling in the philosophy of Aristotle to their assistance, wrote great books of school-divinity, which no man else, nor they themselves, are able to understand" (*B:* 17). He later adds: "The philosophy of Aristotle was made an ingredient in religion, as serving for a salve to a great many absurd articles, concerning the nature of Christ's body, and the estate of angels and saints in heaven" (*B:*

"repugnant to Government," but claims only that the *Ethics* contains much that is said "ignorantly" (*L:* 687).

9 Although it must be admitted that his argument against Aristotle is not especially convincing: "For there are very few so foolish, that had not rather governe themselves, than be governed by others" (*L:* 211). As the Earl of Clarendon was quick to point out, this reply "doth not contradict any thing said by *Aristotle*, the Question being Whether Nature hath made some men worthier, not whether it hath made all others so modest as to confess it" (Hyde 1676: 31).

41).[10] Hobbes's concern is that such doctrines increase the Pope's authority and render him a threat to the sovereign, thus making Aristotle's views responsible for a substantial menace to the peace. When *B* asks "what advantage to them, in these impostures, was the doctrine of Aristotle?" however, *A* answers as follows: "They have made more use of his obscurity than of his doctrine. For none of the ancient philosophers' writings are comparable to those of Aristotle, for their aptness to puzzle and entangle men with words, and to breed disputation, which must at last be ended in the determination of the Church of Rome" (*B:* 41–2).[11] Hobbes's attacks on Aristotle are, therefore, often attacks on the Church's manipulative use of Aristotle rather than on the doctrines of Aristotle himself. In the extended polemic against Rome that constitutes the final part of *Leviathan,* he criticizes the Church not so much for adhering to Aristotelian philosophy as for abandoning philosophy altogether: Since the study of philosophy is there seen as only "a handmaid to the Romane Religion: And since the Authority of Aristotle is onely current there, that study is not properly Philosophy, (the nature whereof dependeth not on Authors,) but Aristotelity" (*L:* 688). He thus objects most not to what Aristotle wrote but to how he wrote and subsequently came to be read.[12] The fact that Hobbes has such harsh words for Aristotle need not detract from the claim that Hobbes and Aristotle have much in common, at least as far as ethics is concerned.

Finally, it must be said that there is little reason to believe Hobbes had an adequate understanding of the theory of virtue expounded in Aristotle's *Ethics.* There are, so far as I have been able to find, three specific claims that Hobbes makes about that theory in his writings, and all three are inaccurate. One is that Aristotle and Hobbes "acknowledge the same Vertues and Vices" (*L:* 216).[13] This is not entirely inaccurate, but it is highly misleading. Aristotle de-

10 This point is also pursued in Part IV of *Leviathan,* in which Hobbes criticizes the Church's use of "the vain and erroneous Philosophy of the Greeks, especially of Aristotle" (*L:* 629).

11 Hobbes also recognizes that Aristotle was not "of such credit with them, but that when his opinion was against theirs, they could slight him" (*B:* 42).

12 It is thus no coincidence that Aristotle's name comes first in Hobbes's famous dictum that "words are wise mens counters, they do but reckon by them: but they are the mony of fooles, that value them by the authority of an *Aristotle,* a *Cicero,* or a *Thomas"* (*L:* 106).

13 Hobbes does not mention Aristotle by name here, but it is clear from the close correspondence between the language here and in the parallel passage in *Behemoth* discussing Aristotle's *Ethics* (*B:* 44–5) that he has Aristotle in mind.

votes a great deal of consideration to the virtue of courage, for example, which does not have a clear counterpart in Hobbes's account. Aristotle's characterization of gentleness as a virtue strays so far from Hobbes's sensibilities that he deliberately omits it from the list of virtues in his translation of Aristotle's *Rhetoric* (*BR:* 1.9). Hobbes insists on the virtues of forgiveness and of acknowledging all others as equal by nature. These virtues have no clear place in Aristotle's ethics. In addition, although there are terms that name virtues in both accounts, it is not clear that they name the same virtues. Aristotle's justice[14] is not the simple promise keeping of Hobbes, and Hobbes's account of what might be called benevolence has an element of Christian charity obviously absent in Aristotle. Hobbes's second claim is that Aristotle maintains that the virtues are good because they are a mean between two vices, or, as Hobbes puts it, because they are a "mediocrity of passions" (*L:* 216, *B:* 44). This is plainly false. Much about Aristotle's doctrine of the mean is subject to dispute, but it is clear that he does not claim that a virtue's lying between two vices is itself the reason that the virtue is good. Hobbes modifies this position in *Behemoth* to the claim that this is only one part of the reason the virtues are considered good on Aristotle's account, and adds as a third claim that they are also considered good because "they are praised" (*B:* 44).[15] This too is wrong. True, Aristotle holds that we can discover what the virtues are by seeing what the virtuous person praises (though not by looking at what just anyone praises), but this is not to say that because the virtuous person praises justice, justice is a virtue. Rather, the virtuous person praises justice because it is a virtue, and we can come to see it is a virtue (though not why it is) by noting that the virtuous person praises it. Hobbes seems to have a deeply misguided view of Aristotle's account of virtue, and this provides a final reason to feel confident that Hobbes's numerous attacks on Aristotle need not cast doubt on the interpretation of Hobbes offered in this work. With this preliminary legitimate concern thus addressed, we may turn to the question of what Hobbes and Aristotle have in common.

5.1.2 Like Hobbes, Aristotle distinguishes between a just person

14 Justice in the narrow sense. See footnote 16.

15 This is also what Hobbes presumably means in complaining of Aristotle and ancient writers in general that "Their Morall Philosophy is but a description of their own Passions" (*L:* 686).

and a just action[16] and insists that being a just person involves more than doing just actions: "Some people who do just actions are not yet thereby just," he says at one point and, similarly, "it is possible to do injustice without thereby being unjust" (1985: 1144a14–15, 1135a16–17). For Aristotle, as for Hobbes, the difference between doing a just act and being a just person is a matter of the agent's condition in performing the act. Several conditions must be met if the agent is to qualify as a just person on Aristotle's analysis, and each of these is just as clearly required by Hobbes.

The most basic feature of Aristotle's position is that, for one to be a just person, one's acts must issue from a certain kind of relatively stable and settled disposition. "Virtue," he says in the *Eudemian Ethics*, is a "disposition . . . from which are done the best functions of the soul and its best affections" (1982: 1220a29–31). In the *Nicomachean Ethics*, he specifies that for an act to be done justly (and not merely to be a just act), the agent must do it "from a firm and unchanging state" (1985: 1105a35). What makes a person just is that his actions proceed from a just character, and thus far the parallel with Hobbes should be clear. The just man, on Hobbes's account, is the one whose manners are just, and the unjust one who has "the disposition, or aptitude to do Injurie" (*L:* 207).

The parallel between the two is even stronger than this, however, for Aristotle's insistence that the just person's acts come not merely from a state of character but from a "firm and unchanging" one is also reflected in Hobbes. In the *Categories*, Aristotle distinguishes between what he calls "habit" and "disposition." "Habit," he says, "differs from disposition in being more lasting and more firmly established." The virtues, he argues, are habits and not mere dispositions: "The virtues, . . . such as justice, self-restraint, and so on, are not easily dislodged or dismissed, so as to give place

16 Also like Hobbes, Aristotle uses the term "justice" in both a narrow and a general sense. Used broadly, "justice" can be understood to encompass all the virtues that concern the agent's actions involving others; it is "complete virtue in relation to another" (1985: 1129b27). This corresponds closely to Hobbes's sense of justice as righteousness, which includes all the laws of nature (although a few of these – e.g., forbidding drunkenness – are purely self-regarding). Understood more narrowly, Aristotle takes "justice" to refer to a kind of fairness (1985: 1130b9–10). Thus for either writer, the term can refer to both a particular virtue and a broad collection of virtues. In treating their analyses of the distinction between a just act and a just person in what follows, I use "justice" in the broader sense, and what is said is meant to apply to each of the virtues.

to vice" (1941: 8b26–34).[17] A disposition firmly established and difficult to replace is a habit, and virtues are good habits, not merely good dispositions.[18] This is at the heart of Aristotle's account of virtue, and it is therefore a significant, if rarely noted, fact that it is repeated, though in different terms, in Hobbes's *De Homine:* "Dispositions, when they are so strengthened by habit that they beget their actions with ease and with reason unresisting, are called *manners.* Moreover, manners, if they be good, are called *virtues,* if evil, *vices*" (*DH:* 13.8). In insisting that ethics focuses on the just person and not merely on just actions, both Aristotle and Hobbes focus our attention on the person whose good acts issue not simply from a good disposition but from a good disposition firmly planted and difficult to uproot.

In Hobbes's account of virtue, as we have already seen, the disposition of the just person is not simply a disposition to do just acts; it is also a disposition to enjoy doing them. The just person is someone who by nature is "delighted in just dealing" (*DC:* 3.5) and "scorns" injustice (*L:* 207). To say that a person is just is to attribute to that person not only a "proneness" toward but an "affection" for justice (*EL* I: 16.4). The same is true for Aristotle: "No one is good if he does not enjoy fine actions; for no one would call him just, e.g., if he did not enjoy doing just actions, or generous if he did not enjoy generous actions, and similarly for the other virtues" (1985: 1099a18–20).[19] Justice, Aristotle argues, is "the state that makes us doers of just actions, that makes us do justice and wish what is just" (1985: 1129a7–9). This is what he means when he summarizes his position by saying that virtue "is about feelings and actions" (1985: 1109b30). To be a virtuous person according to Aristotle is to be disposed both to do the right thing and to enjoy doing it. Aristotle's position is so similar to Hobbes's that typical descriptions of the just person in the literature on Aristotle could also be used to describe the position I have in this work attributed to Hobbes: "Whether one has an excellent character or not depends not merely

17 And again: "Habit differs from disposition in this, that while the latter is ephemeral, the former is permanent and difficult to alter" (1941: 9a8–9).

18 D. S. Hutchinson emphasizes the importance of this distinction. A virtue on Aristotle's account is a *hexis,* and a *hexis* is "a well-entrenched sort of disposition" (1986: 20).

19 For example, "if someone who abstains from bodily pleasures enjoys the abstinence itself, then he is temperate, but if he is grieved by it, he is intemperate. Again, if he stands firm against terrifying situations and enjoys it, or at least does not find it painful, then he is brave, and if he finds it painful, he is cowardly" (1985: 1104b5–8).

on what one does but also on what one likes doing" (Urmson 1988: 26–7); "A moral virtue is itself a disposition to desire or choose and not merely a capacity to know" (Hardie 1968: 101); "A man with a character excellence likes to do the right thing and dislikes doing the wrong thing" (Hutchinson 1986: 86).

An additional feature of Aristotle's analysis concerns the reason why a person with such a character does just acts: "He must decide on them, and decide on them for themselves" (1985: 1105a33–4). The just person is the sort of person who does the just thing *because* it is the just thing to do. If someone consistently chooses to do just acts but does so "because of some other end, not because of the actions themselves," he is not a just person although he does all the same things the just person does (1985: 1144a17–18).

It might be thought that here we would encounter a substantial obstacle to drawing any meaningful parallels with Hobbes. Hobbes is often portrayed as a psychological egoist who maintains that people can only choose an act because it serves their interest to do so. If he believes that, clearly he cannot believe that people ever choose to do an action because it is the right thing to do. As we saw in section 2.3.3, however, Hobbes's science of human nature does not commit him to this form of egoism. It is true that in his analysis of human action every act is seen as an attempt to satisfy some desire of the agent, but this in no way entails that the desire must be self-regarding. People can choose to act for the sake of themselves, for the sake of others, for the sake of knowledge, or for the sake of justice.

Not only does Hobbes acknowledge that people are capable of acting from a respect for the moral law, moreover, but as we saw in Chapter 3, he, like Aristotle, insists that they must do so if they are to count as just people. "That man is to be accounted just," he argues, "who doth just things because the law commands it" (*DC:* 3.5). He does not just say, for example, that a person who makes a promise should keep it; he insists that "he ought to perform for his promise sake" (*DC:* 14.2n). Like Aristotle, he explicitly makes the point that although a person's actions might be identical with those of the just person, if they are not done "for themselves," as Aristotle puts it, then the person is not just: "Although a man should order all his actions so much as belong to external obedience just as the law commands, but not for the law's sake, but by reason of some punishment annexed to it, or out of vain glory; yet he is unjust" (*DC:* 4.21).

Finally, Aristotle, like Hobbes, insists that the sort of character that the just person must have arises from habit. "*Character* (*ēthos*), as the word itself indicates," Aristotle says in the *Eudemian Ethics*, "is that which is developed from habit (*ethos*)" (1982: 1220a38–b1). In the *Nicomachean Ethics*, he says, "Virtue of character results from habit; hence its name 'ethical,' slightly varied from '*ethos*'" (1985: 1103a16–17). The virtues, on Aristotle's account, "arise in us neither by nature nor against nature, but we are by nature able to acquire them, and reach our complete perfection through habit" (1985: 1103a24–26). For Aristotle, as for Hobbes, we become just by doing just actions, and it seems plausible to suppose that Hobbes's use of the music student to illustrate this point is borrowed from Aristotle: We become harpists, Aristotle writes, "by playing the harp; so also, then, we become just by doing just actions, temperate by doing temperate actions, brave by doing brave actions" (1985: 1103a34–b2).[20] Although there are substantive differences between the particular virtues Hobbes and Aristotle defend, there is a fundamental unity in their understanding of the virtuous person: One who wants to do the right thing because it is the right thing to do, and whose wanting to do so is an expression of character, a disposition deeply ingrained as a result of habit that cannot easily be altered.[21] It is good, both Aristotle and Hobbes insist, not merely to do the sorts of acts this sort of person typically does but to be this sort of person.

A number of recent writers have also been attracted by this picture of the virtuous person, and they have urged that moral philosophers return to the task of justifying the claim that it is good to be such a person. These writers have typically turned to Aristotle for inspiration, and their reasons for finding Aristotle's approach compelling will not be considered here. But Hobbes's potential contributions to the current revival of virtue ethics have been neglected, not because they have been considered and rejected, but because they have not yet been recognized. Having tried to establish that moral philosophers attracted by Aristotle's picture of the virtuous person should also be attracted to Hobbes's, we shall now consider

20 In *De Corpore*, as we saw in section 4.4.1, Hobbes notes that the person who "first puts his hand to an instrument" can only learn to play it properly through habit (*Co:* 22.20).

21 Strauss claims that there is a fundamental difference between the two accounts: For Aristotle, a virtue is a kind of state (*hexis*); for Hobbes, it is "solely an intention" (1936: 54). This overlooks, however, the common role that habit plays in both accounts. For both Aristotle and Hobbes, a virtue is not simply a temporary state of mind but a lasting feature of one's character, strengthened by habituation.

what Hobbesian virtue ethics might have to say about the questions these recent writers have raised.

5.2 MODERATE AND RADICAL VIRTUE ETHICS

The first and most general question any proponent of the revival of virtue ethics must ask is, What is the point of this revival? If modern moral philosophers were perfectly content to discuss questions of right and wrong, relegating virtue to the realm of secondary or incidental concerns, what reason can be provided for concluding that they were wrong? Contemporary advocates of virtue have largely broken into two groups on this question, responding with what Kurt Baier has called the moderate and the radical theses of virtue ethics (1982: 57–9; 1988: 126–7). Roughly speaking, the moderate thesis maintains that certain distinctive features of the virtues render them indispensable to the study of ethics; thus, although much of contemporary ethics may prove essentially sound, it must be supplemented by a greater attention to issues concerning the virtues. The radical thesis, on the other hand, insists that mainstream modern ethics is fundamentally misconceived, and that ethics must make questions about virtue the foundation for answering other questions. As Baier puts it, the moderate thesis "regards contemporary ethics as lamentably incomplete but not radically wrongheaded," whereas the radical thesis claims that without "a clear understanding of the virtues and of properly moral motivation, it is impossible to determine what is morally incumbent on us or morally desirable for us" (1988: 126, 127). More must be said about these theses before we can consider which, if either, the Hobbesian virtue ethicist would have us endorse, and this is best accomplished by considering representative arguments from the proponents of each.

Lawrence Becker's article "The Neglect of Virtue" provides an excellent brief in defense of the moderate thesis. Becker's modest claim is that "the philosophical development of the concept of virtue, at least to the level of sophistication we possess for the central concepts of value and obligation, is a matter of considerable importance." He thus seeks to vindicate virtue as "a concept which should be central to moral theorizing" without insisting that it be *the* central concept (1975: 111, 110).[22] His strategy (and the primary

22 An interesting book-length defense of the moderate thesis can be found in Pincoffs (1986).

strategy among moderate virtue ethicists in general) is to identify problems arising from an exclusive focus on actions and rules for actions and to suggest how greater attention to the category of virtue might contribute to their resolution.

The first such problem that Becker identifies, and one that Hobbes also recognizes as crucial, is that there seem to be cases in which it would be inappropriate to call someone a good person despite the fact that her acts were consistently good. If such a person acts entirely out of "blind adherence to authority-training," for example, or because of laziness merely fails to take advantage of opportunities to do evil, we are reluctant to call her good, and we typically take our reluctance to be justified (1975: 113).[23] But if we are right in suspecting that such a person cannot acceptably serve as an exemplar of moral goodness, it is not at all clear how we can account for this fact if we limit our moral inquiry to questions about actions and duties. Such a person consistently does morally good actions, after all, and consistently fulfills her duties. As Becker suggests, we must ask questions about her disposition in order to fully sort things out, and this would focus our attention more pointedly on the issue of virtue.

The problem of distinguishing good people from people who do good acts is perhaps the most familiar justification for renewing our concern with virtue, but it is worth briefly noting a few of the other diverse examples Becker brings to light. One is the problem of specifying appropriate standards of performance given the acceptance of moral duties which have been justified in some virtue-independent way (1975: 114–16). Consider, for example, the duty of care toward others. Such a duty, Becker points out, immediately raises the question of how much care is enough for the duty to be fulfilled. It is difficult to see how this problem can profitably be addressed by an exclusive focus on actions and rules, and as Becker argues, the model provided by tort law suggests that considerations of virtue could be of considerable value here as well. Under tort law, Becker notes, such issues are often resolved by appealing to what a "reasonable person" would have done under the circumstances. It may well seem more plausible to determine the standards of good action by considering what a good person would do,

23 Becker also suggests that there could be a person who consistently does bad acts but whose "tragically accurate self-perception" would make us unwilling to call him bad. This example seems less compelling, but one could imagine other features of such a person (perhaps weakness of will or emotional problems) that might better establish Becker's point.

rather than to decide what a good person should do by first determining the standards of good action. Other problems seem to point toward the same general conclusion. We excuse people for bad actions done out of ignorance, suggesting an ineliminable concern with character and virtue; we hesitate to abandon one person in distress although we can thereby prevent greater harms to unknown others, perhaps reflecting the conviction that ignoring present pain requires a sort of insensitivity incompatible with virtue; our evaluation of the morality of civil disobedience can be substantially influenced by the motives and characters of those involved. We may condemn to different degrees the assassin and the person who hires him, although the two may be equally responsible for the death that results from their cooperation, suggesting that there may be something morally worse about the character of a person who can bring himself to pull the trigger (1975: 116–17, 117–18, 118–20, 120–22). None of these examples purports to show that Kantian or utilitarian ethics is fundamentally flawed, but they make a powerful case for the claim that, at the very least, these moral theories need to be supplemented by a greater concern with the concept of virtue.

Becker's paper offers a compelling plea for virtue, but for the radical virtue ethicist it is far too weak: What is required is not mere refinement of contemporary ethics but a wholesale reconstruction. If the slogan of the moderate theorist is "equal status for virtue," the rallying cry of the radical is "virtue first." As one of the best-known instigators of the movement has put it, "A sound moral philosophy should start from a theory of the virtues and vices" (Foot 1978a: xi).

The most prominent argument in defense of this more radical position remains that of Elizabeth Anscombe in her widely discussed paper "Modern Moral Philosophy." Anscombe's thesis is not merely that virtue should be given equal status with obligation and duty, right and wrong, but that the latter should be "jettisoned" from our moral vocabulary altogether. They are, she claims, "survivals, or derivatives from survivals, from an earlier conception of ethics which no longer generally survives, and are only harmful without it" (1958: 1). Anscombe's argument is this: Christianity embodies a legal conception of ethics, in which what is right and wrong, obligatory and forbidden, is determined by divine law. Because Christianity has dominated Western civilization for so many centuries, "the concepts of being bound, permitted, or excused became deeply embedded in our language and thought"

(1958: 5). They have come to form an important part of our moral intuitions. But the conception of ethics that informs these intuitions, Anscombe insists, makes sense only if there is a divine lawgiver to provide and validate the divine law. Once God is removed from the picture, the notions of moral obligation and moral ought lose the roots that originally gave them meaning. It is, Anscombe says, "as if the notion 'criminal' were to remain when criminal law and criminal courts had been abolished and forgotten" (1958: 6). Modern moral philosophers, in abandoning the pre-Christian paradigm of virtue and attempting instead to work out an ethic of ought and obligation in a posttheistic context, are going down a dead end. Like Joseph K. struggling vainly to understand the meaning of the charges brought against him, they are trying to make sense of a law for which no sense is to be found.[24]

Anscombe's argument is a provocative one, but it seems to rest on some form of the genetic fallacy. The fact that our notions of moral ought and obligation originated in a theistic worldview that we (may) since have abandoned does not entail that they are therefore useless or even unnecessary in the worldview we have subsequently embraced. One could argue that although the concept of laws governing the natural world also originated in a theistic context, this has not prevented it from playing a useful and perhaps necessary role in the subsequent history of science. As Kurt Baier has pointed out in response to Anscombe's position, although the notion of a legal requirement is meaningless in the absence of a legislator, this need not be so in the case of a moral requirement. We can make sense of the claim that the moral law requires a given agent to perform a given action, for example, by understanding it as the claim that there are compelling moral reasons for the agent to so act, and adequate reasons for society to insist that he do so (1988: 128).[25] This is not to say that ethics must proceed in this way, that the concepts of right and wrong, obligation and duty, are essential to any acceptable moral theory. It is simply to say that the radical virtue ethicist has not yet shown that such a theory must be grounded entirely in considerations of virtue. The result of the

24 Richard Taylor makes much the same point: "Modern philosophical moralists do not trace [the distinction between moral right and wrong] to divine command . . . and in the absence of any other source it is difficult to see how the moral laws or principles upon which such distinctions must rest can be presumed to exist at all" (1988: 63).

25 As Baier notes, this is a slightly modified version of Mill's account in Chapter 5 of *Utilitarianism* (1988: 135 n1).

debate thus seems inescapably inconclusive. The best moral theory may yet turn out to center on duty, on virtue, or on both.

The moderate thesis maintains that virtue must play a central role in ethics, the radical thesis insists that it play the central role. Which thesis, if either, would Hobbes have us endorse? It seems clear that, at the very least, Hobbes would agree with the moderate thesis. Becker cites as the primary case in its favor the fact that consistently doing good acts is not sufficient for being called a good person, and as we have noted, Hobbes makes much of the same fact: "The Justice of Actions denominates men, not Just, but *Guiltless:* and the Injustice of the same . . . gives them but the name of *Guilty*" (*L:* 207). This is what motivates Hobbes to distinguish between just acts and just people, and to insist that ethics concentrate on what makes just people. Since Hobbes identifies virtue and vice with the good and bad manners that make for good and bad people, and since he insists that "the science of Vertue and Vice, is Morall Philosophie" (*L:* 216), he goes beyond the moderate position and seems to endorse the radical thesis as well. In equating moral philosophy with the science of virtue and vice, he seems to echo Foot's dictum.

But the matter is not so simple. Anscombe would have us jettison the paradigm of moral law altogether, and have our ethics rely entirely on the concept of virtue. Hobbes's texts are filled with references to the moral law and its requirements. The notion of law seems to play an essential role in Hobbes's argument, since he first tries to determine which general rules of behavior are required by reason, and only then uses the content of the rules to justify the goodness of the dispositions to follow them. The radical virtue ethicist is committed to the view that we can only determine what a just act is by first discerning what a just person is and then considering what sorts of acts such a person would typically perform. Hobbes, by contrast, seems to believe we can only determine what a just person is by first deciding what a just act is and then considering what a disposition to perform such acts would involve. Although virtue ends up being the crucial category in Hobbes's ethics, there is, nonetheless, a sense in which it fails to be the most fundamental. In terms of this sense, Hobbes cannot accurately be placed in the radical camp.

Yet this account, too, is unsatisfactory. It suggests that Hobbes is something more than a moderate and less than a radical, when it would be better to say that he is different from both. The difficulty of locating him within the moderate–radical spectrum may in the end suggest a way for the virtue ethicist to transcend it. The moderate views virtue and law as important but largely autonomous concepts any sound moral theory must accommodate; there can be duties that make no reference to virtues, and virtues that make no reference to duties. The radical claims that ethics must start with virtue, and that virtue is all that is needed. Hobbes is not a moderate; he does not merely want to add virtue to an eclectic list of equally important moral categories. And he is not a radical; he does not think that virtue is all that is needed for ethics to be done properly. He does not start with virtue, but he does not start with law either. He starts with something more fundamental than both.

Hobbes's moral philosophy starts with the ideal of living well, of avoiding premature and unpleasant death in the brutal state of nature and enjoying "peaceable, sociable, and comfortable living" (*L:* 216). It poses, as its fundamental problem, the question of how such living can best be secured given the nature of human beings. It answers that the cultivation of the virtues offers the best means to such living, and the goodness of the virtues is grounded in this fact. Ethics is thus concerned above all else with understanding the goodness of the virtues, and I have maintained in this work that Hobbes is best understood as a virtue ethicist in this sense. In justifying this answer, Hobbes does not find the concepts borrowed from the law tradition in ethics to be dispensable. He begins by recognizing that acts can be right or wrong, and that there are moral laws governing them. Bad acts are those that tend toward the agent's detriment, and these are principally those disruptive and antisocial forms of behavior that threaten to cause retaliation (or at least noncooperation) on the part of others. But, crucially, Hobbes appreciates that this analysis does not go far enough, since acts alone are not what elicit such responses. Promises broken under stress may be forgiven, and promises kept out of base motives may fail to elicit trust. Thus Hobbes is forced by the logic of his position to press further, to consider not merely acts, but the dispositions from which they arise. If what is good is what tends to promote the agent's prospects for living well, then it is good not simply to do just acts, but to be a just person. It is not, therefore, that Hobbes gives virtue a role more important than that of the moderate but less than that of the radical. It is that he gives it a role different from both. We began this section by asking what the point of the revival of virtue ethics is. Hobbes seems to provide an answer more compelling than that of the moderate, and more defensible than that of the radical: The vindication of virtue should again be made the central goal of ethics; it should be attempted by following the ancient strategy of justifying the virtues by revealing the contribution they make to living well, and this should be done in a way that exploits some of the conceptual tools that ethics has developed since then.

5.3 THE GENUS OF VIRTUE

A second question any advocate of the new virtue ethic must address concerns the nature of the virtues themselves. What sort of thing are they? What is their genus? The number and diversity of possible answers to this question are immense. The virtues have been held at one time or another to be skills, passions, perceptual abilities, and more. A full consideration of this question would thus go beyond the scope of the present work and would, after a point, offer only limited illumination of the Hobbesian position in particular. This section will therefore concentrate instead on the position that has been taken by one contemporary writer on this question, and on some of the criticisms aimed at it. The position is essentially Hobbes's, and therefore its place in the contemporary debate may serve as an indication of what Hobbesian virtue ethics can contribute to this discussion.

Richard Brandt's important paper "Traits of Character: A Conceptual Analysis" is concerned with character traits in general and not simply with virtues, but since he explicitly identifies the moral virtues as an important class of character traits, we can with fairness take his comments on character traits to form a proposed analysis of the nature of virtue (1970: 23–4). Brandt begins by rejecting what he calls the "summary view" of virtues as dispositions. To say that a person has a certain trait is not simply to say that under certain conditions he would, or would be likely to, perform the acts associated with the trait. We can justifiably draw inferences about character from single acts, Brandt insists, in a way that is incompatible with the summary view (1970: 26). Nonetheless, Brandt does endorse a more refined sort of dispositional analysis, and his primary refinements each have a clear counterpart in Hobbes.

Most generally, Brandt maintains that character traits "are relatively permanent features of a person," so that a correct dispositional account of a virtue "must begin with some such phrase as 'It is a relatively stable and permanent feature of *X* that, were he . . . , he would . . . '" (1970: 27, ellipses in original). This stipulation clearly corresponds to Hobbes's claim that virtues are not just dispositions, but dispositions that "are so strengthened by habit that they beget their actions with ease and with reason unresisting" (*DH:* 13.8). Brandt also argues that such traits "are relatively permanent dispositions *of a specific kind* – the kind of dispositions that wants and aversions are" (1970: 27). Brandt's analysis is somewhat complex, but the essential point seems to be that to attribute a character trait to a person is to say not merely that under certain conditions he would (or would be likely to) do something, but that he would (or would be likely to) *want* to do it, would feel disappointment or joy depending on how things went. Thus, for example, to call a person sympathetic would involve making claims about conditions under which he would not only act in certain ways but would feel certain ways, disturbed, or relieved, or guilty (1970: 29, 30). A trait of character can therefore be understood "as a *set* of dispositions; not only as a disposition to act, but, under certain conditions, to have certain emotions relatively frequently" (1970: 31).[26] This element of Brandt's position is also clearly echoed in Hobbes. To speak of a man's virtue is to speak of his manners, which is to speak of his endeavors, which is to speak of his appetites and aversions. As we have repeatedly noted, the just person on Hobbes's account is one who is "delighted in just dealing" (*DC:* 3.5) and who "scorns" injustice (*L:* 207). We should be careful not to attribute to Brandt all Hobbes's views on virtue, but the two seem to be largely in agreement on the question of what sort of thing a virtue is.

What can be said against Brandt's (and thus Hobbes's) position? In one of the seminal works in the revival of virtue ethics, Georg von Wright argues that virtues are not dispositions at all. A disposition in the relevant sense, von Wright argues, is best understood as a habit, a "certain acquired regularity of acting" which "manifests itself in the doing of a characteristic act or in the performing of a characteristic activity under recurrent conditions" (1963: 143). For a person's actions to be understood as manifestations of habit, they must all be instances of the same act; one can make a habit of "washing one's hands before eating" or "leaving a tip in restaurants," because these expressions designate a uniform set of acts.

26 This view can be found in other recent discussions of virtue. Pincoffs, for example, emphasizes that in characterizing traits of character in general and virtues in particular as dispositions, he means by the term "not just tendencies to act in certain ways but also to feel, to think, and to react and to experience 'passions' " (1986: 81).

But, von Wright argues, the virtues do not pick out kinds of acts in this way. "'To be courageous' or 'to show courage' do not name an activity in the same sense in which 'to breathe' or 'to walk' or 'to chop wood' name activities. . . . There is no art of 'couraging', in which the brave man excels" (1963: 139). We can pick out all the acts of "walking a dog" without making reference to the disposition of the agent who engages in this activity, but the same cannot be said of virtuous acts. Virtuous acts are those acts that are done virtuously by virtuous people. And therefore, von Wright concludes, virtues cannot be dispositions.

Von Wright's attack is susceptible to several important objections. In the first place, his claim that the virtues do not pick out single sets of activities can be denied. Although the acts subsumed under the category of acting equitably are on the face of it far more eclectic than the act of brushing one's teeth, for example, there is nonetheless an underlying unity that enables them to be grouped together sensibly. The Hobbesian virtue ethicist can insist that virtue play a central role in ethics while at the same time allowing that the acts required by virtue, however diverse, are united by the categories under which they fall. Thus, although we may accept von Wright's analysis of the prerequisites of habit, we may also persist in the claim that virtues are habits. Perhaps more important, von Wright's stipulation about habits seems somewhat arbitrary. Even if we were to allow that there is no specific activity at which, say, the kind person excels, this would not provide a clear reason to deny that some people perform kind acts regularly out of habit, unless by doing so we mean to redefine the word "habit." Finally, there is a serious question as to whether we can draw as clear a distinction as von Wright assumes between such activities as being courageous and those more easily described as manifestations of habit. Von Wright says, for example, that "there is no specific activity at which, say, the courageous man must be good – as the skilled chess-player must be good at playing chess" (1963: 139). But when he explains why courageous acts as a group do not compose a single set of activities, what he says seems to apply equally to chess playing: He notes that courageously performed acts need not have any external feature in common, and that the result of any courageous act could also have been achieved through some noncourageous act (1963: 141). But a person might produce checkmate by moving a rook forward because he thought it would look nicer there. There is no physical similarity between all good chess moves that distinguishes them from all bad ones. One may wonder about even such a simple case as brushing one's teeth. One can produce the external movements typically associated with that activity while attempting to do something quite different (perhaps trying to remove some pasty material from the bristles of a brush by scraping it off with one's teeth), and one might discover ways to fulfill the aim of the activity in a variety of physically dissimilar ways. Von Wright's distinction may thus prove unable to get his argument off the ground, providing yet another reason to reject his rejection of the claim that virtues are dispositions.

In "Character and Thought," Lester Hunt attempts to adduce some additional arguments in support of von Wright's position (1978: 178). We consider it odd when a person acts out of character, Hunt notes, so if we find a person who is not brave acting bravely, we are likely to seek some explanation for this. Yet there is nothing per se odd, he maintains, about a person doing something he is not in the habit of doing: "Today I drank tea at 3:00, though I am not in the habit of doing so, and no one found it odd at all." Hunt claims that this represents an important asymmetry between traits of character and habits, and that (again assuming that virtues are character traits) virtues cannot be habits as Brandt and Hobbes claim.

It is important that even if Hunt's alleged asymmetry obtains, this need not overturn the claim that virtues are habits. It may show that there are different kinds of habits, some of which we find it odd to break and others of which we do not. Virtues might be understood as habits of a particularly important sort, so that for them, but not for more trivial sorts of habits, there could be a legitimate presumption that breaking the habit required an explanation. Hunt's argument, in any event, rests on a misleading comparison. The person who acts out of character does not merely perform an act he does not characteristically perform; he performs an act he characteristically abstains from performing. A more accurate comparison between habits and character traits would require us to compare him to the person who does something that he, as a matter of habit, would not do, and not just to a person who does something he does not as a matter of habit do. Once the comparison is set straight in this way, the alleged asymmetry vanishes. It is not odd for Hunt to drink tea at three o'clock if he has no habits about such matters at all, just as it is not odd for a person to make a modest contribution to charity if he is neither extremely stingy nor especially generous. If a miser were to make such a contribution, we might well wonder what the reason for his change of heart was, but we might equally well wonder about Hunt's behavior had he in the past revealed a long-standing habit of drinking only coffee. This argument, too, therefore fails to cast doubt on the claim that virtues are habits.

Finally, Hunt attempts to articulate what he takes to be the "most intuitively obvious" difference between character traits and habits. When a person does something out of habit, there is a sense in which he has no reason for doing it; he does it because it is a habit. When a person acts out of a character trait, the trait suggests that he has a reason for so acting. A person who helps another out of kindness does not do so blindly, but because he recognizes an opportunity to be kind and he seeks to be kind. Thus, there is a sense in which character traits "involve our intelligence in some important way, while habits seem to be unintelligent by nature."

As Hunt himself concedes, however, we can have habits that are informed by reason: I am in the habit of brushing my teeth, but this does not mean that I brush my teeth for no reason at all. Similarly, I can be in the habit of being just, but do so for a reason. Hunt maintains that this does not impugn his criticism, since the connection between reasons and habits is at least sometimes weaker than that between reasons and traits of character. This merely shows that habits may not be a uniform group; there may be mindless habits and rationally informed habits. According to the Hobbesian account, at least, the virtues are a subset of the latter. The just person is one who by nature is inclined to do, and to enjoy doing, the just thing, but to do so because it is just. The criticism suggested by Hunt therefore fails.

What shall we conclude about the Hobbesian position with respect to this second important issue in the modern revival of virtue ethics? It seems capable of surviving much of the criticism aimed at it, yet it also seems hard to justify the claim that Hobbes has anything especially original to contribute to the debate over what kinds of things the virtues are. The general schema of Brandt's position, that a virtue is a deeply rooted habit of a certain kind, is Hobbes's but it is also a familiar one which can as easily be identified with Aristotle and a number of other philosophers.[27] Nor should this come as a great surprise. Hobbes's goal is not to criticize the traditional understanding of what the virtues are, but to provide an

27 Stephen D. Hudson, for example, identifies Brandt's analysis with some of the central beliefs of Plato, Dewey, Butler, and Bradley among others (1980: 539–40).

innovative and more acceptable account of what it is that makes the virtues good. With respect to the question of virtue's genus, the Hobbesian must therefore be content not to play the role of the innovator but to join in the project of Brandt and others in defending a largely familiar picture from a variety of criticisms.

5.4 THE GOODNESS OF VIRTUE

Finally, we come to the crucial question, What makes the virtues good? Other questions about the nature and goals of virtue ethics are undeniably important, but the theory will be rendered useless unless it can provide an account of why we should praise the virtues and criticize the vices. There is substantial disagreement about the best approach to this question within the virtue ethics literature, and this provides perhaps the greatest opportunity for the Hobbesian to make a lasting contribution to its revival. In one sense, more or less everyone agrees about the nature of the goodness of the virtues. As Foot puts it, "virtues are, in some general sense, beneficial. Human beings do not get on well without them" (1978d: 2). The question lies in what sense the virtues are taken to be beneficial, and in who is taken to be the beneficiary when a given individual cultivates them.

Perhaps the most ambitious contribution to the revival of virtue ethics in recent years is James Wallace's *Virtues and Vices*. In one of the few systematic, book-length studies on the subject, Wallace attempts to develop a neo-Aristotelian account of virtue that preserves much of the form of Aristotle's argument while revising some of its content. The catalogue of the virtues is not identical with Aristotle's, and the human *ergon* of activity in accordance with reason is replaced by the notion of "a social life informed by convention," but the central contention remains the same: Certain character traits must be cultivated in order for human beings to flourish. The virtues, Wallace argues, "tend to foster good human life in extensive and fundamental ways," and without them "human life – the form of life characteristic of our kind – would be impossible" (1978: 37, 153).

Wallace's argument thus follows the form familiar to the virtue ethics tradition, but there is a crucial difference. Wallace's argument is not that an agent should cultivate the virtues because doing so will have beneficial consequences for him. Rather, it is that general cultivation of the virtues is enormously beneficial to society as a whole, and that since these benefits are widely distributed and the costs to the individual relatively small, it is reasonable for society to inculcate them in its citizens or to enforce the behavior they recommend (1978: 115). In thus defending the virtues of honesty and fairness, which he groups under the term "conscientiousness," Wallace argues that practices such as honoring promises, refraining from cheating, doing one's share, and so forth "are absolutely necessary in order to have communities, and thus they are necessary for the sort of life we regard as characteristically human," but he does not maintain that it is necessary for an individual to be conscientious in order to enjoy the benefits of these practices, or that his doing so is sufficient to ensure that he will enjoy them (1978: 110, 115). Wallace would have us make sense of the claim that human beings do not get on well without the virtues by arguing that society as a whole would not survive without them and using this as a justification for their applicability to individuals.

The strength of Wallace's position is that, at least with respect to some of the virtues, his central contention is almost impossible to deny. Although it is more difficult (as Wallace acknowledges) to demonstrate the indispensability of such virtues as magnanimity and benevolence, it does seem clear that society, and thus social beings, could not survive without at least some measure of honesty and fairness. Since Wallace's argument centers around the benefits to society of a general cultivation of the virtues, he is spared the daunting task of convincingly demonstrating that individuals always benefit from being virtuous. He need not convince the Foole that *he* would benefit from being just, only that he would benefit from others' being just. Yet this very feature that makes Wallace's argument plausible seems also to render it inadequate. By focusing on the reasons we have for wanting the virtues to be prevalent, Wallace's argument risks leaving unanswered the question, Why should *I* be virtuous? That society may have a reason to encourage me to be virtuous need not entail that I have a reason to comply.[28] It is one of the great merits of the virtue ethics tradition that it has the potential to unite morality and individual rationality through the notion of human flourishing, but that potential is left unrealized when the cultivation of the virtues is tied only to social, and not individual, well-being.

The most obvious remedy for this problem is to stick with the more traditional response to Thrasymachus' challenge: to maintain

28 Arthur Flemming presses this point persuasively in a joint review of Wallace's and Foot's books (1980: 592–3).

that since no one can be truly happy without being virtuous, it is good for each agent to be virtuous; it is not simply good for that person that others are virtuous. This position is most famously represented in the modern virtue literature by Foot's "Moral Beliefs." Foot agrees that we cannot consider justice to be a virtue unless we can show that for every person it is more profitable to be just than to be unjust, and she explicitly argues that this is the case. Those who would recommend the life of the unjust person who masquerades as just, she insists, overlook the "colossal" costs involved in successfully maintaining a respectable veneer; even though justice may in certain cases bring misfortune to those who respect it, it is nonetheless necessary if the individual is to flourish (1978b: 128–9). This position does indeed resolve the difficulty with Wallace's position, but it does so at the cost of credibility. As Foot's critics have been quick to point out, history teems with examples of vicious individuals who seem to have flourished quite successfully,[29] and Foot herself has since come to renounce her original position, settling instead for the claim that character traits must be beneficial to someone, though not necessarily to the agent who cultivates them, in order to qualify as virtues (see, e.g., 1978b: 130, endnote 6; and 1978c: 168, endnote 6). Yet this brings us back to Wallace's position and thus to Wallace's problem. If it is unnecessary for me to cultivate the virtues in order for me to flourish, how does the notion of human flourishing provide me with a reason to be virtuous? The strong relationship between virtue and human flourishing suggested by Foot's early position seems untenable, but once that relationship is severed, the relationship between virtue and reason threatens to become unbridgeable.

This is perhaps the greatest single problem facing proponents of contemporary virtue ethics. What relationship can be posited to exist between individual virtue and individual flourishing that is both weak enough to avoid entailing the unrealistic claims of Foot's early position and strong enough to play the justificatory role lacking in Wallace's? The answer suggested by the Hobbesian approach is this: Being a virtuous person is neither a necessary nor a sufficient condition for human flourishing. It is possible that a resourceful villain could escape detection and punishment (although it would be unreasonable for him to rely on this happening), and it is possible that a fully virtuous person could lead a miserable life.

29 Sarah Conly constructs a particularly spirited critique of Foot around the figure of Lorenzo the Magnificent (1988: 92–3).

There is, nonetheless, an important relationship between virtue and flourishing: The person who cultivates the virtues minimizes the chances that she will fail to flourish. This is a weaker claim than the assertion that only virtuous people flourish and is thus significantly more plausible. It allows for the possibility that an unjust person might prosper, while insisting that such a person nonetheless runs a higher risk of failing to flourish than does the just person. It is a stronger claim than the observation that society as a whole benefits when virtuous characters are prevalent, and it provides a justification for virtue that applies at the individual level. The fact that eating sensibly reduces my vulnerability to certain health problems provides me with a reason to eat sensibly, although some people who do not eat sensibly manage to remain healthy and some people who do eat sensibly nonetheless become unhealthy.

Present-day moral philosophers have tended to look for inspiration to the writings of Kant, on the one hand, and to those of the utilitarians, on the other; those who have grown disenchanted with this limited menu in recent years have, by and large, sought an alternative in the works of Aristotle. As this study is an attempt to show, however, moral philosophers in general, and virtue ethicists in particular, might do well to widen their view even further and take more seriously than they have in the past the often misunderstood views of the virtue ethicist of Malmesbury. Kant once remarked that "there is nothing more common than the title of moral philosopher, and nothing rarer than a man who has really earned it" (1989: 28). Hobbes was rarely accorded the title of a true moral philosopher in his own time, and it has often been denied to him since, but he has earned it.

References

WORKS BY HOBBES

An Answer to Bishop Bramhall's Book, called "The Catching of the Leviathan." In W. Molesworth, ed., *The English Works of Thomas Hobbes* (*EW*), Vol. IV. London: John Bohn, 1840 (published posthumously in 1682).

"Answer to the Preface to Gondibert." In *EW* IV (1650).

"Appendix to [the Latin edition of] *Leviathan*" ("*AL*"). Trans., with Introduction and Notes, by George Wright, *Interpretation*, Vol. 18, No. 3 (Spring 1991), pp. 323–413 (1668).

Behemoth, or The Long Parliament (*B*). Ed. by Frederick Tonnies. Chicago: University of Chicago Press, 1990 (published posthumously in 1680).

A Briefe of the Art of Rhetorique (*BR*). In John T. Harwood, ed., *The Rhetorics of Thomas Hobbes and Bernard Lamy.* Carbondale: Southern Illinois University Press, 1986, pp. 33–128 (1637).

"Considerations upon the Answer of Doctor Wallis to the Three Papers of Mr. Hobbes." In *EW* VII (1672).

"Considerations upon the Reputation, Loyalty, Manners, and Religion of Thomas Hobbes of Malmesbury." In *EW* IV (1662).

De Cive (*DC*). In Barnard Gert, ed., *Man and Citizen*. Gloucester, MA: Peter Smith, 1978 (1642).

De Corpore (*Co*). In *EW* I (1655).

De Corpore Politico (*EL* II). In Frederick Tonnies, ed., *The Elements of Law, Natural and Politic*. Cambridge: Cambridge University Press, 1928 (1640).

De Homine (*DH*). In Gert, ed., *Man and Citizen* (1658).

Decameron Physiologicum, or Ten Dialogues of Natural Philosophy (*DP*). In *EW* VII (1678).

A Dialogue between a Philosopher and a Student of the Common Laws of England (*D*). Ed. by Joseph Cropsey. Chicago: University of Chicago Press, 1971 (published posthumously in 1681).

"An Historical Narration concerning Heresy, and the Punishment Thereof." In *EW* IV (published posthumously in 1680).

The History of the Grecian War Written by Thucydides (translated by Hobbes). In *EW* VIII (1628).

Homer's Iliads (translated by Hobbes). In *EW* X (1675).

Homer's Odyssies (translated by Hobbes). In *EW* X (1675).

Human Nature (*EL* I). In Tonnies, ed., *The Elements of Law* (1640).

"The Last Sayings or Dying Legacy of Mr. Thomas Hobbs of Malmesbury, who Departed this Life on Thursday, Decemb. 4, 1679." London: Printed for the Author's Executors, 1680.

Letter to Mr. Cavendish (LC). In Ferdinand Tonnies, *Studien, Studien zur Philosophie und Gesellschafftslehre im 17. Jahrhundert*, ed., by E. G. Jacoby. Stuttgart: Bad Cannstatt, 1975, pp. 94–5.

Letter to the Duchess of Newcastle (LD). In Tonnies, p. 105.

Letter to Edward Howard (LEH). In Edward Howard, *The Brittish Princes: An Heroik Poem*. London, 1669.

Letter to Marin Mersenne (LMM). In Harcourt Brown, "The Mersenne Correspondence: A Lost Letter by Thomas Hobbes," *Isis*, 34 (1943), pp. 311–12.

Letter to Lord Scudamore (LS). In Perez Zagorin, "Thomas Hobbes's Departure from England in 1640: An Unpublished Letter." *The Historical Journal*, 21, 1 (1978), pp. 159–60.

Letter to Samuel Sorbière (LSS). Trans. [from Latin] by Howard Warrender, in Warrender, ed., *De Cive: the Latin Version* (Oxford: Clarendon Press, 1983), pp. 310–12.

Leviathan (*L*). Ed. by C. B. MacPherson. Harmondsworth: Penguin, 1968 (1651).

"The Life of Thomas Hobbes of Malmesbury" ("LTH") Trans. by J. E. Parsons, Jr., and Whitney Blair, *Interpretation*, 10, 1 (January 1982), pp. 1–7 (published posthumously in 1681).

Manuscript on the Law of Heresy (MH). In Samuel I. Mintz, "Hobbes on the Law of Heresy: A New Manuscript." *Journal of the History of Ideas* 29 (July–September 1968), pp. 409–14.

"Mr Hobbes Concerning ye Compression of Aire" ("CCA"). Reproduced as the appendix (pp. 296–8) to Simon Schaffer, "Wallifaction: Thomas Hobbes on School Divinity and Experimental Pneumatics," *Studies in the History and Philosophy of Science*, Vol. 19, No. 3 (September 1988), pp. 275–98.

"Objections to Descartes' *Meditations*" ("O"). In John Cottingham, Robert Stoothoff, and Dugald Murdoch, eds. and trans., *The Philosophical Writings of Descartes*, 2 vols. Cambridge: Cambridge University Press, 1985, Vol. II, pp. 121–37 (1641).

Of Liberty and Necessity (*LN*). In *EW* V (1654).

"Of the Life and History of Thucydides." In *EW* VIII (1628).

A Physical Dialogue of the Nature of the Air (*Dialogus Physicus, sive de Natura Aeris*) (*PD*). Trans. Simon Schaffer. In Steven Shapin and Simon Schaeffer, *Leviathan and the Air-Pump: Hobbes, Boyle, and the Experimen-*

tal Life (Princeton: Princeton University Press, 1985), pp. 345–91 (1661).

Principia et Problemata aliquot Geometrica (Some Principles and Problems in Geometry) (PPG). Trans. by Venterus Mandey. In Mandey, *Mellificium Mensionis: or, the Marrow of Measuring*. London, 1727 (1672).

The Questions concerning Liberty, Necessity, and Chance (LNC). In *EW* V (1656).

Seven Philosophical Problems (SPP). In *EW* VII (published posthumously in 1682).

"A Short Tract on First Principles" ("ST"). In Tonnies, ed., *The Elements of Law*. Cambridge: Cambridge University Press, 1928. (See Chapter 2, footnote 5, in the present volume.)

Six Lessons to the Savilian Professors of the Mathematics (SL). In *EW* VII (1656).

Thomas White's De Mundo Examined (DME). Trans. by Harold Whitmore Jones. London: Bradford University Press, 1976 (1973).

OTHER WORKS

Alexandra, Andrew. 1992. "Should Hobbes's State of Nature be Represented as a Prisoner's Dilemma?" *The Southern Journal of Philosophy*, Vol. 30, No. 2 (Summer), pp. 1–16.

Annas, Julia. 1981. *An Introduction to Plato's Republic*. Oxford: Clarendon Press.

Anonymous. 1679. "An Elegie upon Thomas Hobbes of Malmesbury, Lately Deceased." London.

1680. "Mr Cowley's Verses in Praise of Mr Hobbes Oppos'd by a Lover of Truth and Virtue." In *The True Effigies of the Monster of Malmesbury: or Thomas Hobbes in his Proper Colours*. London.

Anscombe, G. E. M. 1958. "Modern Moral Philosophy." *Philosophy* 33 (January), pp. 1–19.

Applebaum, Wilbur. 1964. "Boyle and Hobbes: A Reconsideration." *Journal of the History of Ideas*, Vol. 25, No. 1 (January–March), pp. 117–19.

Aristotle. 1941. *Categories*. Trans. by E. M. Edghill. In Richard McKeon, ed., *The Basic Works of Aristotle*. New York: Random House, pp. 3–37.

1982. *Eudemian Ethics* (Books I, II, and VIII). Trans. by Michael Woods. Oxford: Clarendon Press.

1985. *Nicomachean Ethics*. Trans. by Terence Irwin. Indianapolis: Hackett.

Aubrey, John. 1957. *Brief Lives*. Ed. by Oliver Lawson Dick. Ann Arbor: University of Michigan Press.

Baier, Annette. 1987. "Commodious Living." *Synthese*, Vol. 72, No. 2 (July), pp. 157–85.

Baier, Kurt. 1982. "Virtue Ethics." *Philosophic Exchange* 3, Summer, pp. 57–70.

1988. "Radical Virtue Ethics." *Midwest Studies in Philosophy* 13, pp. 126–35.

Baier, Lee S. 1965. "*Gondibert* and Its Debt to Hobbes." Diss., Columbia University.

Becker, Lawrence C. 1975. "The Neglect of Virtue." *Ethics*, Vol. 85, No. 2 (January), pp. 110–22.

Bernhardt, Jean. 1990. Review of Rogers and Ryan, eds., *Perspectives on Thomas Hobbes*. "Bulletin Hobbes II," *Archives de Philosophie* 53, 2, pp. 21–4.

Bertman, Martin. 1979. "Hobbes: Language and the Is-Ought Problem." *Philosophical Studies* [Ireland] 26, pp. 146–58.

Bobbio, Norberto. 1993. *Thomas Hobbes and the Natural Law Tradition*. Trans. by Daniela Gobetti. Chicago: University of Chicago Press.

Bowle, John. 1951. *Hobbes and His Critics: A Study in Seventeenth Century Constitutionalism*. London: Alden Press.

Brandt, Frithiof. 1928. *Thomas Hobbes' Mechanical Conception of Nature*. Copenhagen: Levin & Munksgaard/London: Libraririe Hachette.

Brandt, Richard B. 1970. "Traits of Character: A Conceptual Analysis." *American Philosophical Quarterly*, Vol. 7, No. 1 (January), pp. 23–37.

Brown, Clifford W., Jr. 1989. "Thucydides, Hobbes and the Linear Causal Perspective." *History of Political Thought*, Vol. 10, No. 2 (Summer), pp. 215–56.

Brown, K. C. 1962. "Hobbes's Grounds for Belief in a Deity." *Philosophy*, Vol. 37, No. 142 (October), pp. 336–44.

Cantalupo, Charles. 1991. *A Literary Leviathan: Thomas Hobbes's Masterpiece of Language*. Lewisburg, Pa.: Bucknell University Press.

Carmichael, D. J. C. 1988. "Natural Right in the *Leviathan*." *Canadian Journal of Philosophy* 18 (June), pp. 257–70.

Catlin, George E. G. 1922. *Thomas Hobbes as Philosopher, Publicist and Man of Letters: An Introduction*. Oxford: Basil Blackwell.

Catteneo, Mario A. 1965. "Hobbes's Theory of Punishment." In Keith Brown, ed., *Hobbes Studies*. Oxford: Blackwell.

Collins, James. 1972. *Interpreting Modern Philosophy*. Princeton: Princeton University Press.

Conly, Sarah. 1988. "Flourishing and the Failure of the Ethics of Virtue." *Midwest Studies in Philosophy* 13, pp. 83–96.

Cottingham, John, Robert Stoofhoff, and Dugald Murdoch, eds. and trans. 1985. *The Philosophical Writings of Descartes*, 2 vols. Cambridge: Cambridge University Press.

Danford, John W. 1978. *Wittgenstein and Political Philosophy*. Chicago: University of Chicago Press.

Davenant, William. 1970. "The Author's Preface To his much honour'd Friend Mr Hobs." In *Gondibert: An Heroick Poem*. London, 1651, rpt. by Scholar Press, Menston.

Descartes, René. 1984. "Author's Replies to the Third Set of Objections [to the *Meditations*]." In Cottingham, Stoothoff, and Murdoch, trans., *Philosophical Writings of Descartes*, Vol. II, pp. 121–37.

1985. *Principles of Philosophy* (abridged). In Cottingham, Stoothoff, and Murdoch, trans., *Philosophical Writings of Descartes*, Vol. I, pp. 179–291.

Dewey, John. 1974. "The Motivation of Hobbes's Political Philosophy." In

Ralph Ross, Herbert W. Schneider, and Theodore Waldman, eds., *Thomas Hobbes in His Time*. Minneapolis: University of Minnesota Press, pp. 8–30.

Dietz, Mary G. 1990. "Hobbes's Subject as Citizen." In Dietz, ed., *Thomas Hobbes and Political Theory*. Lawrence: University Press of Kansas, pp. 91–119.

Dowlin, Cornell March. 1934. *Sir William Davenant's Gondibert, Its Preface, and Hobbes's Answer: A Study in English Neo-classicism*. Philadelphia: University of Pennsylvania.

Eliot, T. S. 1964. "John Bramhall." In Eliot, *Selected Essays*, New Edition. New York: Harcourt, Brace & World, Inc., pp. 311–19.

Ewin, Robert E. 1991. *Virtues and Rights: The Moral Philosophy of Thomas Hobbes*. Boulder, Colo.: Westview Press.

Flathman, Richard E. 1993. *Thomas Hobbes: Skepticism, Individuality and Chastened Politics*. Newbury Park, Calif.: Sage Publications.

Flemming, Arthur. 1980. "Reviving the Virtues." *Ethics* 90 (July), pp. 587–95.

Foot, Philippa. 1978a. "Introduction." In Foot, *Virtues and Vices and Other Essays in Moral Philosophy*. Berkeley: University of California Press, 1978, pp. xi–xiv.

1978b. "Moral Beliefs." In Foot, *Virtues and Vices*, pp. 110–31.

1978c. "Morality as a System of Hypothetical Imperatives." In Foot, *Virtues and Vices*, pp. 157–73.

1978d. "Virtues and Vices." In Foot, *Virtues and Vices*, pp. 1–18.

Forsberg, Ralph P. 1990. *Thomas Hobbes' Theory of Obligation: A Modern Interpretation*. Wakefield, N.H.: Longwood Academic Press.

Gauthier, David. 1969. *The Logic of Leviathan: The Moral and Political Theory of Thomas Hobbes*. Oxford: Clarendon Press.

1979. "Thomas Hobbes: Moral Theorist." *The Journal of Philosophy*, Vol. 76, No. 10 (October), pp. 547–59.

1986. *Morals by Agreement*. Oxford: Oxford University Press.

1988. "Hobbes's Social Contract." In G. A. J. Rogers and Alan Ryan, eds., *Perspectives on Thomas Hobbes*. Oxford: Clarendon Press, pp. 125–52.

1990a. "Introduction." In Gauthier, *Moral Dealing: Contract, Ethics, and Reason*. Ithaca: Cornell University Press, pp. 1–8.

1990b. "Thomas Hobbes and the Contractarian Theory of Law." *Canadian Journal of Philosophy*, Supplementary Vol. 16, pp. 5–34.

Gert, Bernard. 1965. "Hobbes, Mechanism, and Egoism." *Philosophical Quarterly* 15 (October), pp. 341–9.

1967. "Hobbes and Psychological Egoism." *Journal of the History of Ideas* 28 (October–December), pp. 503–20.

1978. "Introduction." In Gert, ed., *Man and Citizen*. Gloucester, Mass.: Peter Smith, pp. 3–32.

1988. "The Law of Nature as the Moral Law." *Hobbes Studies* 1, pp. 26–44.

Goldsmith, M. M. 1966. *Hobbes's Science of Politics.* New York: Columbia University Press, 1966.

1969. "Introduction to the Second Edition." In Frederick Tonnies, ed., *The Elements of Law, Natural and Politic,* 2nd ed. New York: Barnes and Noble, pp. v–xxi.

Graham, Catherine Sawbridge Macaulay. 1767. *Loose Remarks on Certain Positions to be found in Mr. Hobbes's Philosophical Rudiments of Government and Society.* London.

Gray, Robert. 1978. "Hobbes' System and his Early Philosophical Views." *Journal of the History of Ideas,* Vol. 39, No. 2 (April–June), pp. 199–215.

Hampton, Jean. 1986. *Hobbes and the Social Contract Tradition.* Cambridge: Cambridge University Press.

1989. "Hobbes's Science of Moral Philosophy." In Marcelo Dascal and Ora Gruengard, eds., *Knowledge and Politics: Case Studies in the Relationship Between Epistemology and Political Philosophy.* Boulder: Westview Press, pp. 48–67.

Hardie, W. F. R. 1968. *Aristotle's Ethical Theory.* Oxford: Clarendon Press.

Hardin, Russell. 1991. "Hobbesian Political Order." *Political Theory,* Vol. 19, No. 2 (May), pp. 156–80.

Harwood, John T. 1986. "Introduction." In Harwood, ed., *The Rhetorics of Thomas Hobbes and Bernard Lamy.* Carbondale and Edwardsville: Southern Illinois University Press, pp. 1–32.

Herbert, Gary B. 1989. *Thomas Hobbes: The Unity of Scientific and Moral Wisdom.* Vancouver: University of British Columbia Press.

Heyd, David. 1982. "The Place of Laughter in Hobbes's Theory of Emotions." *The Journal of the History of Ideas* 43 (April–June), pp. 285–95.

1991. "Hobbes on Capital Punishment." *History of Philosophy Quarterly,* Vol. 8, No. 2 (April), pp. 119–34.

Hinnant, Charles H. 1976. "Hobbes on Fancy and Judgment." *Criticism,* Vol. 28, No. 1 (Winter), pp. 15–26.

1977. *Thomas Hobbes.* Twayne's English Authors Series. Boston: G. K. Hall.

Holmes, Stephen. 1990. "Introduction." In Thomas Hobbes, *Behemoth, or The Long Parliament,* ed. by Ferdinand Tonnies, rpt. by Chicago: University of Chicago Press.

Hood, F. C. 1964. *The Divine Politics of Thomas Hobbes.* Oxford: Clarendon Press, 1964.

Hudson, Stephen D. 1980. "Character Traits and Desires." *Ethics* 90 (July), pp. 539–49.

Hume, David. 1975. *An Enquiry Concerning the Principles of Morals.* Ed. by L. A. Selby-Bigge, rev. by P. H. Nidditch. Oxford: Clarendon Press.

Hunt, Lester. 1978. "Character and Thought." *American Philosophical Quarterly,* Vol. 15, No. 3 (July), pp. 177–86.

Hutchinson, D. S. 1986. *The Virtues of Aristotle.* London: Routledge & Kegan Paul, 1986.

Hyde, Edward (Earl of Clarendon). 1676. *A Brief View and Survey of the Dangerous and Pernicious Errors to Church and State, in Mr. Hobbes's Book Entitled Leviathan.* Oxon.

Jackson, Dudley. 1973. "Thomas Hobbes' Theory of Taxation." *Political Studies,* Vol. 21, No. 2 (June), pp. 175–82.

Jacob, James R. 1983. *Henry Stubbe, Radical Protestantism and the Early Enlightenment.* Cambridge: Cambridge University Press.

James, D. G. 1949. *The Life of Reason: Hobbes, Locke, Bolingbroke.* London: Longmans, Green.

Johnson, Laurie M. 1993. *Thucydides, Hobbes, and the Interpretation of Realism.* DeKalb: Northern Illinois University Press.

Johnson, Paul J. 1974. "Hobbes's Anglican Doctrine of Salvation." In Ross, et al. eds., *Thomas Hobbes in His Time,* pp. 102–25.

1989. "Death, Identity and the Possibility of a Hobbesian Justification for World Government." In Airaksinen and Bertman, eds., *Hobbes: War Among Nations,* pp. 70–8.

Johnston, David. 1986. *The Rhetoric of Leviathan: Thomas Hobbes and the Politics of Cultural Transformation.* Princeton: Princeton University Press.

Jones, Harold Whitmore. 1976. "Introduction." In Thomas Hobbes, *Thomas White's De Mundo Examined,* ed. by Harold Whitmore Jones. London: Bradford University Press, pp. 1–20.

Kant, Immanuel. 1989. "Report on the Organization of His Lectures for the Winter Semester of 1765–1766." Trans. and pref. by Eugene Kelly. *American Philosophical Association Newsletter on Teaching Philosophy* 89:1 (Fall), pp. 24–8.

Kavka, Gregory S. 1983. "Right Reason and Natural Law in Hobbes's Ethics." *The Monist* 66 (January), pp. 120–33.

1985. "The Reconciliation Project." In David Copp and David Zimmerman, eds., *Morality, Reason and Truth: New Essays on the Foundation of Ethics.* Totowa, N.J.: Rowman & Allanheld, pp. 297–319.

1986. *Hobbesian Moral and Political Theory.* Princeton: Princeton University Press.

Kay, Carol. 1988. *Political Constructions: Defoe, Richardson, and Sterne in Relation to Hobbes, Hume, and Burke.* Ithaca: Cornell University Press.

Kemp, John. 1970. *Ethical Naturalism: Hobbes and Hume.* London: Macmillan.

1982. "Hobbes on Pity and Charity." In J. G. van der Bend, ed., *Thomas Hobbes: His View of Man.* Amsterdam: Rodopo, pp. 57–62.

Kidder, Joel. 1983. "Acknowledgement of Equals: Hobbes's Ninth Law of Nature." *The Philosophical Quarterly* 33 (April), pp. 133–46.

King, Preston. 1974. *The Ideology of Order: A Comparative Analysis of Jean Bodin and Thomas Hobbes.* London: George Allen & Unwin.

Klosko, George, and Daryl Rice. "Thucydides and Hobbes's State of Nature." 1985. *History of Political Thought,* Vol. 6, No. 3 (Winter), pp. 405–9.

Kraynak, Robert P. 1990. *History and Modernity in the Thought of Thomas Hobbes*. Ithaca: Cornell University Press.

Laird, John. 1934. *Hobbes*. London: E. Benn.

Lamprecht, Sterling P. 1940. "Hobbes and Hobbism." *American Political Science Review* 34 (February), pp. 31–53.

Lloyd, S. A. 1992. *Ideals as Interests in Hobbes's* Leviathan: *The Power of Mind over Matter*. Cambridge: Cambridge University Press.

Locke, John. 1960. *The Second Treatise of Government*. In Locke, *Two Treatises of Government*, ed. by Peter Laslett. Cambridge: Cambridge University Press.

Lott, Tommy L. 1989. "Hobbes on International Relations." In Airaksinen and Bertman, eds., *Hobbes: War Among Nations*, pp. 91–8.

Lowde, James. 1694. *Discourse Concerning the Nature of Man*. London: T. Warren.

Lynch, William T. 1991. "Politics in Hobbes' Mechanics: The Social as Enabling." *Studies in the History and Philosophy of Science*, Vol. 22, No. 2 (June), pp. 295–320.

Machamer, Peter, and Spyros Sakellariadis. 1989. "The Unity of Hobbes's Philosophy." In Airaksinen and Bertman, eds., *Hobbes: War Among Nations*, pp. 15–34.

MacIntyre, Alasdair. 1966. *A Short History of Ethics*. New York: Macmillan.

McNeilly, F. S. 1969. *The Anatomy of Leviathan*. New York: St. Martin's Press.

Macpherson, C. B. 1962. *The Political Theory of Possessive Individualism: Hobbes to Locke*. Oxford: Oxford University Press.

Malcolm, Noel. 1981. "Hobbes, Sandys, and the Virginia Company." *The Historical Journal*, Vol. 24, No. 2 (June), pp. 297–321.

1988. "Hobbes and the Royal Society." In Rogers and Ryan, eds., *Perspectives on Thomas Hobbes*, pp. 43–66.

Martinich, Aloysius. 1981. "Translator's Commentary." In Thomas Hobbes, *Computatio Sive Logica* (Part I of *De Corpore*), ed. by Isabel C. Hungerland and George R. Vick. New York: Abaris Books.

1992. *The Two Gods of* Leviathan: *Thomas Hobbes on Religion and Politics*. Cambridge: Cambridge University Press.

Midgley, Mary. 1993. "Virtuous Circles." *Times Literary Supplement*, No. 4707 (June 18), pp. 3–4.

Mill, John Stuart. 1974. *Utilitarianism*. In Mary Warnock, ed., *Utilitarianism and Other Writings*. New York: New American Library, pp. 251–321.

Mintz, Samuel I. 1969. *The Hunting of Leviathan*. Cambridge: Cambridge University Press.

Moore, G. E. 1903. *Principia Ethica*. Cambridge: Cambridge University Press.

Moore, Stanley. 1971. "Hobbes on Obligation, Moral and Political (Part I: *Moral Obligation*)." *Journal of the History of Philosophy* 9 (January), pp. 43–62.

Murphy, Mark C. 1993. "Hobbes' Shortsightedness Account of Conflict." *The Southern Journal of Philosophy,* Vol. 31, No. 2 (Summer), pp. 239–53.

Nagel, Thomas. 1959. "Hobbes on Obligation." *Philosophical Review* 68 (January), pp. 68–83.

Norrie, Alan. 1984. "Thomas Hobbes and the Philosophy of Punishment." *Law and Philosophy* 3, pp. 299–320.

Nunan, Richard. 1989. "Hobbes on Morality, Rationality, and Foolishness." *Hobbes Studies* 2, pp. 40–64.

Ogilby, John (trans.). 1660a. *Homer, his Iliads.* London: Thomas Roycroft.
1660b. *Homer, his Odysses.* London: Thomas Roycroft.

Oxford English Dictionary, The. 1971. Oxford: Oxford University Press.

Pacchi, Arrigo. 1988. "Hobbes and the Problem of God." In Rogers and Ryan, eds., *Perspectives on Thomas Hobbes,* pp. 171–87.

Pence, Gregory E. 1984. "Recent Work on Virtues." *American Philosophical Quarterly,* Vol. 21, No. 4 (October), pp. 281–97.

Peters, Richard. 1956. *Hobbes.* Harmondsworth: Pelican Books.
1967. "Hobbes, Thomas." In Paul Edwards, ed., *The Encyclopedia of Philosophy.* New York: Macmillan and The Free Press.

Peters, Richard, and Henri Tajfel. 1972. "Hobbes and Hull: Metaphysicians of Behavior." In Maurice Cranston and Richard Peters, eds., *Hobbes and Rousseau: A Collection of Critical Essays.* Garden City, N.Y.: Doubleday.

Pincoffs, Edmund L. 1986. *Quandaries and Virtues: Against Reductivism in Ethics.* Lawrence: University of Kansas Press.

Plato. 1974. *The Republic,* trans. by G. M. A. Grube. Indianapolis: Hackett.

Pocock, J. G. A. 1971. "Time, History and Eschatology in the Thought of Thomas Hobbes." In Pocock, *Politics, Language and Time: Essays on Political Thought and History.* New York: Atheneum Press, pp. 148–201.

Pope, Alexander (trans.). 1967. *The Iliad of Homer* (2 vols.), ed. by Maynard Mack. New Haven: Yale University Press.

Popkin, Richard H. 1992a. "Hobbes and Scepticism I." In Popkin, *The Third Force in Seventeenth-Century Thought.* Leiden: E. J. Brill, pp. 9–26.
1992b. "Hobbes and Scepticism II." In Popkin, *The Third Force,* pp. 27–49.

Prokhovnik, Raia. 1991. *Rhetoric and Philosophy in Hobbes' "Leviathan."* New York: Garland.

Rapaczynski, Andrzej. 1987. *Nature and Politics: Liberalism in the Philosophies of Hobbes, Locke, and Rousseau.* Ithaca: Cornell University Press.

Raphael, D. D. 1977. *Hobbes: Morals and Politics.* London: George Allen & Unwin.

Rawls, John. 1971. *A Theory of Justice.* Cambridge, Mass.: Harvard University Press.

Regan, Tom. 1986. *Bloomsbury's Prophet: G. E. Moore and the Development of His Moral Philosophy.* Philadelphia: Temple University Press.

Reik, Miriam M. 1977. *The Golden Lands of Thomas Hobbes*. Detroit: Wayne State University Press.

Riddehough, G. B. 1958. "Thomas Hobbes' Translations of Homer." *The Phoenix*, Vol. 12, No. 2 (Summer), pp. 58–62.

Robbins, Caroline, ed. 1938. *The Diary of John Milward*. Cambridge: Cambridge University Press.

Robertson, George Croom. 1886. *Hobbes*. Philosophical Classics for English Readers, 240. Edinburgh: W. Blackwood.

Roesch, Eugene J. 1963. *The Totalitarian Threat: The Fruition of Modern Individualism, as Seen in Hobbes and Rousseau*. New York: Philosophical Library.

Rogow, Arnold A. 1986. *Thomas Hobbes: Radical in the Service of Reaction*. New York: W. W. Norton.

Ross, Ralph. 1974. "Some Puzzles in Hobbes." In Ross et al., eds., *Thomas Hobbes in His Time*, pp. 42–60.

Ross, Ralph, Herbert W. Schneider, and Theodore Waldman. 1974. Introduction. In Ross et al., eds., *Thomas Hobbes in His Time*. Minneapolis, University of Minnesota Press, pp. 3–7.

Rossini, Gigliola. 1987. "The criticism of rhetorical historiography and the ideal of scientific method: history, nature and science in the political language of Thomas Hobbes." In Anthony Pagden, ed., *The Languages of Political Theory in Early Modern Europe*. Cambridge: Cambridge University Press, pp. 303–24.

Rudolph, Ross. 1986. "Conflict, Egoism and Power in Hobbes." *History of Political Thought*, Vol. 7, No. 1 (Spring), pp. 73–88.

Sarasohn, Lisa T. 1985. "Motion and Morality: Pierre Gassendi, Thomas Hobbes and the Mechanical World-View." *Journal of the History of Ideas* 46 (July–September), pp. 363–80.

Scally, Thomas. 1981. "The Fool's Heart and Hobbes' Head." *Dialogue* 20 (December), pp. 674–89.

Schlatter, Richard. 1975. "Introduction." In Schlatter, ed., *Hobbes's Thucydides*. New Brunswick: Rutgers University Press, pp. xi–xxviii.

Schneider, Herbert. 1974. "The Piety of Hobbes." In Ross et al., eds., *Thomas Hobbes in His Time*, pp. 84–101.

Shafte, J. 1673. *The Great Law of Nature, or Self-Preservation, Examined, Asserted, and Vindicated from Mr. Hobbes his Abuses*. London.

Shapin, Steven, and Simon Schaffer. 1985. *Leviathan and the Air-Pump: Hobbes, Boyle, and the Experimental Life*. Princeton: Princeton University Press.

Shapiro, Alan E. 1973. "Kinematic Optics: A Study of the Wave Theory of Light in the Seventeenth Century." *Archive for History of Exact Sciences*, Vol. 11, Nos. 2–3, pp. 134–266.

Shelton, George. 1992. *Morality and Sovereignty in the Philosophy of Hobbes*. New York: St. Martin's Press.

Silverman, Morris, ed. 1951. *High Holiday Prayer Book*. Hartford, Conn.: Prayer Book Press.

Skinner, Quentin. 1963. "Thomas Hobbes and His Disciples in France and England." *Comparative Studies in Society and History* 8 (January), pp. 153–67.

1966. "The Ideological Context of Hobbes's Political Thought." *The Historical Journal*, Vol. 9, No. 3 (September), pp. 286–317.

1969. "Thomas Hobbes and the Nature of the Early Royal Society." *The Historical Journal*, Vol. 12, No. 2 (June), pp. 217–39.

1991. "Thomas Hobbes: Rhetoric and the Construction of Morality." *Proceedings of the British Academy* 76, pp. 1–61.

Smart, J. J. C. 1973. "An outline of a system of utilitarian ethics." In Smart and Bernard Williams, *Utilitarianism: For and Against*. Cambridge: Cambridge University Press, pp. 3–74.

Smith, Adam. 1976. *The Theory of Moral Sentiments*. Oxford: Oxford University Press.

Sneath, E. Hershey, ed. 1898. "Introduction." *The Ethics of Hobbes*. Boston: Athenaeum Press.

Sommerville, Johann P. 1992. *Thomas Hobbes: Political Ideas in Historical Context*. New York: St. Martin's Press.

Sorell, Tom. 1986. *Hobbes*. London: Routledge & Kegan Paul.

1988a. "Descartes, Hobbes and the Body of Natural Science." *The Monist*, Vol. 71, No. 4 (October), pp. 515–25.

1988b. "The Science in Hobbes's Politics." In Rogers and Ryan, eds., *Perspectives on Thomas Hobbes*, pp. 67–80.

1990. "Hobbes's Persuasive Civil Science." *The Philosophical Quarterly*, Vol. 40, No. 3 (July), pp. 342–51.

1993. "Hobbes without Doubt." *History of Philosophy Quarterly*, Vol. 10, No. 2 (April), pp. 121–35.

Spragens, Thomas A., Jr. 1973. *The Politics of Motion: The World of Thomas Hobbes*. Lexington, KY: University of Kentucky Press, 1973.

Stephen, Leslie. 1904. *Hobbes*. English Men of Letters Series, 243. London: Macmillan.

Stoffel, Brian. 1987. "Hobbes's Conatus and the Roots of Character." In C. Walton and P. J. Johnson, eds., *Hobbes's 'Science of Natural Justice.'* Dordrecht: Martinus Nijhoff, pp. 123–38.

Stone, Christopher D. 1987. *Earth and Other Ethics: The Case for Moral Pluralism*. New York: Harper & Row.

Strauss, Leo. 1936. *The Political Philosophy of Hobbes: Its Basis and Its Genesis*. Oxford: Clarendon Press.

Stubbe, Henry. 1840. "An Extract of a Letter Concerning the Grammatical Part of the Controversy Between Mr. Hobbes and Dr. Wallis." In *EW* VII, pp. 401–28.

Talmor, Sascha. 1984. *The Rhetoric of Criticism: From Hobbes to Coleridge*. Oxford: Pergamon Press.

Taylor, A. E. 1908. *Thomas Hobbes*. London: A. Constable.

1965. "The Ethical Doctrine of Hobbes." In K. C. Brown, ed., *Hobbes Studies*. Oxford: Blackwell, pp. 35–55.

Taylor, Paul W. 1975. *Principles of Ethics: An Introduction*. Belmont, Calif.: Wadsworth.

Taylor, Richard. 1988. "Ancient Wisdom and Modern Folly." *Midwest Studies in Philosophy* 13, pp. 54–63.

Thorpe, Clarence DeWitt. 1940. *The Aesthetic Theory of Thomas Hobbes*. Ann Arbor: University of Michigan Press.

Tonnies, Frederick. 1928. "Preface." In Tonnies, ed., *The Elements of Law, Natural and Politic*. Cambridge: Cambridge University Press.

Tricaud, François. 1988. "Hobbes's Conception of the State of Nature from 1640 to 1651: Evolution and Ambiguities." In Rogers and Ryan, eds., *Perspectives on Thomas Hobbes*, pp. 107–23.

Tuck, Richard. 1979. *Natural Rights Theories: Their Origin and Development*. Cambridge: Cambridge University Press.

1988a. "Hobbes and Descartes." In Rogers and Ryan, eds., *Perspectives on Thomas Hobbes*, pp. 11–41.

1988b. "Optics and sceptics: the philosophical foundations of Hobbes's political thought." In Edmund Leites, ed., *Conscience and Casuistry in Early Modern Europe*. Cambridge: Cambridge University Press, pp. 235–63.

1989. *Hobbes*. Oxford: Oxford University Press.

1993. *Philosophy and Government, 1572–1651*. Cambridge: Cambridge University Press.

Urmson, J. O. 1988. *Aristotle's Ethics*. Oxford: Basil Blackwell.

Verdon, Michel. 1982. "On the Laws of Physical and Human Nature: Hobbes' Physical and Social Cosmologies." *Journal of the History of Ideas* 43 (October), pp. 653–63.

von Wright, Georg Henrik. 1963. *The Varieties of Goodness*. London: Routledge & Kegan Paul.

Waldman, Theodore. 1974. "Hobbes on the Generation of a Public Person." In Ross et al., eds., *Thomas Hobbes in His Time*, pp. 61–83.

Wallace, James D. 1978. *Virtues and Vices*. Ithaca, N.Y.: Cornell University Press.

Wansbrough, Henry, ed. 1985. *The New Jerusalem Bible*. Garden City, N.Y.: Doubleday.

Warrender, Howard. 1957. *The Political Philosophy of Hobbes: His Theory of Obligation*. Oxford: Clarendon Press, 1957.

1987. "Hobbes and Macroethics: the Theory of Peace and Natural Justice." In Walton and Johnson, eds., *Hobbes' 'Science of Natural Justice,'* pp. 297–308.

Watkins, J. W. N. 1965. *Hobbes' System of Ideas: A Study in the Political Significance of Philosophical Theories*. London: Hutchinson.

Willman, Robert. 1970. "Hobbes on the Law of Heresy: A Further Note." *Journal of the History of Ideas*, Vol. 31, No. 4 (October–December), pp. 607–13.

Wilson, John F. 1979. "Reason and Obligation in 'Leviathan.'" *Interpretation*, Vol. 8, No. 1 (January), pp. 30–57.

Wolin, Sheldon S. 1960. *Politics and Vision: Continuity and Innovation in Western Political Thought*. Boston: Little, Brown.

1970. *Hobbes and the Epic Tradition of Political Theory.* Los Angeles: Clark Memorial Library, 1970.

Woodfield, Richard. 1980. "Thomas Hobbes and the Formation of Aesthetics in England." *British Journal of Aesthetics,* Vol. 20, No. 2 (Spring), pp. 146–52.

Wootton, David. 1988. "Lucien Febvre and the Problem of Unbelief in the Early Modern Period." *Journal of Modern History,* Vol. 60, No. 4 (December), pp. 695–730.

Zagorin, Perez. 1990. "Hobbes on Our Minds." *Journal of the History of Ideas,* Vol. 51, No. 2 (April–June), pp. 317–36.

1993. "Hobbes's Early Philosophical Development." *Journal of the History of Ideas,* Vol. 54, No. 3 (July), pp. 505–18.

Zaitchik, A. 1982. "Hobbes's Reply to the Fool: The Problem of Consent and Obligation." *Political Theory,* Vol. 10, No. 2 (May), pp. 245–66.

Index